Kenny's Shoes

A Walk Through the Storied Life of
The Remarkable Kenneth W. Monfort

By Walt Barnhart

Copyright © 2008 by Walt Barnhart

All rights reserved. No part of this book shall be reproduced or transmitted in any form or by any means, electronic, mechanical, magnetic, photographic including photocopying, recording or by any information storage and retrieval system, without prior written permission of the publisher. No patent liability is assumed with respect to the use of the information contained herein. Although every precaution has been taken in the preparation of this book, the publisher and author assume no responsibility for errors or omissions. Neither is any liability assumed for damages resulting from the use of the information contained herein.

ISBN 0-7414-5035-6

Published by:

INFINITY
PUBLISHING.COM
1094 New DeHaven Street, Suite 100
West Conshohocken, PA 19428-2713
Info@buybooksontheweb.com
www.buybooksontheweb.com
Toll-free (877) BUY BOOK
Local Phone (610) 941-9999
Fax (610) 941-9959

Printed in the United States of America

Printed on Recycled Paper

Published October 2008

For my late father,
Alvin E. Barnhart

Books aren't written about all remarkable men.

Table of Contents

Preface: The Shoes --- i
Foreword: Hank Brown --- iii
1: The Detour --- 1
2: The Patriarch --- 11
3: The Foundation: 1930-1960 --------------------------------- 29
4: The Growth: 1960-1975 -------------------------------------- 43
5: The Politics --- 75
6: The Businessman -- 117
7: The Help -- 139
8: The Man -- 153
9: The Conscience -- 179
10: The Roller Coaster: 1975-1987 -------------------------- 193
11: The Deal: 1987-1991 --------------------------------------- 229
12: The Columnist --- 245
13: The Educator -- 251
14: The Conclusion 1991-2001 ------------------------------- 261
Epilogue: The Gift --- 271
Sources --- 275
Acknowledgments -- 281
Ken Monfort's Awards and Honors ------------------------- 285
Ken Monfort's Philanthropy ---------------------------------- 287
Index --- 289

Preface
The Shoes

It's an old joke. But Ken Monfort's friends insist it happened. As Rich Gebhardt recalls, it was in the spring of 1968 at a Denver campaign fundraising party for Mark Hogan who was considering a run for governor of Colorado in 1970. Held across the street from the governor's mansion, it was hoped that well-heeled invitees would pony up for what looked to be an expensive campaign.

Guest of honor was Jay Rockefeller, member of the esteemed Rockefeller family who continues to be an important office holder in West Virginia. Another of the invitees, Ken Monfort, had been called to a meeting at work and was late to arrive, but was his usual sociable self when he got to the event. Gebhardt, Rockefeller, Kenny and other guests were chatting when suddenly there was a hush and all the attention was on Kenny's feet. On one foot he had a brown shoe and on the other he had a black one. Kenny was nonplussed. He must have been in a hurry, he said. That was O.K., though; he was sure he had another pair just like 'em at home.

Many of the more than 90 friends, associates and family members interviewed for this book remembered the story in different settings and in different ways. But most of those who knew him would agree: That sounds like Kenny.

The mismatched shoes point to Kenny's famous indifference to fashion and his engaging, self-deprecating sense of humor. Both of these were part of his charm and suggestive of his enormous people skills, which could rival those of Dale Carnegie.

That story (or any like it) is not the most important aspect of this book. That's because the mismatched shoes event says nothing about sides of Kenny that were equally fascinating. For instance, it doesn't address his incredible intelligence and business sense, which helped turn a successful and respected cattle feeding business into a meat industry giant. It doesn't reveal his compassion for people and totally unprejudiced nature, or his vision and willingness to take risks to help shape the future. It doesn't explain his unwavering integrity, loyalty and uncompromising honesty. It doesn't touch on his love for his kids and for the community in which he grew up.

Events that follow in this book are true; as they say, you can look 'em up. The excerpts from his columns in the *Greeley Tribune* and the *Town & Country News* help shed some light on his views, from his brain to his typewriter to you, almost. The stories about incidents in Kenny's life are also true, as told by the people involved. Time may have blurred or embellished some of the specifics, but no one who really knew Kenny would deny they took place, or could have. For every event related, many readers who knew him well will have two that just as vividly describe Kenny Monfort, who was a colorful, compelling and complex man.

The precise time I met Ken Monfort is lost in my memory. It must have been the summer of 1974, after my sophomore year at the University of Northern Colorado. I was working as a host at the visitor's center at the original Monfort feedlot north of Greeley, a city boy doing my best to pick things up as I went along so I could pass them on to others. Kenny would occasionally bring customers by to show them how things got started and tell them why the operation started by his family was different from others.

Though the first meeting didn't stick in my mind it must have been pleasant. In the six years I worked for the Monfort organization Kenny never talked down to me. He always greeted me warmly by name and treated me with respect, as if I was important to him and his company. That's the way I saw him treat everyone.

Throughout the process of researching and writing this biography I found that trying to accurately understand – let alone explain – the person who filled Ken Monfort's shoes was a difficult task. It's my hope this book will at the very least help demonstrate why those shoes seem so very hard to fill.

Walt Barnhart
July 2008

Foreword

This portrait of a true giant of the West is long overdue. Ken Monfort was an innovator. He helped change the beef and lamb industries and played a key role in revolutionizing how meat is processed. He was an environmentalist before there was an environmental movement and was fair to all because it was right. Kenny epitomized the best of the Colorado spirit – a pioneer who truly cared about his neighbors.

He was also one of a kind, an extraordinarily kind and generous man in a hard and uncompromising business. His business ethics were beyond reproach, and some of his personal habits were occasionally beyond belief. He was, as Walt Barnhart calls him, a remarkable man, and I was proud to call him my friend and colleague.

Barnhart does a great job of pulling together many of the stories and facts that give readers a look not only at Kenny's amazing life, but the lives of family members. It's a compelling tale that will be fascinating to anyone who lived in Colorado during the Monfort era. It will also be of tremendous interest to those in animal agriculture, as well as to students and people in business or government.

It's a wonderful work that captures many of the details about Kenny some of us had forgotten and many people never knew. A few of the stories in the book I shared with Barnhart; a few of the others I remember a little differently. They all make me smile, though, as I remember the kind of man Kenny Monfort was and what he meant to me and so many others.

His heritage lives on in the industry he molded, the family foundation he helped endow, the four children he adored, the thousands who had a job as a result of his work, the scores who were inspired by being associated with him.

Kenny would never have allowed this book to be written while he was alive. But, his modesty aside, his life should be an example for all of us. That example will only last as long as we are wise enough to remember it. This outstanding book helps chronicle the life of an exceptional human being who deserves to be both praised and emulated. And, surely, never forgotten.

Hank Brown

A long-time employee of Monfort of Colorado, Hank Brown served 10 years in the U.S. House of Representatives and 6 years in the U.S. Senate. He also served as president of both the University of Northern Colorado and the University of Colorado.

Chapter 1
The Detour

Ken Monfort could be charming and urbane, but most of the time he appeared to have gotten dressed while blindfolded. He was exceedingly bright but in many ways simple, a college dropout that was well-read and thoughtful, able to converse on any number of subjects. He was a war dove but a business hawk; an opinionated, open-minded patriotic peacenik with a serious stubborn streak. He had a diet some would consider lethal yet consistently worked rings around his employees. He was a Democrat – wait, Republican – who sought out people who had diverse views; a corporate cowboy who was fiercely loyal and expected the same in return. He was a gentle giant who made his living from death that provided life. He was as at home chatting with company janitors as he was visiting with bank presidents and dignitaries.

Ken Monfort, or Kenny, as he encouraged others to call him, was a contradiction in terms, a contrarian in views, a contrast in styles. In short, while he wasn't easy to classify he was a fascinating study in business acumen, common sense, humanity, character and fashion. (Well, maybe not fashion.) His complex personality and varied life offers an intriguing look at how relationships, politics, community and history come together to help shape our lives.

It was a unique life, lived with a sense of personal style no one else could possibly duplicate. While that life diverted from the course on which it started, it is a rare individual who is permitted to live out his or her early dreams. Fate has a way of making decisions without regard for how we see ourselves as we're growing up. After all, we can't all be astronauts or policemen. Most people make the best of what life hands them.

There was an age when the life's work of the father dictated the life's work of the son. The 20th century helped bury that concept in the United States. But that didn't mean sons couldn't follow their fathers into business. In this respect, life handed Kenny some tremendous opportunities, but he didn't always see them as *his* opportunities. While he was given the chance to occasionally stray from the path, it may have been that an invisible hand kept nudging Kenny back toward the road he must have known would take him home.

Gene Meakins was tired. Painting houses is no picnic, but he was glad to have the work. It was 1949 and competition for summer jobs for college students was aggressive. The weather in Fort Collins, Colorado, was hot this week before school started and he wasn't much in the mood for idle chit chat.

Meakins put down his paint brush and listened to his tall, lanky friend and fraternity brother. Now, in addition to being hot and tired, Meakins was slightly miffed and more than a little disappointed. Ken Monfort had decided not to come back to school. He was going to get married and go to work with his father near Greeley.

A year older than Ken, Meakins had been in the Navy the last year of World War II, getting out in 1946 and landing at Colorado A&M (now Colorado State University). Ken and Gene had become friends and both had joined the Sigma Phi Epsilon fraternity. As the editor of the Rocky Mountain Collegian, A&M's weekly newspaper, Meakins had also taken Monfort under his wing and had been hoping to make him his managing editor during this, their senior year.

Ken wanted to be a writer and Meakins thought he was good at it. Sure, Ken couldn't spell worth a damn. But he was a good communicator and reported with rare candor and honesty. His time on the Collegian staff as a sports editor had been good practice for his future career as a sports writer, and Meakins thought Ken would make a great managing editor. His heart was in it.

Meakins considered the problem Ken faced and believed a compromise could be crafted. Why not just get married and go back to school? What's wrong with that? You can always go to work after you have your degree.

But Ken felt that if he got married, he had other obligations. It wasn't right to make his father pick up the tab for Ken's family while he was in school.

For Gene it was a disappointing conclusion. He had looked forward to their last year in school together and the fun times, both as fraternity brothers and editors. At the same time Gene was impressed with the integrity revealed by the decision. Ken's father wasn't a poor man, nor was he a miserly one. And his parents were devoted to their youngest child. Many students would have jumped on the opportunity, taken the money from mom and dad and not looked back.

Sure, Ken, I'd be happy to be in your wedding. I'll be darned if our friendship will end here.

In fact, the careers of Ken Monfort and Gene Meakins would cross again nearly two decades later, and in interesting ways.

Wedding Bells

Ken and Patricia Ann McMillen of Greeley formally announced their engagement on Sept. 24, 1949. The wedding was a grand affair, held two months later on Nov. 20 at the Park Congregational Church in Greeley, Colorado. It was two days before Kenny's 21st birthday. About 300 people attended the ceremony.

Pat had been a pretty and popular student at Greeley High School, two years behind Kenny. From a prominent Greeley family, she was president of the Pep Club and a cheerleader, and very active in school activities. She had gone on to become a cheerleader and a member of the Kappa Alpha Theta sorority at the University of Colorado, where she majored in fine art.

Though they had known each other in high school, they hadn't actually dated then. It was while they were both in college that they truly got together. It was a short courtship; after her freshman year Pat was ready to get married.

It was no surprise to people who knew them that she and Kenny Monfort would marry, even though the city kids felt the country boy had stolen one of theirs. Tall and good looking – not to mention from a prominent and wealthy family – Kenny attracted the girls.

The *Greeley Tribune* the next week called the wedding "one of the most beautiful of the season," with an all-white color motif and pompons and chrysanthemums. Kenny's sister Margery was one of the bridesmaids, while Gene Meakins was one of the ushers. Another fraternity brother in Sigma Phi Epsilon, Jack Crane of Fort Collins, was his best man and many other fraternity brothers were among the guests.

Kenny and Pat honeymooned for 2½ weeks in Miami Beach, Florida, and Havana, Cuba, then came back to live in town on 19th Avenue in Greeley at a home that Kenny had purchased shortly before the wedding. The home was near Pat's parents' house on 14th Avenue and very close to the high school they both had attended.

Kenny wasn't a city boy, though, and both he and Pat knew it. He was becoming a cattle feeder, like his father. They were a two-man team now, he and dad. It hadn't started out that way, but that's the way it needed to be.

High Hopes

Living up to the expectations of a demanding father isn't easy. But how do you live up to the memory of a favorite older brother, especially one who's your hero and who gave his life in the service of his country?

Richard Lee Monfort was almost six years older than Ken, born Feb. 11, 1923. Feeding cattle was his passion, not Kenny's. Dick had been about 7 when his father started his feeding operation and enjoyed being part of the growing business.

With his father's help, Dick began participating in 4-H fed cattle contests when he was about 10. Each year for at least five he meticulously filled out the contest books, which required monthly reports on feed costs, cattle weights and costs of gain. His efforts earned him many blue ribbons.

Kenny loved and respected his older brother. In fact, he believed he owed him his life.

On the original Monfort family feedlot was a feed mill, which had a grinder powered by an old Fordson tractor. Feeding the grinder was a square grain elevator, with corn flowing to the center opening at the bottom. One day Dick and Kenny were supposed to be cleaning the corners of the elevator, but in reality they were just "messing around," covering each other up with shell corn and then crawling out. But all of a sudden the suction of the grain heading toward the grinder had Kenny and he couldn't get out. Dick quickly grabbed Kenny's arm and wouldn't let go. Luckily, the Fordson quit and Dick was able to pull Kenny to safety. It was something he would never forget.

Dick was a great brother to Kenny and the first son of a proud father. He had graduated from Greeley High School in 1939 and went off to study agriculture at Colorado A&M in Fort Collins where he was a member of Sigma Phi Epsilon, the same fraternity at the same school his brother would later join and attend. He had been a prominent fixture and well respected in the Weld County cattle industry. It was clear Dick was being groomed as the heir to the Monfort family business.

That was fine with Kenny, who aspired to be a journalist anyway. Or maybe a teacher. Dick could run the business, as Kenny was planning to head down a different career path. Besides, Kenny thought the cattle business was too much work.

World War II intervened, though. At age 19 and after being at Colorado A&M for two and a half years, Dick was called to serve in the Army Air Force in December 1942. His primary training was at Ellington, Texas, and he was commissioned as a second lieutenant Aug. 5, 1943. He later received training as a B-17 "Flying Fortress" heavy bomber navigator, and had been stationed in England with the 401st Army Air Force Bomb Group starting in December 1943.

With a wing span of nearly 104 feet, a dozen machine guns and a bomb payload of almost 10,000 pounds, the B-17 was a superb weapons system. The crews loved it, and Dick felt privileged to be serving his country through his work on one. Of the 1½ million tons of bombs dropped on Germany during the war, about a third were dropped from B-17s.

Despite their incredible durability and tales of survival during devastating counter-attacks, many B-17s were lost during World War II. A total of 43,742 members of the U.S. 8th Army Air Force were killed during raids in World War II. One of those stood out for the Monfort family.

Richard Lee "Dick" Monfort

It was Jan. 29, 1944, and Dick was on a bombing raid over Frankfurt, Germany, when the crew's aircraft came under fire. In the crew of 10, one man was killed on the plane; the others parachuted before it crashed. Initially, Dick's status was unknown and he was reported missing Feb. 13, 1944. The news was later delivered to the family that Dick had indeed died on the day his plane was shot down.

Dick left behind not only his parents, sister and brother, but a new bride, the former Viola Swanson of Farmers Spur, Colorado, a small community midway between Greeley and Windsor. They had been married in Houston on March 27, 1943.

His death devastated the entire Monfort family, no one more so than Kenny, who had looked up to his older brother and known little but Dick's hand-me-down clothes throughout his early life. A sophomore at Greeley High School at the time of Dick's death, Kenny couldn't even watch war movies for a long time. The event would forever color how he would think about war and its tremendous toll on society and the world.

Kenny completed his high school education as World War II waned. He was a popular student who was not exceptional in all of his studies. For example, he got a C in first year Spanish, which must have frustrated his mother who had taught five languages. But he was bright in many classes and involved in several school activities, including student council and thespians. He worked as the sports editor of the *High Light*, the school newspaper, and was on the National Activities Committee, which compiled names of Greeley High School students killed while serving their country in World War II.

Because he was working in the cattle industry and knew how to ride a horse, Kenny did give rodeo a shot while in high school. Two tries at bareback bronc riding, however, resulted in one second place at Gill and a broken arm in Estes Park. That was all for the rodeo circuit. He played basketball in 4-H and tried out for the sport early in high school, but found that he was lacking a necessary ingredient called coordination.

His growth spurt actually happened later in high school, as early on he wasn't that large. Coming into his junior year he was only 5 feet 8 inches and 140 pounds; by his senior year he had grown to 6 feet and 165 pounds. He did play football and lettered as a senior, but didn't appear to help the Wildcats much. Number 86 played on a team that didn't win any of its eight games, getting outscored 153-40 in those contests and going scoreless in four of them. He was also on the Boys Athletic Association for three years.

He went off to school at Colorado A&M, sometimes called the Aggies, and joined the football team but lasted all of three days of workouts. There were some large 20-year-old military veterans coming back from the service to play football, Kenny found, but part of it was his tremendous distaste for getting hit. He had experienced the same feeling while in high school. Apparently he hadn't outgrown it. All in all, Kenny discovered he enjoyed watching and writing about sports more than he enjoyed participating competitively in them.

He had gone off to school with some reluctance, but with the full support of his parents. He knew his father was expanding the business and needed his help. Kenny also had other interests he wanted to pursue, however. His parents, who both had college degrees, encouraged his interests – especially his mother, who could appreciate Kenny's more scholarly pursuits. They both urged him to get his degree.

The first year at A&M Kenny took and passed the Army Reserve Officers Training Corps (ROTC) test, and was sworn into the corps. The ROTC would pay for his first year's tuition, but as the sole surviving son of a family with a war casualty he would never serve in the military.

His college major was animal nutrition. A&M was the state's agricultural school and he was from an agricultural family. It could have been nothing else. But he wouldn't limit himself to that area of study or activity. In fact, Kenny wanted to live his life to its fullest while he had the chance.

They were young and carefree. But in post World War II boys grew up quickly because some never had the chance to grow up at all.

Roy Romer had the itch to go to Europe, and his fraternity roommate Ken Monfort said he would like to go along. It would be a great adventure, and the way they had it planned it wouldn't be very expensive, either.

Warren and Edith Monfort weren't exactly thrilled with the idea. They had already lost one son in Europe, and not that many years earlier. It was now 1948, and their grief had not yet been buried some 3½ years after the death of their oldest son. Their only requests of Kenny were that he be careful and that he make a side trip to the cemetery in France where Dick Monfort's body was buried.

Roy and Kenny threw together a few essentials and hitched a ride to the East Coast, taking turns driving in exchange for the trip. There they caught a tramp steamer to Le Havre, France, south of the English Channel. They purchased bicycles and flipped a coin to see in which direction they would ride. It was north.

They took only what they could carry in packs on their backs, stopping when they got tired in the evening. They knocked on the door of the nearest farmhouse and asked about lodging. It wasn't often that they were refused or sent on their way. Europeans had become accustomed to seeing Americans in their midst.

They spent three months biking around the countryside. They headed south to the Riviera, then north again, spending time mountain climbing in the Alps. They climbed a small mountain, looking longingly at the Matterhorn in the distance. Now there was a peak! Romer said he wanted to try it, but Kenny had promised his parents he wouldn't take unnecessary risks while in Europe. The Matterhorn was an unnecessary risk. Romer remembers making the trek alone.

They had a few scrapes along the way. Europe was far from stable this soon after the war. In bars they would make note of the distance to the door – just in case. Coming out of Italy they smuggled Italian money in the frames of their bikes for no other reason than it was a challenge and they were kids.

Finally, at a military cemetery near Nancy, France, about 40 miles from the German border, Roy went with Kenny to find his brother's grave. There were 14,000 identical graves and an "out to lunch" sign on the door of the visitor's center. Kenny knew it would take a long time to search for and find the right grave. But it didn't. Within a few minutes he had found his brother's marker.

Kenny and Roy fought across Europe, discussing their future plans. They argued about which of them would be the first to become a senator, a governor, a president. They clashed over politics and war and the state of the world.

It was a special summer in the lives of both Kenny Monfort and Roy Romer. They had spent about $200 the entire summer on what would end up being a trip of a lifetime. It created a special bond that would never be closer than it was right then.

Kenny Monfort was a very bright guy in college, but not tremendously disciplined or motivated. He was an average student with a relaxed attitude toward study. You know the type; someone who might ditch that 3 p.m. psychology class because the teacher went by the book and common sense would get you a C. After all, it was spring and the lure of the mountains was awfully strong. Capable of straight A's, he never applied the kind of work ethic he would be famous for in later life.

Yes, education was important to Kenny. But school? At that time, not so much. Or, it could have been that Kenny already knew where his life was headed.

He'd get an education, all right. Though it wouldn't involve formal schooling, it would be a good one.

Chapter 2
The Patriarch

There are those who say Kenny Monfort didn't start his successful run in business from a standstill. They are absolutely right. In fact, the Monfort business was a growing concern and highly successful before Kenny was even old enough to hold a manure shovel.

His father Warren was the patriarch of the business, a very intelligent and successful businessman. He taught Kenny not only much of his cattle business acumen but his people skills as well. It would be an understatement to say the two were close. In his eulogy to his father Kenny would call him "not only a good father but the finest man I have ever known."

There would not have been a Monfort legacy in the cattle industry if it had not been for Warren Monfort. As the only child of Charles K. and Pella Monfort, much of the responsibility of keeping things afloat in the later years of his father's life fell on Warren. Charles apparently wasn't that good of a farmer and didn't think much of cattle raising as a business. Though they would run their operation as a partnership, Warren and his father didn't always see eye-to-eye on what it really took to make a living.

The Monfort family had first moved to the Greeley area from Charleston, Illinois, in 1906. The Charleston farm wasn't a productive one. Warren's ancestors had landed there in the first half of the 19th century from Kentucky with a wave of settlers moving northward, but were too late to get any of the good land. They were left with hilly and bottom land that had to be grubbed out before it could be farmed.

Charles was born in 1870 and Warren's mother in 1873. Warren came along Dec. 1, 1892. As a youngster he was no stranger to animals, because in addition to crop farming they raised hogs. Warren was in charge of making sure the animals stayed in their pens. It was a tough job that he detested. The animals were crafty and determined, and seemed to get out at will.

Warren's father was an amiable and easy-going man who longed for the better life he was sure he could find "out West." Tales were wistfully shared by neighbors over horseshoes about the virgin lands of Nebraska, Kansas and especially Colorado, with its majestic mountains and fertile rolling hills. Charles was just one of the many men in those days who wanted to see if there were indeed greener pastures on the other side of the plains.

His angst was made no easier by the hard work in the hot, sweaty Illinois summers. The crops weren't doing well for him and the machinery seemed to break down when it was needed the most. These were the last straws for Charles Monfort, who decided his family needed to get out of the Midwest.

After a meager harvest in the fall of 1906 the family sold its unneeded possessions and loaded up a freight car with their farm machinery and furniture. Warren was about 14 and thrilled to be making the move. It would be his grand adventure and he joined his father in the excitement of a new life. They were determined to make the move work.

But Illinois ties were strong, especially for Charles's wife Pella. Before they actually made the Colorado move permanent they would have second thoughts and move back to Illinois. They had already sent Warren back to Charleston to attend the Normal School there. He lived with relatives and did odd jobs for his room and board before his parents rejoined him.

The family soon discovered, however, that Illinois wasn't really the wonderful place they thought they had left. In 1908 they came back to Colorado and purchased an 80-acre farm near the one they had owned previously. There they would have a farm, raising beets, potatoes, corn and some alfalfa – as well as chickens. As they weighed the benefits and disadvantages of their move, they finally came to the conclusion that Colorado really was just the right spot for the Monfort clan.

A Proud Agricultural Tradition

Greeley was founded in 1870 in Weld County at the confluence of the Cache la Poudre and South Platte Rivers about 50 miles north of Denver. Its founder was Nathan Meeker, who had been the agricultural editor of Horace Greeley's *New York Tribune* and had visited the Colorado territory in 1869. He was taken by its clean air, moderate temperatures and "perpetual sunshine." As a result Meeker wrote a flattering article about the area in the Dec. 14, 1869, issue of the *Tribune* and invited others to move west and join him in a new joint stock colonization company to be called the Union Colony of Colorado.

Of the more than 3,000 people who responded, 700 were selected and paid $155 apiece to purchase land in the Union Colony. The approximately 1,200 people who eventually joined Meeker in the move were predominantly white, Anglo-Saxon, Republican individuals who were thrifty, hard-working and had high moral standards. All shared Meeker's vision of a cooperative utopia that would be based on temperance, religion, education, agriculture, irrigation and family values.

Not everyone in the Colorado Territory was enamored with the city's original constitution. Sometimes called "City of Saints," "City of Churches" or the "City of Hayseeds and High Morals," others would sometimes poke fun of the community's squeaky clean image.

But the new colony's inhabitants were proud of their community and pleased with its reputation and limited crime. In fact, for lack of residents the new city jail was rented to store buffalo hides in the 1870s.

The city was incorporated in 1886 with a population of 2,177 and it rode a boom in agriculture into the 20th century. A new sugar factory was built in 1902, a canning company for vegetables in 1907. By 1910 the population had risen to 8,179, and by 1920 to 10,598.

Also by 1920, Colorado was producing a quarter of the nation's sugar, with Weld County, the state's third largest county covering more than 4,000 square miles, playing a predominant role in that production. Sugar beets had surpassed potatoes as the region's major crop. Thanks to the local sugar factory, this provided farmers a steady supply of beet tops and pulp for feeding to their cattle and sheep, one of several crops used in this manner.

Warren as a young man

While it isn't known whether Charles had seen information about Greeley before the family's move, it certainly fit his family's needs at the time. Warren was able to transfer to the Colorado State Normal School (later to become the University of Northern Colorado), which was only about three miles south of their home. The Normal School had a good program and reputation and fit Warren's interests and long-term teaching goals.

Warren could balance chores at home with his school work. He would travel to school using the family's horse and buggy, working long hours at both ends of his classes. While attending school he had little time for extra-curricular activities but did manage to work on the school's literary publication, *The Crucible*, at one time serving as its editor. He graduated from Normal in 1914 with a degree in history.

At the end of his studies Warren found employment in Weldona, about 25 miles due east of Greeley, in the junior and senior high school. He was a social studies teacher, as well as a basketball and track coach. He secured a room at the Weldona Hotel, and although he was primarily focused on his teaching and coaching he found time to become an excellent checkers player. It was this talent, he believed, that later helped him become a successful cattle feeder.

"Plan the moves, evaluate the obstacles, continually check the procedures and don't become impatient. Sometimes you get cornered and lose, but other times everything works out just like you wanted it to and there's clear sailing," he said. "In later years in working in the cattle industry I learned that you have to remain calm and keep your wits about you, just as in a tight checkers match or you'll lose your shirt."

After beating one of the local "checkers champions," he would receive another lesson he would never forget. "It's harder to be a good winner than a good loser," his opponent said. "When you are winning people get envious and they figure out all sorts of ways to try and cut you down to their size. They'll start foolish stories to belittle you, so I say it takes a great man to be a real champ."

In the summer of 1915 he returned home to work on the farm, but he hadn't finished his teaching career. Through some excellent contacts he had established at the Normal School and thanks to research he had done in education that had gained statewide attention, he was hired by the high school in Sterling, Colorado, as a social studies and history teacher. At the time the school system in Sterling, about 100 miles northeast of Greeley, was considered among the best in the state and Warren was pleased to get the assignment.

The Scholars

It was in Sterling that Warren met Lillian Edith Shrum of Omaha, Nebraska. Shrum was a Greek, Latin, German, French and English teacher at Sterling High School. Her family was originally from Indiana, but had moved to the Missouri Valley in Iowa, then later to Omaha. That's where Edith, who always preferred her middle name to her first, was born Dec. 31, 1890, and grew up.

Her father was a bricklayer and contractor who went where he thought work would be easiest to find. Although his family got by, he wasn't a tremendous success. To make ends meet Edith's mother was a seamstress and did sewing for many of the more well-to-do families in Omaha.

Edith had demonstrated her studious nature early, graduating from college Phi Beta Kappa in just three years. She was the middle of five children and her parents encouraged all of their offspring to study hard and do well in school. All five went to college, which was unusual in the early 1900s.

After she graduated from the University of Nebraska in 1913 she returned to Omaha, starting her teaching career in the small town of Bancroft, about 40 miles northwest of the city. She also spent two summers at the University of Wisconsin in Madison furthering her studies of languages. While there the second summer she learned about a vacancy for a language teacher in Sterling and decided to give it a try.

Warren met and got to know Edith in Sterling at a boardinghouse where they both ate their meals. Edith thought Warren looked young for his age, but appreciated his thoughtful manner and intellect. Warren, meanwhile, was smitten with Edith's good looks, keen sense of humor and intelligence.

They began dating soon after meeting, but those dates were hardly extravagant. For amusement they would walk down the streets, window shopping or stopping to read the ads at the local movie house. They each made only about $900 a year, which after room and board, clothing and incidentals didn't leave much money for recreation or entertainment. In addition, Warren was trying to set some funds aside to help his folks on the farm. It just didn't seem that his parents were that successful in making ends meet from year to year.

Warren and Edith, 1916

In the spring of 1916, at the end of the school year, World War I loomed and Warren headed to Denver to enlist in the war effort. His father Charles really needed him on the farm, both as a manager and a laborer, and Warren probably could have gotten a deferment. But like many of the young men at the time he felt a duty to serve his country. He was also interested in aviation and thought he could get training in this field, which he believed would come to be a key means of transportation in future years.

Unfortunately, Warren's eyesight let him down and he failed all of the tests for pilot training or aviation duty. The Army did use him as a staff sergeant, however, and later as a mechanic. He started his service in Texas and soon was moved to North Carolina, New York City and Kentucky, where he entered officers' training school. Throughout his service he continued to correspond with Edith, so when the war ended in November 1918, he was mustered out of the service and ready to get married.

Warren in World War I

Edith was ready, too. On March 15, 1919, they took a train to Boulder and got married in a small ceremony witnessed by Edith's mother, who had come by train from Omaha, and a close teacher friend from Sterling. Warren's father didn't think much of this idea, preferring that Warren finish out the school year in Sterling and come back to the farm with a little cash. Among others not happy with the timing of the wedding was the principal at Sterling, who disliked losing a teacher as good as Edith before the end of the school year. Warren and Edith honeymooned in Denver, Colorado.

They went back to the farm north of Greeley, living with Warren's parents until new quarters could be built nearby. He didn't consider going back to teaching the next year. Although he liked the students, teaching didn't seem to appeal to him that much. He thought farming was more challenging and more fun.

About a year and a half after they were married Warren and Edith had their first child, a girl they named Margery Jane. Born Oct. 28, 1920, Margery had dark hair like her mother. Then came Richard Lee, who they nicknamed Dick, on Jan. 11, 1923. Their youngest, Kenneth Warren, came along many years later, on Nov. 22, 1928.

The farm continued to struggle. Warren thought his father didn't display the necessary agricultural aptitude. The fact was, other than raising chickens Charles didn't show a lot of interest and really put little into making things work better. And if it hadn't been for the chickens, they might have all starved during the 1920s. "During the 20s we thought we would go under about every year, but somehow we managed to hang on," Warren told an interviewer.

Others in the community, however, saw Charles – known as C.K. to his friends – a little differently. One fellow farmer was impressed with Charles' ability to produce seed potatoes and thought he was indeed the "county's best poultryman." He had been the first president of the Weld County Agricultural Advisory Council, formed in the 1920s to protect the county agent's office from an economy drive by the county commissioners.

Charles had kept a few cattle and sheep to graze on the farm, but didn't think much of them as a business entity. In fact, the cattle industry nationally was a disaster in the 1920s. Virtually the entire industry went broke and some farmers and ranchers took bankers with them. It took most of the decade to get out of the mess.

A New Industry

For the majority of farmers in the West cattle were owned primarily to manage the excess grasses that grew on the property, and were used for milk and meat for the family. In 1921 Warren decided he would feed a few, but from the beginning his father was against the idea. Charles told his son that if he wanted to feed the cattle it would be on his own dime. Other people, too, thought it was a get-poor-quick strategy. Several told him trying to feed cattle would break him quicker than a Depression. When it came to most farmers, they were right.

On June 2, 1930, Warren's father died of an intestinal blockage following surgery. Charles was 60 years old and the Depression was in full swing. When Warren took over the farm, the mortgage on the property was $16,000 – about $192,000 in 2007 dollars – which was more than the farm was worth. Declaring bankruptcy was one option, an option many people were deciding to take during those tough economic times. He considered going back into teaching, but because he hadn't enjoyed it that much he decided to give cattle feeding a try to see if he could turn things around.

Warren purchased 18 head of cattle and studied what he needed to do to get them fattened and marketed properly. He decided to stop cash cropping, instead just raising food for the family and his animals. It was the start of a true revolution in beef production, and a milestone in the Monfort family. Kenny was not yet 2; his brother Dick was 7 and his sister Margery was 9.

Although the kids weren't old enough to be of much help, Edith offered tremendous support to Warren in his feeding efforts. As he would add a pen to his lot she would encourage him, unlike his mother who would tell him he was on his way to the poorhouse. Edith was indeed a valuable "farm wife" and partner. She had given up teaching to take on this role, something with which she was not familiar, having been part of a "town family" all her life. But she took to the new responsibilities with tremendous energy and enthusiasm. This was the life she had chosen.

Soon the whole family was involved in the operation. Dick became old enough to help with the cattle. In addition to her farm wife duties Edith would help Warren with the farm's books. Warren was meticulous about keeping extremely accurate records about his cattle and how they were doing. Later Kenny would help with the books, too, even though he was only about 8 or 9 years old when he got started. His mother and he made a great team when it came to working with the numbers.

It was unheard of at that time to feed cattle year-round, but through perseverance and physical exertion from sunrise to sunset and beyond, Warren was making it work. The relatively mild winters, at least by Midwestern standards, and pleasant summers made it somewhat easier. But it was still backbreaking work seven days a week, and both Warren and Edith knew it would take exceptional luck as well as talent to make it all come together.

After a day's work Warren would slump his sturdy, 5-foot-10-inch frame into one of the kitchen chairs, physically exhausted, and think about ways he could make things work more effectively and efficiently. Though his health was good and he was ready to put everything he had into the effort, he knew it would take more than physical effort to have a successful business.

Edith was a great farm wife, but one thing she never got the hang of was cooking. It wasn't just that she didn't enjoy it; she was not a good cook and knew it. After the business got going she and Warren would eat away from home for most of their evening meals, often at The Hut, a converted Quonset hut in Eaton, or at the Farm Fare (later called the Red Steer) on Highway 85 in Lucerne, just north of their home.

John Matsushima had never seen Warren Monfort this incensed. All this over a hamburger?

Warren looked down at his plate and angrily told the Red Steer waitress that he had a special guest and they should be served a decent meal. This scrawny hamburger just wouldn't do. There should be more meat and less bun. Take it back, he told her, and bring us something that's more appropriate. So the chef had put together a 1/2-pound burger for the diners, which would serve as Warren Monfort's hamburger whenever he wanted one. When other diners saw what Warren was being served, they wanted one, too. So the Monfort Burger went on the Red Steer menu from then on.

Certainly success would also require an attitude and approach to business that made others want to do business with them. (This same attitude and approach would be taken up by Kenny when he got more involved in the operation.) One attribute Warren showed was a trust for his fellow man. Far from being suspicious in business dealings, he was a trusting soul and believed what people told him. Occasionally he would get burned by this approach, but more often he found that people were honest and appreciated being treated as though they were.

He was also more than fair to his hired help. He would pay his Hispanic help the same as any of his other workers, and during World War II caused a stir among his neighbors by hiring a Japanese-American man. He just thought these were the right things to do. But as his son Kenny – who thought his father was "tough and smart with a heart of gold" – said, if the government had required him to do these things, he would have had a fit.

Much of this social conscience was probably derived from one of Warren's professors at Colorado State Normal School, Gurdon Miller, Ph.D. Miller was widely recognized as a champion of worker rights and was highly critical of industry's corporate giants who would get rich at the expense of their help.

While teaching at Weldona and Sterling, Warren had stressed to his students that all American citizens should have an opportunity to share in the bounty of democracy, as long as they were willing to work for it. Warren carried this philosophy over to the help he hired in his farm and feeding operation. His wages were often the best in the area, and his feedlots were the first in the nation to offer profit sharing. Some other benefits he offered were less conventional but appreciated just as much.

He didn't need to spell it out, but workers knew that when he hired someone it was on a probationary basis. Always known as Mr. Monfort or affectionately as "Boss," Warren would send the new hire to a task to see how well he would perform and how he would handle himself. It may have been scooping manure from a pen or moving cattle, or sweeping excess grain from under the elevators. When the man had finished, he would report back to The Boss, who would send him back out on another task.

This would go on for a period of time – solely determined by Mr. Monfort – until such time as he was deemed a good worker. At that time he would be told to go get a milk pail, which meant he was on staff permanently.

Fringe Benefits

The milk pail was more than just a symbol; it was another benefit to the new employee. Hired hands got a free pail of milk every day to take home to their families. Each morning they would return with their pails to get them filled again. The milk came from dairy cows on the farm (Kenny helped milk the dairy cows when he was as young as 10). Later, when dairy cows were eliminated from the farm, the Monforts contracted with a local dairy to provide the milk in bottles for their employees.

Full-time workers were also given a free hot lunch. Warren and Edith Monfort believed well nourished employees who had balanced diets could work harder and longer and were more alert. By providing their employees a good lunch the Monforts would make sure they got at least one healthy meal during the day. In later years employees could fill up their gas tanks from feedlot supplies, paying a reasonable price on the honor system, signing a log book for how much they took.

In the house, The Boss wasn't always the boss. In fact, what Edith said was the law when it came to matters of the family. And even with employees Edith made key decisions when it came to their welfare and benefits.

If not working beside his hired hands, The Boss would make sure he stopped by to see each of them during the day if he could, asking about their families, their health and chatting casually about the work and the events of the day. If they had ideas for improving efficiency or the overall operation of the lots, they knew those ideas would be accepted and appreciated. In fact, Mr. Monfort was quick to pass credit for new ideas or innovations back to the employees who first came up with them.

For example, The Boss and his employees were one day discussing how much work it took to mix the feed for the animals before taking it to their pens. The feed was being mixed at a central site, then hand-scooped into a truck to be taken to the cattle. Mr. Monfort had been to a feedlot in Kansas and seen an automatic mixer that worked pretty well. He didn't see why this kind of mixer couldn't be attached to a truck body so the feed could be mixed in transit. Then they came up with an idea for adding a chute to the mixer, allowing the feed to be fed into the troughs without any scooping at all.

They came up with other ideas, including storing corn ensilage in pits in the ground and a Caterpillar manure loader. While these were "Monfort inventions," Warren Monfort never claimed ownership of the ideas, instead describing them as a collaborative effort among employees – including himself – for being more effective and efficient in their work. He was quick to offer praise to his staff and gave credit where credit was due.

If not dressed in work clothes The Boss would be outfitted in dark slacks and a matching coat or light jacket, with a favorite tan felt hat he preferred for outdoors. By farming standards it was a businesslike appearance, giving an air of authority without a hint of arrogance.

He knew everything that was going on in the feedlot and would patrol the feedlots on horseback or in a car to assure things were going well. He could get mad on occasion but was sincere and selected his words carefully. He was almost always even keeled and his workers respected him for that.

His employees always felt a special closeness to him and knew they could go to him with any problem or idea. The relationship was more like teacher and student than boss and worker; they looked up to and respected him but never feared him. He didn't expect anything from his employees in return for employment, other than an honest day's work.

This didn't stop them from wanting to show their respect and gratitude. One year in the late 1950s the feedlot workers collectively came up with something they thought he would appreciate. Each of them had their photo professionally taken and pasted on a board with their names underneath. An aerial photo of the feedlots was pasted in the center top. A casual glance would cause an observer to mistake it for a teacher's class, except the photos were of 20- to 60-year-old men and women. Warren was moved and displayed the board proudly.

Mr. Monfort never had a secretary, as he didn't believe he needed one. He rarely wrote letters as he thought they were too slow. Most of his communications were done by telephone, as a delay of a few days or hours in his business could mean a loss of profits. It was the difference in getting cattle or supplies at the right price and the right time or losing out. His agreements on the phone meant he had to rely on his trust in people, but that was all right with him. He just didn't do business with people he didn't trust.

In addition to paying excellent wages, Mr. Monfort insisted on paying higher than market prices for the grain and feed he bought. By doing so he would assure that his sources were reliable and consistent. Plus, he thought it was just the fair way to do business.

Bill Benton had some hay to sell and knew who might be interested. Warren Monfort had regularly purchased corn ensilage from Benton's father Wilbur for the cattle at his growing feedlot. So Benton visited with Mr. Monfort and they agreed on a price for the hay.

Because they weren't able to get the hay chopped right away, it was left at Benton's and picked up a week or two later. When Benton went to get his check he noticed something wasn't right.

Didn't we pay you enough? asked Mr. Monfort. Just the opposite, said Benton. This check is for more than the price we agreed on.

Well, the price of hay has gone up since then, said Mr. Monfort. That's what the hay is worth to me now. Just take the check.

Benton had no doubt if the tables were turned and the price of hay had decreased, Mr. Monfort would have lived up to his original agreement without a second thought.

Business arrangements were always done either over the phone or on a handshake, and he rarely had issues with them. If he did, it was only once; if cheated, he would never do business with that person again.

He was also a good neighbor, pioneering efforts to reduce odors at the feedlots. (See Chapter 9.) As his operation got larger this issue got bigger and bigger for him. He worked diligently to keep his yards clean and reduce his impact on the environment and his fellow citizens. His employees at the time described him as a "fussy" person when it came to how things were done on the feedlots to increase cleanliness and reduce odors.

Mistakes by his employees were tolerated and forgiven, but negligence? Never. Mr. Monfort was especially committed to the welfare of the animals on the operation. If he saw one of the employees mistreating a horse, that person wouldn't be there the next day – or ever again. He liked the cattle and wanted to make sure they were moved in an orderly and calm manner, and wouldn't allow his men to use excessive force to get them going in the right direction.

Other animals around the farm did well, too. Chris, the company watchdog and a Doberman, had the run of the house, even though he also had a heated dog house. Warren's trusted pet in the 1940s was Henry, a St. Bernard. (Kenny's St. Bernard Sarge would later join the family.) Cats were everywhere. Larry Knee, the bookkeeper in the 1950s, would throw them out of the office only to have Warren let them back in.

A simple, humble and behind-the-scenes leader, Mr. Monfort disliked flashy displays of wealth – a trait his son would also adopt and later often exhibit to the extreme (see Chapter 8). "In my way of thinking, to be a good winner a man must never immodestly display his winnings," Mr. Monfort told his biographer. "He should play fair and never be dishonest or take unfair advantage of another."

Warren and Edith were not drinkers or smokers and the strongest drug in the Monfort household was the coffee, but that was plenty strong. Though they didn't drink, they weren't prudes and Warren was known to buy men drinks on occasion. They had no ashtrays for their visitors, though, because they didn't allow smoking in the house.

In addition to the activities of their children, many of which were focused on school or raising cattle, Warren and Edith enjoyed socializing with friends over a game of bridge, although Edith didn't consider herself very good at cards. (Edith, in fact, was known to say their hobby was work.) Warren served on the board of directors of the Buell School, where his children were enrolled. They also occasionally got involved in the activities of their church, the Park (later First) Congregational Church of Greeley, where Warren served as a church trustee and chairman of the building committee.

Warren was a huge part of local agriculture, serving as a member of the Weld County Agricultural Advisory Council and as an officer of the Weld County Farmer's Institute. He was one of the original directors of the Colorado Cattle Feeders Association, an organization that would become incorporated in 1955 with Warren's son Ken as a director. Warren was also a charter member in 1938 of the T-Bone Club, a group of local feeders who got together regularly to discuss issues of common interest.

He was on the Colorado Board of Agriculture from 1949 to 1959, which governed Colorado State University, and was instrumental in helping the university acquire land for the College of Veterinary Medicine and Biomedical Sciences and the Equine Teaching and Research Center. He was one of the driving forces behind getting a new dormitory built after World War II.

Because he believed the Social Security program was there only for people who needed it, Warren never took benefits. Taking that cue from his father, Kenny never did, either. And believing that community involvement was a key responsibility of any of its citizens, Warren was a member of Rotary International and secretary of the school district. In 1948 Warren was also named to the board of the Greeley National Bank, a position he would hold until January of 1964. Warren served as chairman of the bank's executive committee from 1959 to 1964.

Edith was also involved in the community, having chaired the county Junior Red Cross and serving as a member of the Weld County Health Organization and American Association of University Women. She was also a 4-H Club leader.

His parents' years of public and community service, as well as their uncommon compassion for their fellow man, weren't lost on Kenny. They had set the stage and he would follow their lead.

Warren and Edith's senior years in the late 1960s and 70s were far from comfortable. Still working uncommon hours, Warren would take a half-hour nap each day to gain some strength. Humped over from severe arthritis and with poor eyesight, Warren was as involved as he could be to the end.

When he got sicker Warren's nurses would take him in his car to patrol the feedlot, and the employees would look on in reverence. To a large extent he and Edith could only watch in amazement at their son's emergence as the new family chief.

It was an educated family in a field known more for honest, hard working people than for the use of science and economics. The Monforts were certainly honest and hard working. But they also were adopting strategies that would bring them a unique reputation.

Chapter 3
The Foundation: 1930-1960

Intelligence and incredibly hard work were only two elements that led to the success Warren Monfort found in the cattle feeding industry. As he readily admitted, there was a degree of luck involved as well. Being in the right place at the right time was crucial to his growth and accomplishments.

Weld County, Colorado, was just a perfect place to get started in cattle feeding. Feed was plentiful and the weather was ideal. The winters were relatively mild, especially when compared to those in the Midwest. Because the humidity is low, both winter and summer temperatures seem less severe. The summer temperatures usually range from 72 to 90 degrees. The average winter temperature is 30.

It snows in Weld County, but the average yearly snowfall is less than 34 inches. The average high temperature in July is 90°F, and the average low in January is 16°F. Total annual precipitation is just over 13 inches, so there is generally little mud for the workers to worry about. And there are 340 days of sunshine a year.

Warren found that the best term that could be used for the overall climate was benign. It had none of the tornados of the Midwest, none of the hurricanes of the Southeast, none of the blistering heat of the Southwest, and none of the icy, bone-chilling cold of the North.

Then there were the benefits of water. Even though it didn't get the rainfall, it did enjoy plentiful water from the Rockies, with the foothills only 30 miles to the West. This was beneficial not only for the cattle – each animal drank about 10-15 gallons a day – but for the nearby crops. Weld County today is one of the largest crop producing counties in the country, thanks to the irrigation that is prevalent throughout the region. It continues to help produce the crops and crop byproducts that make cattle feeding a logical, and successful, business.

The Monfort operation itself was well situated. The lots were just a half mile from the rail line that would bring grain to the elevators and allow the operation to obtain cattle from a larger area. It would also provide a means for sending cattle to market. The operation was close to the city, which at the time was advantageous because numerous building and other supplies would be needed as the feedlots grew. (It would later prove to be less than fortunate. More in Chapter 9.)

Timing? Again, it couldn't have been more perfect. Technology was helping push ahead all kinds of industries throughout the world. Whether it was manufacturing or farming, businessmen were finding they could increase productivity tremendously by using available knowledge and equipment. Plus, since horses that ate were being replaced by tractors that didn't, there was more food available for feeding livestock. As Warren Monfort was proving, these were perfect conditions for establishing a cattle feeding operation.

It took only a small amount of calculating for Warren to figure out cattle feeding might just make sense from a business standpoint. Feed products were very cheap – hay at $4 to $5 a ton, grain at 25 to 50 cents a bushel, wet pulp during harvest at 10 cents a ton. And feeder cattle cost only 4 to 6 cents a pound. Warren was sure he could make these numbers work.

In fact, it didn't take long for Warren to discover how profitable his new business could be. In 1933 the Depression was still going strong and many other farmers were struggling, but Warren had a great year in cattle feeding and farming. He was able to pay off the mortgage in January of the next year. It was definitely a sign he was onto something.

Warren had been doing business with the Greeley National Bank, but the financial resources from that institution were limited and he was always pushing for more money. He had been doing well and had audited financial statements that confirmed a solid, successful business. So he went to the 1st National Bank of Denver in the early 1930s to see if he might be able to expand with their help. After his pitch, one of the directors of the bank took him *aside to his safety deposit box, removed $200,000 in cash and handed it to Warren. Take this; here are my terms. Warren did, they shook hands, and he was off and running.*

    Warren Monfort was taking advantage of opportunities to feed cattle on a greater scale. It was no longer necessary to feed your animals by hand with a scoop shovel, a horse-drawn wagon and a hand cart. With the innovations he and his help were able to devise, they could feed thousands more animals in a day, and without any additional manpower. But his basic philosophy remained the same: Have a big checkbook and a big shovel, and don't be afraid to use either.

    Warren's kind of brainstorm wasn't happening throughout the cattle industry. After all, other traditional cattlemen were still going broke. But Warren and local feeders like him were figuring out how to make money from this new line of work. Among these in the area were W.D. Farr and Bert Avery, who together with Warren had figured out that if you bought some heifer (unbred female) cattle in the fall and fed them through the winter, you could market them in the early summer at lighter weights when few other cattle were available to meat packers and prices were higher. Good money could be made then.

    All of these conditions allowed them to conduct year-round feeding, something that was virtually unheard of at the time. If they could purchase animals and feed at lower prices, they could keep the animals alive and their lots busy through the winter and market animals to packers when they were at their slowest and needed the animals to keep their plants running. The "buy low, sell high" philosophy really worked for year-round cattle feeding.

    There was one more thing: The product being produced was superior and more consistent. The meat was more flavorful and tender than that from cattle right off grass. Warren had done his homework and researched the available information about the science of cattle feeding, which at the time wasn't much. He knew that by giving the animals a consistent ration on a regular timetable they would fatten at about the same rate and produce beef that had little nonconformity.

He had also seen information about what Germans had done to fatten geese for market. Not only was it an efficient system, but the meat turned out more succulent. He believed – rightfully so – that some of the same principles would apply to cattle fed in confinement operations.

Hard work and intelligence in Warren's case also included keeping very meticulous books on how well the cattle were doing, something few farmers raising cattle were doing at the time. He would know how much each pen of cattle was eating and what the average weight gain was. He liked to tell people he was more than a cattle feeder. He was producing a product: Beef.

In 1941 his carloads of cattle outsold others in the Chicago market 23 times; in 1942 it happened 26 times, and another 25 times in 1943. Over that three year span he had topped the Chicago market an unprecedented 74 times, more than any other cattle seller. Buyers liked what he was selling, and more importantly, consumers liked the meat from the animals he was

Warren Monfort (left) receives the Skelly Agricultural Achievement award. With him is (from left) his wife Edith, his mother Pella, his daughter-in-law Viola and his son Kenny. The family wouldn't know until February that the day this picture was taken, January 29, 1944, Dick's B-17 was being shot down over Germany.

raising. He knew that he was onto something good.

World War II was also a spur for the industry, raising demand for food – especially this new kind of beef – and increasing cattle prices, making cattle feeding highly profitable. Now feeding both steers (castrated males) and heifers, this new breed of cattle feeder could stretch marketing throughout the year to capture the best markets and assure a good income.

Slow and Steady

Warren didn't build his lots all at once. Instead, he would buy young cattle when he sold fattened ones ready to go to market, purchasing cattle by the carload (about 25 head) in Denver at about 600 to 750 pounds each. He would use the profits from the group he sold (at about 1,150 pounds), if any, to increase the number of animals he had in the lots at the time. When the market was not as favorable, he would buy fewer cattle; when he made good money, he'd buy more.

Though he had workers by the late 1930s, and though one son (Dick) was at an age that he was of significant help, it was still basically a one-man operation. Kenny was not only too young to provide assistance, for a substantial time he had a serious health problem that would require daily attention from Edith and influence Warren's concentration on the business (Chapter 8).

By the time World War II had begun the number of animals in Warren's operation had risen to 3,000 head, which was enormous by the day's standards. In 1942 he fed animals that produced about 5½ million pounds of beef; he had increased that to 7 million pounds by 1943. Warren Monfort was establishing an outstanding reputation in the cattle feeding business, both for size and quality. (Because of price controls and to assure a market for his animals, during the war Warren fed cattle for National T Packers. Many packers at the time were doing this.)

Meanwhile, a marketing philosophy was being established for the Monforts, one that would serve the family well. They would sell the cattle when they were ready to go to market, not when they believed the market was best. Warren believed he was a cattle feeder, not a speculator.

Through the years he and Kenny were able to use this strategy to modify their feeding with little lead time to better meet the needs of consumers. When the consuming public wanted heavily marbled beef that often graded Prime, and beef packers didn't mind excess fat, they could feed the animals the extra days necessary. As the public moved to leaner, less marbled beef with less waste fat, they reduced the feeding time accordingly.

Another philosophy was to grow as much as the market and their lenders would allow – but not get over-extended in the process. They would make enough on the good markets to weather the bad, then come back stronger after that. It was a conservative, slow and steady growth that, viewed from a historical perspective, proved to be a wise business strategy. Warren had increased the size of his lot to about 4,500 by the time World War II ended, then nearly doubled the capacity of his Greeley lot to 8,000 by 1950, when his son Ken joined him in the business. There were fewer than 10 employees with the company at that time.

Involving the Family

When Warren was first getting started he and Edith's eldest son Dick was old enough to help out to an extent. He was the heir-apparent to the operation, with both the aptitude and the desire for this kind of business, and getting a valuable education as he grew older. Only 7 years old in 1930 when his father got started in the cattle feeding business, he was well into his teens by the time the operation reached the thousands. At that time he was able to assist with feeding animals and other aspects of the farming operation.

Dick had shown skill in 4-H in cattle feeding, winning ribbons for his feeding efficiency of groups of animals. His feeding journals from the 1930s show a conscientious attention to detail when it came to amounts of feed and cost of weight gain – as well as evidence of his father's oversight and direction. Warren obviously knew more about what it took to be a good cattle feeder and was more than willing to share that knowledge with his son.

As he got older, Kenny was also thrust into the family's cattle feeding endeavor, although he showed less interest in it than his brother.

It was a miserable, icy winter morning; must have been at least 20 degrees below zero with the wind chill. The year was 1936 and Kenny was in third grade. He was responsible for feeding his 4-H calves before going off to school, and he wasn't much up for it this time.

He rationalized that it was so cold there was no way the calves would eat that day. So he stomped around in his mother's chicken house for the appropriate amount of time, shivering violently, then went back into the house to have breakfast and finish getting ready for school. Did you feed the calves? his father asked. Sure did, Kenny said, and hurried out the door for the mile hike to the Buell School.

At about 10:30 the door to his classroom opened, and there stood Warren Monfort, his angry eyes burning a hole in his son. He didn't have to say a word. Off they went to feed the calves. When they finished, they hopped back into the pickup for the very quiet ride back to school. Don't you ever do that again, was his father's only comment.

Born in 1928, Kenny was up with the chickens by the age of 10 to help milk the cows and feed the cattle. He went to school for eight years at the Buell School, about a mile northwest of their home, then continued his education at Greeley High School on 14th Avenue in Greeley. As a youngster he enjoyed reading, stamp-collecting and other solitary pursuits. He was an easy-going child, and would carry that trait throughout his life.

Young Kenny

Knowing that his older brother would inherit management of the farm and feedlot, he didn't always put his full effort into the business. "The ranch looked the right size for one son, and Richard was going to be the rancher," Kenny said. Although Kenny showed cattle at the county fairs and eventually at the

National Western Stock Show, it was more at his father's insistence than at his own initiative. Often he couldn't have cared less about showing cattle; it was Warren that demanded he do the best he could and put in the proper amount of effort to be successful at it. It was this paternal oversight, in fact, that contributed much to Kenny's later dedication to work and his ability to focus on tasks at hand.

It was the Weld County Fair, and time for the presentation of the animals. Participants were busily preparing their animals for the ring, and Kenny was nowhere to be found. Warren Monfort was beside himself, as Kenny's and Dick's friend and fellow competitor John Matsushima looked on in amusement. Where could that boy be? Warren finally found him and both had to work hard to get the animals ready for the competition.

Sometimes when Kenny misbehaved it resulted in a spanking from Warren. His mother, however, would rarely even scold him. (His grandmother didn't hesitate in doing it, though.)

It turned out Kenny was good at doing manual labor; he just wasn't that personally invested in it. He would rather do something cerebral, like read. His brother Dick, on the other hand, was a hard worker. He won numerous local, regional and national awards for his cattle feeding, including Reserve Champion and 2nd Premium ribbons from the National Western Stock Show in Denver for his carload of fed animals in 1937. He and his brother were prominent in the winners circles of these kinds of events, earning cattle feeding ribbons in 1932, 1936, 1937, 1938 and 1940, both at the National Western and the Colorado State Fair in Pueblo.

It was Kenny, though, who took the spotlight. At the tender age of 12 he took top honors with the Grand Champion Hereford steer at the 1941 National Western Stock Show. At that time he was the youngest ever to get this award. For his efforts he received a wristwatch from the Standard Oil Company of Indiana and the proceeds from the sale of the steer, which went for the princely sum of $1 a pound, or $1,055, to K & B Packing Co. for the Melnick Bros. Market.

He would then spend all of his prize money the next day when he and Dick, then 18, bought a carload of Reserve Champion Feeder Herefords at the show for $21 a hundredweight. And in 1942 Dick and Kenny would show the Grand Champion Carload of Fat Steers at the National Western, earning $18.25 a

Kenny and Slit Ear at the National Western Stock Show

hundredweight for the animals – $2 a hundredweight above the previous year's winners. For some it would seem selling at a per pound price lower than what was paid for the animals would be less than successful. Because of the low cost of putting each additional pound on the animals, though, the return on the Monfort brothers investment was significant. They discovered for themselves that this business could be highly profitable.

Warren was ever-present at all of the events, as he was a judge at the National Western, but not the events in which his sons participated. He was proud when the youngsters did well and was quick to offer suggestions for how they could improve.

The year had been a good one for young Kenny Monfort on the cattle show circuit. He had purchased the National Western calf at the 1940 Stock Show from the T.O. Ranch in Raton, New Mexico, with money from two other calves he had owned that he sold for $75, plus a $30.50 loan from his father. He had named the calf "Slit Ear." That calf had earlier won the blue ribbon at the 4-H Club feeding contest and proved to be a wise purchase on Kenny's part. He had also won the champion 4-H heifer contest at the state fair in August 1940. "Boy, am I happy," was all he could muster upon accepting the Grand Champion ribbon and check in Denver.

Dick's death just three years later devastated the entire family and threw a wrench into Kenny's career plans. His father's enterprise was growing rapidly. While he was dabbling in things like journalism in school, Kenny knew at some point he would have to either rejoin his father or allow the business to eventually be sold.

In his mind – and his father's – the latter was not an option. Furthermore, Kenny believed it was his responsibility not only to his father but to his late brother, who had once saved his life in a grain elevator, to keep the Monfort feedlot in the family.

After dropping out of school to join his father in late 1949, the father/son business never lost a step. Kenny started at the bottom, riding the pens, feeding cattle or pouring cement to line the feed bunks of new cattle pens. He went on to become a cattle buyer, putting as many as 70,000 miles on an old Pontiac in one year to find the right kind of cattle for their operation.

By 1955 they had doubled the size of the feedlots to 16,000, and by 1960 had doubled again to 32,000. They had utilized the same philosophy of hard work and reinvesting profits that had worked so successfully for Warren in the 1930s and 1940s, and maintained the operation's reputation for fair dealings and high quality.

Kenny and Pat lived in Greeley but a home on the northwest edge of the family property was being built for them later in the 1950s. They were also busy starting a family. During the decade he and Pat would have two girls and two boys; Kyle the oldest was born in 1952; Dick, named after Kenny's late brother, was born in 1954; Kaye came along in 1958; and Charlie was born in 1959.

Kenny and Pat with Kyle and Dick, circa 1956

Kenny and Warren made an excellent cattle feeding team for many reasons, not the least of which is they agreed on many business philosophies. Kenny also highly respected his father's experience in and knowledge of cattle feeding and what it took to produce cattle that would sell at the highest price. One of the few disagreements they had in this area was in sorting. Kenny preferred to sort by pen and Warren insisted on sorting frequently by animal. Kenny thought too much sorting tended to reduce the weight of the animals, and, well, was just too much work.

It was much more than just a business relationship, though. His father always impressed on Kenny the values he felt were important as you got older. Those never left Kenny, and as a youngster he held the kind of admiration for his father that made him want to follow his lead.

Go FISH

In 1946 Warren had incorporated the family business, allowing him to both protect personal assets and obtain legal tools for financially managing expanded operations. He had wanted to defer taxes, if possible, so he explored different approaches to reporting business finances. One of the tools for doing this is called LIFO accounting, a useful technique for determining inventory value and the cost of goods sold. For the purposes of a feedlot, it assumes that the last animal purchased is the first one sold. LIFO would later become extremely significant for the company.

LIFO – or Last In, First Out – seems counterintuitive to these kinds of operations. After all, the last animals into the feedlot aren't the first ones out. In essence, cattle purchased in 1951 were still in the inventory when the company sold in 1987, at least according to the books. Later this led the accounting practice to become known affectionately as FISH, or First In, Still Here.

The Internal Revenue Service accepts LIFO as a method of inventory evaluation. In inflationary times LIFO keeps the value of inventory lower and increases the cost of goods sold. With a lower inventory value and a larger cost of goods sold, the earnings would be lower, reducing both taxable income and, consequently, taxes that needed to be paid.

Generally, the difference between the value determined by LIFO and the value determined by a First In, First Out (or FIFO) accounting method was put into what was known as a "LIFO Reserve." This difference initially was not permitted to be shown in a company's audited financial statements. Later, though, accounting rules were changed so that the LIFO and FIFO values could both be reflected in the "Notes to Financial Statements" in an annual report.

It was an exciting but frustrating time for the growing business. As Warren had shown in topping the Chicago markets, the cattle being produced at the giant feedlot near Greeley were recognized for quality. But they weren't always given the highest respect by buyers in terminal markets like Chicago, Kansas City and Omaha. Warren worked hard to purchase high quality feeder cattle, sort them properly and feed them a good diet, treating the animals almost like show cattle. Often, however, to boost their perceived value Chicago buyers would claim the animals were from Iowa or somewhere else in the Midwest. This disturbed Warren, who was justifiably proud of the animals he had been producing for decades. Kenny, too, thought the work they were doing was going unrecognized.

As their operation kept growing Ken and Warren Monfort were exhibiting the chemistry of a great team. They were also becoming frustrated by the lack of options they had for marketing their increasing supply of fat cattle. This would lead to one of the most significant changes to the Monfort empire. The Monforts would no longer be just cattle feeders. They would become true beef producers.

Chapter 4
The Growth: 1960-1975

At the very least, the Monforts needed some way of reducing their marketing costs. Packing plants were merciless – and the Monforts thought unscrupulous – when it came to how they treated their cattle suppliers. For one thing, they would charge a yardage fee for the animals being purchased, whether those animals actually spent any time in a yard or not. It was, Warren and Ken thought, a huge injustice.

Furthermore shrinkage, the amount of weight the cattle lost on their way to plants or to the terminal markets, was always more than they thought it should be, partially because they had to go off feed during transportation. If they had to be shipped long distances, they were bruised more. It was costing about $6 a head to market animals through terminal markets like Chicago, and the cattle feeders were picking up a significant portion of that. Changing the process could reduce those costs to $1-$1.50, which multiplied by thousands of animals a week meant huge savings. Because so much cattle feeding was now being done in the West, it just made sense that plants should start moving their way.

Warren assigned Kenny the job of finding out if there were any packing companies willing to locate a plant closer to the Monfort operation. Even if those plants still charged yardage charges, it would help with the shrinkage and provide a more reliable and consistent market for their animals.

Though the concept was a good one, the major packers were not willing to participate. They already had established plants in Chicago or other "points East," and they thought it made more sense to just go on doing business the way they had for decades. There was a substantial and consistent labor pool in the cities, and that was important. Getting the fresh beef to the customers quickly was also crucial, and those customers were in the cities, too. Better to ship the cattle than find new employees and ship the meat long distances.

It was a no-go, Kenny told his father, but I've come up with another idea. There's a firm in Denver, Capitol Pack, that's willing to run a plant if we'll build it. We'd be partners, and have a dependable market for our animals.

Kenny also saw value in the family having control over its own product. In the mid-1950s Swift and other companies were proudly proclaiming to cattle feeders that more than 73 cents of the average sales dollar of beef went back to pay for livestock and other agricultural products. All Kenny could see was the 27 cents the packer was keeping for himself.

Warren was unimpressed and told Kenny to keep looking. Kenny's idea wasn't for them, he thought; we're expert cattle feeders, not beef packers. He believed the family should focus on what it did best and let others concern themselves with how to convert the animals to beef. Besides, the margin for packing operations was less than 2 percent, while margins for cattle feeders were more often in the 5 percent range.

Kenny kept pressing his case, though, and continued to emphasize to his father the drawbacks of shipping cattle long distances and the advantages of having more control over how those animals went to market. Another benefit was that the beef could age while in transit; beef doesn't age while it's part of the animal. It also would allow the company to ride out the highs and lows of the cattle cycle. When cattle prices were good, the feedlots would make money at the expense of the packing plant. But when cattle prices were low, the packing plant could make up the difference by showing a profit. In essence, they could become a "one company industry."

Finally, in 1959 Warren gave in and agreed the family could get into the packing business – at least in a limited way. Capitol Pack, run by Meyer and Dave Averch, would have to hold up its end of the arrangement and agree to help process and market the products. Monfort would still be considered primarily the cattle supplier for the plant. Construction on the plant began in the summer of 1959.

On May 16, 1960, Greeley-Capitol Pack, Inc. began operations. It was certainly well-situated, located just a mile south

Kenny hands a check for the first load of cattle at the new packing plant to Lee Dalton. At left is cattle buyer Bud Middaugh; at right is Lee Dalton's brother Arnold.

of the feedlots along the east side of business Highway 85, adjacent to the Cache La Poudre River and along the rail lines for additional convenience. It was a state-of-the-art plant. Comprising about 92,000 square feet, it cost about $2 million to build and was to have the capability of processing about 600 cattle and 240 lambs a day. Its weekly sales volume would be about $1 million.

While it was Capitol Pack's name on the building, it was really a Monfort operation, with Kenny Monfort leading the way. He helped hire most of the people who would work in the facility and worked beside them as they got the hang of how to slaughter and process the animals. It was slow going and few of them knew what they were supposed to be doing.

The investors in Capitol Pack also thought it was a good idea to process lambs, so lamb harvesting was also being included in the plant, starting in August 1960. It did make some sense, as lamb feeding in the region was significant and provided a huge supply of animals for the operation. The Greeley plant would become one of the largest lamb slaughter facilities in the country.

While the plant was well constructed, what was going on inside among its approximately 300 employees was a disorderly mess, at least initially. No animals were processed the first day, with the workers cleaning and getting used to the facilities. On May 17 only 16 cattle were officially slaughtered. Some put the number closer to 11.

Kenny discusses plant operations with Niles Campbell (left) and Wayne Tritt

For the first several months it was learn-as-you-go. In fact, this business was new to everybody in Greeley. The Monforts had hired a dozen experienced meat packers from Lincoln Packing in Lincoln, Nebraska, to help get them off the ground, then let it be known around town that the company was hiring. And it was paying good wages, better than almost any in a farming community like Greeley.

Bill Boekel was the fifth of 12 men hired – employee #00005 – and went to work in the coolers. Kenny and Boekel had been friends in school, Kenny one year ahead of him at Greeley High, and Kenny's wife Pat one year behind. Now 14 years out of high school, their wives were good friends and played bridge together.

Boekel had been working at the Post Office and wasn't happy. When the chance came to work with Kenny, he jumped at it, especially at the wages being offered.

The camaraderie was wonderful when the plant first opened. Because it was such a new experience, everyone helped everyone else and there were few petty arguments and jealousies. At the end of each plant shift, Kenny and key workers would meet in the office to discuss the highs and lows of the day, laughing and telling stories about the work and the challenges they were facing. It was without a doubt an extended family. Kenny was a perfect boss – relaxed, open to suggestions and fun to be around.

People enjoy having a good time at work, of course, but that isn't why they were there. As far as Kenny and some of his employees were concerned, money always had a way of complicating perfectly good working relationships.

Meat packing – or in today's vernacular "harvesting" – is a very nasty business by any standards or terminology. Even though far from the conditions described in Upton Sinclair's *The Jungle*, it is still a very difficult way to make a living. Men in rubber aprons stand in pools of blood, carrying huge blades and moving awkwardly from animal to animal. The heat and odor is oppressive. Cattle bellow from the ramp in the background.

Meanwhile, carcasses hanging from massive overhead hooks move at an uncompromising speed. Though built with safety in mind, complicated machinery makes moves that threaten to sever limbs – or worse. Standing along row after row of conveyor belts, hundreds of people carry impressively sharp knives or whirling saws, moving as fast as their muscles and joints will allow. The noise would allow little communication even if the workers had time to communicate.

Hundreds of animals an hour. Thousands and thousands of individual beef cuts. Eight hours a day. Viewed when at its best, it's a well-oiled machine; at its worst it's a three ring circus. It's slippery and messy, foul smelling and depressing. It's tiring and dangerous. Many adjectives can be used to describe the working conditions. Enjoyable and pleasant are not two of them. Still, it's exciting to learn something new and get a business running effectively. Everyone wanted to pull his weight.

It was a rocky start for the packing plant economically, though. Money was pouring into the operation and little was coming out. The Capitol Pack investors were getting nervous. In fact, they wanted out. Right away. After six months Kenny went to his dad and asked if he didn't really want to see the Monfort name on the front of the plant. He didn't.

Again, though, Kenny kept talking and Warren finally consented. He agreed to sign his share of the papers buying out the Averch interests in October 1960 and creating what would be a cattle feeding/packing operation controlled completely by the Monfort family. Success was by no means guaranteed, and Warren had his doubts. If the packing plant went under, it could pull the feedlots with it. After the papers were signed Warren looked at Kenny and with a smile told him, "At least I still have my teaching certificate. I don't know what you'll do."

The Capitol Pack people packed up and went home. Monfort Packing was born. The feedlot was still in control, though. It owned the Monfort Packing facility, with Monfort Packing Co.

Monfort Packing in the early 1960s

leasing it from the feedlots. Warren was primarily in charge of overseeing what took place in the feedlots, and Kenny – whose idea it was to get into this silly sideline – would be in charge of making the packing plant work.

It was touch-and-go for more than a year. The family would have to go to the bank and beg for additional capital to keep things afloat, and there were times when it wasn't known whether they would be able to make payroll the next week.

Thank heaven for Maurice Feldman.

Morrie Feldman was a salesman, and a good one. He was loud, profane, aggressive and sometimes abrasive, but he knew how to sell meat. Kenny had hired him out of New York City and put him in charge of beef sales for the company. It was one of the best moves Kenny made in the early months of the packing plant. With his contacts back East and his refusal to take no for an answer, Feldman was getting the job done. During those very early years he kept the doors of the packing plant open by making key sales.

Still, it was a difficult start and Kenny knew he would need the support of the people in the plant if he was going to make the packing element of the operation work.

Kenny came walking toward the north end of the plant, pant legs tucked into the tops of his cowboy boots. He looked beaten. He was wearing a flattop haircut, because that's what you wore in the early 1960s. He called the workers together. It was the first speech Jay Boeddeker, a plant worker at the time, could remember Kenny making.

Kenny climbed up into the cherry-picker basket, which raised him up so that he could look out over workers collected below. He wasn't looking forward to this, you could tell.

Kenny stammered and stumbled, telling the workers that the plant was going through some very tough times and might need to be shut down. It wasn't a smooth speech, but it was from the heart. Everyone was quiet.

While the workers expected the worst, they knew the Monfort family would do whatever they could to keep the plant open and save their jobs. They would just have to suck it up and get through it a day at a time.

Things were beginning to lighten during the second year, but barely. The plant was still in the red, and Kenny was doing some fast talking to calm the bankers and convince them to keep on board for just a little while longer. Funny thing, though; the workers never missed a paycheck. They might have been willing to do so if they had been asked, but they never were.

In 1962 the Amalgamated Meat Cutters and Butchers Workmen of North America (Local 641) approached Kenny and said it wanted to talk with his employees about unionizing. Kenny, a good Democrat, saw nothing wrong with it. (The union would later merge with the United Food and Commercial Workers Union.) Other packers were unionized, and the union, his employees and he would all be working toward the same goal: a successful company. Some of his executives tried to tell him it was a mistake to let the union in, but at the time it seemed a natural step for the company.

Kenny Monfort, 1963

And it was. The workers felt more confident and were beginning to get the hang of this packing business. The sales crew was securing new customers. Monfort Packing Company, in 1963, was making money. Kenny first knew he could be a success that year on the day the packing plant made enough profit to pay off its debt.

It was just the beginning of Monfort's meteoric rise, however. And it was very unprecedented. No one had taken this strange approach to beef production. Feeders and packers were just different animals, and most of the time didn't get along at all.

Cattle feeders hated packers because they paid too little for the animals, which obviously couldn't be stockpiled and sold when the markets got better. They also believed packers would manipulate production to get the animals at the lowest price possible.

Packers, meanwhile, thought feeders would raise animals for maximum weight gain and cared nothing for their quality and composition needs. They had razor thin margins and to keep their plants running they would sometimes need to take what they could get.

As the cattle feeder in the family, Warren fell in with the feeders, and Kenny often would take the packer side of the argument. (Kenny would later jokingly say his father became just like the other feeders: "He learned to hate me.") Kenny could see all sides of the arguments, however, and recognized that there needed to be some balance. He also firmly believed in the logic of what their company was trying to do.

Others thought packers had no right to be in the cattle feeding business, and feeders had no business processing their own animals. Bert Bandstra was a one-term Democratic Iowa congressman who introduced a bill in 1966 that, had it passed, would have prohibited packer feeding of livestock.

Many cattlemen thought that was a tremendous idea. They agreed with Bandstra that the cattle industry should not go the way of the poultry industry, which at the time was about 95 percent vertically integrated. "Experience has shown that vertical integration in any particular industry must be stopped in its early stages or it will not be stopped at all," Bandstra said. "Fortunately, insofar as the livestock industry is concerned, it is not too late."

The legislation made Kenny nervous. He considered their family to be feeder-packers, not packer-feeders. "It is rather obvious what HR-12115 would do to us," Ken Monfort told the House Agriculture Subcomittee in testimony Oct. 6, 1966. "It would force us to either sell our packing plant to someone else or to shut the plant down."

He also believed this kind of legislation set a bad precedent. If it had been in effect before 1960, the Monfort family couldn't have done what it did and the modernizations and positive changes in the packing industry would not have taken place. Packers may not have seen the need for improvements in refrigeration and fabrication, and the industry might not have been able to expand as it did.

He told the subcommittee that thanks to his firm's ability to start its own packing plant, "other packers have been forced to modernize and improve both their facilities and their buying techniques." Other feeders were now getting the idea and following their lead. "New packing plants have now opened in Fort Morgan and Sterling (Colorado), financed and operated by cattle feeders. Very simply, the trend in Colorado is not packer-feeding but, conversely, feeder-packing."

In 1966 only 60-70 percent of the production at the Monfort packing plant was supplied by the company's own feedlots, and that presented another issue for the government to consider. Because Monfort had been able to start processing, a new outlet had been created for other feeders in the area. That amounted to about 85,000 cattle yearly.

Kenny certainly understood why the legislation was being introduced – and if he was only in one business or the other, it would probably help him by limiting his competition. And he realized that cattle in Iowa weren't raised the same way they were in Colorado, with Iowa featuring many more small farmer-feeders and very few large feeding operations.

But Kenny believed a feeder or group of feeders should have the "freedom to improve their economic position by further processing of their production," he testified. "If I believe this, it then follows that I must believe that the packer should have the right to assure himself a supply of livestock of a proper quality by feeding some of them himself if necessary, as it is in many areas of our country."

The U.S. Department of Agriculture at the time was supporting the Bandstra effort. The agency suggested that if packers were allowed to own cattle it would reduce cattle prices for farmers. But Kenny disagreed and didn't think this argument had a leg to stand on.

"I am sure that a larger percentage of the cattle slaughtered in Colorado are packer owned than in any other large feeding state in the nation," Monfort testified. "I am even more sure that our live cattle market is higher, considering freight differentials, than any other live cattle market in the country."

If other packers owned cattle, they wouldn't want low prices either, he told the subcommittee. "Can any of you possibly believe that in our operation, where we have 10 times as much money invested in inventory of cattle in our feedlots as we have invested in our packing business, we are interested in low prices?" he asked. "We are interested in a higher market. A healthy market."

Kenny thought legislation that interfered with a marketing avenue for cattle feeders and told beef packers in what form it could acquire their supply was bad legislation. More than that, though, he believed it was a bad idea to allow government to tell you how to run your business. That philosophy would get even stronger as his business got bigger and the government got more involved.

Among the other controversies in the mid-1960s was beef imports. Many in the industry hated them, but Kenny didn't think they were that harmful – especially if the industry wanted to increase its exports. "I honestly believe that the net effect of imports and exports on the cattle industry is a plus," he said. He noted that the export of hides alone brought $4 more per animal, and in an industry with such small margins that was significant. "I can't believe that beef imports have hurt us that much."

In 1966 there were other advances in the beef industry Monfort was helping pioneer. For instance, shipping beef and lamb carcasses had been the tradition in the industry, but like shipping cattle it had its drawbacks. There was tremendous inefficiency, for one thing, as hanging carcasses, while somewhat uniform, were not shaped in such a way that they fit well in truck trailers.

The hanging carcasses were sides of beef, each cut into a forequarter and hindquarter weighing about 150 to 175 pounds. These quarters that had to be manually carried into the refrigerated trailers and hung on hooks. When shipped, they were often called swinging beef because that's exactly what the carcasses would do on their way down the road: swing. It was not good for the meat and increased product losses at the other end.

The plants were also shipping lots of bone and fat that couldn't be used by the customers purchasing it. If kept at the packing plant, though, these "by-products" could be collected to be sold and transformed into useful products instead of being thrown away. Finally, the customers had to buy an entire carcass whether that's what they wanted or not. It was then up to them how to best market some beef items that may not sell well in their areas, but might have sold well in others.

As a result, Monfort became one of the key proponents of cutting up, or fabricating, at the site of slaughter and selling the beef in boxes. They began the process in 1964 with a new freezer and fabrication facility that increased the workforce to 425. In 1966 they spent $2.25 million on an 88,000-square-foot addition, nearly as large as the original plant, to further fabricate the carcasses into primal and subprimal cuts and ship the meat. By dividing the carcasses into the primal cuts – chuck, loin, round, rib, plate, brisket and flank – the company decided it could better allocate its production.

While this didn't completely do away with carcass shipping, it had many advantages. About 85 percent of their product was going to the East Coast and the change allowed the company to sell products where they were needed or wanted and to keep about 30 percent of the product in Greeley for more efficient processing.

Monfort even came up with a way to more effectively package and ship the smaller cuts in a process they called MOPAC. MOPAC was a program designed to supply different retailers with the primal cuts of beef they wanted in boxed form. The company would give each box an application of carbon dioxide, or "CO_2 snow," which was odorless and colorless but chilled the product to 30 degrees both internally and externally and inhibited bacteria growth. Now in addition to cooled trailers they had cooled boxes, too.

The process increased shelf life and maintained the bloom in the meat, and saved labor at the store or warehouse. Other packing companies had moved more to a vacuum packaged product, but Monfort believed their process eliminated liquid loss to maintain product weights. Later, because of cost advantages, the company would join others in selling primarily vacuum packaged beef.

One of the reasons fabricating at the plant of origin didn't do away with carcass beef involved labor issues in the East. Supermarket beef cutters were unionized and wanted to keep working, so they had to be kept busy. They didn't want the jobs they were doing to be done at the plants, no matter how efficient and logical it sounded.

These unions were powerful and went to great lengths to protect their workers. In 1957, for instance, the Amalgamated Meat Cutters and Butcher Workmen union declared that fresh meat would only be sold between 9 a.m. and 6 p.m. Monday through Saturday. Under a threat of a strike, the union forced about 9,000 retailers to comply with this edict. Jewel Tea Company, one of the chains affected, sued for restraint of trade and the case went all the way to the Supreme Court. It ruled in 1964 that it was a matter that belonged in negotiations, not in the courts. Modernization and efficiency weren't high priority for the unions; if it meant the unemployment line for their workers, it was apparently a bad idea.

As the packing plant began expanding and making improvements, the company was becoming even more of a presence in the Greeley community. The company paid the city's best hourly wages in 1964: $3.21 an hour for luggers (those who carried carcass sections) and $3.89 for slaughter floor workers. The annual impact on the Greeley-area economy was now about $85 million.

Feeding Improvements

At the same time, the company was improving its effectiveness in its feeding operations. In June of 1966 Monfort spent about $750,000 on a system at their feedlot that would steam and then roll shelled corn into moist, palatable flakes. The plant featured 16 steam chests, with flakers powered by four 10-ton, 700 horsepower Caterpillar engines that supplied the 1,800 kilowatts of energy needed for the operation.

It was an elaborate and revolutionary idea. Very few feedlots were using this technique, developed by John Matsushima at Colorado State University, and none on this scale. But the Monforts believed the financial risk was worth the potential feed gain reward.

The corn was heated to about 250°F for approximately 18 minutes, then sent through rollers that would flatten the kernels. About 6 percent moisture was added by the steam, and the starches and sugar molecules were fractured, making the corn more digestible to the cattle.

Through testing that had started in about 1964 the Monforts had found the cattle would gain weight 10 percent faster with this method of feed treatment. The company liked to boast that at the peak of its feedlots in the 1970s, it would use about 1.3 billion pounds of corn a year, which at the time was four times as much as Kellogg used for its cornflakes.

In 1966 the feedlot held about 75,000 head of cattle on pens that spanned 320 acres. They were marketing about 150,000 head a year to Monfort Packing, which at the time was about 60 percent of the plant's capacity of 250,000 head a year. Most of the animals were Hereford or Angus crosses, purchased at about 750 pounds and fattened for 140 days until they reached 1,200 pounds.

Each of the pens could hold about 400 head of cattle. Fed twice a day via 5-6,000 pound feed trucks, the animals would gain about 2.6 pounds a day on the flaked corn ration that was supplemented with corn ensilage and alfalfa, as well as dried sugar beet pulp, a by-product from the nearby sugar factories.

Two years later the family would invest another $400,000 to expand on the other end of the production chain. It established the Monfort Provision Co., a 17,000-square-foot operation on 20th Street and Highway 85 Bypass in Greeley. Its employees cut larger cuts sent from the packing plant into steaks and roasts for the hotel, restaurant and institution (HRI) trade, especially in Wyoming, northern Colorado and western Nebraska.

The Monforts had been conducting similar work since 1962 on a much smaller scale at their Poudre Provision Co., located at 7th Street and 11th Avenue in Greeley. But this new facility gave the Monfort products a much-needed identity and brand name in the HRI trade, which required an even higher degree of consistency and quality.

The company was also increasing its international exposure. Through its Monfort International division, Monfort in 1969 reached a five-year agreement to provide technical assistance in the construction of a new meat packing plant and modernization of current facilities for one of the largest food processing companies in Argentina. Kenny believed this was more than just a business deal; it was an act of global kindness because many people in South America were living on unhealthy diets. By improving food processing in Argentina people in another country would eat better, he reasoned.

In 1971 the company also participated in a pilot program that involved feeding 3,000 cattle in the Republic of Ireland. The 6-month venture, with partners from Ireland and Continental Europe, was unlike anything conducted in Greeley, with different feeds and the cattle fed under roof. The cattle from the project were marketed in the U.K. and in other European countries.

Monfort of Colorado was hired for this because of the reputation it had developed in both its feeding and packing operations. Meat producers from around the world were impressed with the history the family had established in the feeding business. And the efficiency at the Greeley packing plant was state-of-the-art. The entire process from slaughter to cooling took only 28 minutes for cattle, and even less time for lambs.

In 1968 tragedy struck the packing plant when a mentally disturbed employee in the shipping department, George "Rosie" Osborne Jr., asked the plant's personnel manager, Harold Adcock, to his home and subsequently stabbed him to death. Adcock had been a fellow Democratic legislator with Kenny, and had been an industrial arts, journalism and social sciences teacher at Greeley High School when Kenny was going to school there.

Osborne had a connection to Kenny, too. His father, George Sr., had worked for Kenny. Adcock had felt a tremendous responsibility to Rosie, a large man who was troubled by several personal issues, and thought he could help him. It cost him his life, and Kenny and many others in the company were devastated.

By early 1969 the packing plant had increased its fabrication capabilities to the point it could bone its entire production of loins and rounds from a weekly cattle slaughter of between 6,000 and 7,200 head. Its capabilities in the lamb department had increased, too. The company was now able to break and bone more than half of the daily slaughter of about 3,000 lambs. Both Monfort beef and lamb were gaining greater acceptance in the marketplace.

The Monfort family was proving that their ideas about beef packing made sense. They had invested about $6.5 million in plant facilities during the plant's first 10 years, and the company looked forward to making about $13 a head in 1969. The Monforts were now a leader of the pack, rather than a follower.

> "After World War II, when the big packers (Swift, Armour, Wilson) should have modernized, they didn't. When they should have changed locations, they didn't. They continued operating high-cost plants in areas where cattle weren't – which allowed new people into the business. They chose to spend their money diversifying – which again allowed us into the business. We've proved money can be made in modern plants, operated well, in the right locations."
>
> Ken Monfort Interview
> *Business Week* Magazine
> Aug. 30, 1969

In October 1969 Monfort made what would turn out to be a significant acquisition to broaden the company's marketing capabilities. The company merged with Mapelli Bros. Co. of Denver, which was a key purveyor and distributor of quality meats. The company had 125 employees and had been supplying Monfort beef and lamb to customers across the country for years. As Kenny would tell the *Denver Post* that year, adding the Mapelli operation "is certain to play a major role in our goal of distributing Colorado beef to all of America." One of the principals in that company, Roland L. "Sonny" Mapelli, would eventually become chairman of Monfort of Colorado and Kenny's closest friend and confidant.

A first-ever night shift at Monfort Packing was being contemplated, and plans were put in place in 1969 to start it at the beginning of 1970. Plans for a second feedlot north of Gilcrest, about six miles southwest of Greeley, were already in the works. Obviously, the company wanted to get even bigger.

> It is apparent that if we are to compete we must be able to continue our industry leadership and growth. It appears that this will be impossible UNLESS we broaden our source of funds. Hence, we are exploring and negotiating the possibility of becoming a publicly-held company. If this materializes, as I believe it will, new money will be raised by selling stock to the public.
>
> Ken Monfort
> Letter to Employees
> Company Newsletter
> April, 1969

The company was a family corporation at the time, and it was thought $12 million or more could be raised if shares were sold to people outside of the family. The "new" company would be called Monfort of Colorado, Inc., and Kenny told his employees that the present owners – mostly family, but a few managers – would continue to own about 75 percent of the stock.

He wrote that he hoped that employees, customers, cattle and lamb producers and neighbors in the community would take the opportunity to invest in the company – if they wanted. He knew it was a tough business and didn't want to mislead investors into believing this would be anything like a get-rich-quick scheme.

The money raised from the public sale of stock would be used in three areas: Increasing feeding capacity (the Gilcrest lot), an increase in slaughter capacity (preferably at the Greeley plant) and construction of a consumer products facility near Lucerne, just north of the original feedlots. That facility was never built. He told his employees that the family had mixed emotions about this approach, but it was better than being bought out by a conglomerate.

While the emotions might have been mixed, the only disagreement going on behind the scenes about selling public shares was between Kenny and his father. Warren Monfort was against the strategy.

Mr. Monfort had an idea to put a stop to talks of going public. He would give Kenny a raise. He called Larry Knee, the comptroller for the feedlots, and Burke Hurt, comptroller for the packing plant, together for a meeting. Each paid Kenny a salary out of their side of the business. Added together the pay totaled no more than what a good teacher today makes.

He would have none of Kenny's big ideas, Warren told Hurt and Knee. It was a family business and should stay a family business. Instead, he wanted each to increase Ken's salary by a specific amount. And they did just that – or tried to.

Because Kenny didn't have much use for checks, his pay was automatically deposited. Knee never mentioned the pay increase from the feedlots to Kenny and if he noticed, Kenny never mentioned it to Knee. But Hurt was a character and couldn't resist a little ribbing.

He called Kenny into a private room at the plant and said, Kenny, you're doing such a fine job I've decided to give you a raise. And he told him what it was. Like hell you are, Kenny fired back, and stalked out of the room. Kenny Monfort could take a joke as well as anyone, but that isn't the way you talk to him – especially about money. He did not accept the raise.

Warren did not prevail in keeping the company private. Eventually Kenny convinced him that to expand the way they wanted to, they would need outside money. When the decision finally was made, Warren was solidly in Kenny's corner.

There were many issues to be considered as the price of the stock was established. One of those was the company's responsibility to employees, and Kenny wasn't about to compromise the relationship that had been built with the workers. A profit sharing plan that had been started at the feedlots and in which packing plant workers also participated was off limits, Kenny said. Even if the price of the stock was a couple of dollars cheaper, he said, the profit sharing plan was the right thing to do. "It isn't only the stockholders who should profit from our success," he wrote to employees, "it's those who worked hard for a year to provide that success.

"And, as we soon become a public company, help me remember that although earnings are important and the 'action' of our stock is critical – it is people that make it possible, it is people that are important," he wrote.

The company went public with the sale of 1 million shares on Jan. 22, 1970, with a stock price of $16 per share. No dividends were expected to be paid; all of the money made would be retained to help expand the business.

Of the $16 million raised, the company would receive about $12 million; of the rest about $3 million would be going to directors of the family corporation. Warren and Edith Monfort would sell about $1.7 million of their shares in the company, but would remain the largest shareholders with nearly a million shares. Their son would sell about $625,000 of stock, but still own about the same number of shares as his parents.

The family's shares were to be turned in so the public sale could take place. Warren Monfort, who owned millions of shares worth about 25 percent of the business, didn't necessarily agree with the public offering, but he wasn't going to stand in its way.

But when it came time to hand it over to Holland and Hart, the company's law firm, the certificates were nowhere to be found. This was a legal and corporate problem. While the shares weren't legal tender or negotiable instruments, if they fell into the hands of someone who claimed ownership and decided to press it, serious legal costs could be incurred.

Highly concerned about the potential consequences, the lawyers got all of the principals together to re-enact the original distribution of the certificates and see if it could jog some memories.

When you were given the certificates, what did you do with them? the lawyers asked Warren. Well, I put them in my blue suit, he replied.

So Hank Brown was dispatched to the Monfort house to look in the blue suit. The job was harder than he thought. On opening the closet there were about 15 nearly identical blue suits. Though a careful search was done of each one, no certificates were found.

Finally, the lawyers decided to add a note in the prospectus saying the family was indemnifying the company from any problems that arose if the shares ever turned up in the wrong hands, and placed an equivalent number of shares in escrow.

The mystery still wouldn't go away, however. Kenny went to the feedlots and discreetly told a select group of his employees to find those certificates. I don't think my father would have thrown them away, he said, but we need to turn over every stone. Do what you have to.

Where do you start? After looking in the usual places, about eight or nine of them headed over to the Monfort dump, which was about a mile from the feedlots. There they spent an afternoon looking for stock certificates. Still no luck.

After Warren died the case of the missing certificates was solved when the dining room bureau was taken from the house. When the silverware drawer was removed, underneath were the certificates, placed with care for safe-keeping by Warren or Edith Monfort.

Altogether, the Monfort family still controlled 77 percent of the stock in the company, so it remained in a position to control the policies of the company even after the stock sale. The family consisted of Warren and Edith, Kenny and his four children and Margery Monfort Wilson and her husband, Lloyd Wilson, and their child.

The company that was going public looked nothing like the operation Warren Monfort had started some 40 years earlier. In 1970 the company was huge, at least by Greeley standards. It included one feedlot north of town with another on the way to the south, and a beef and lamb packing plant that processed 350,000 head of cattle and 600,000 head of lambs a year. It had just acquired Mapelli Brothers, a purveyor operation that supplied a full-line of meat products to the HRI trade as well as to supermarkets. It also had a grain elevator business in Cozad, Nebraska, operated by Kenny's brother-in-law, Lloyd Wilson, and sister Margery, as well as one in Goodland, Kansas.

Monfort of Colorado had signed a pact with Mapelli-Linder-Sigman Co. of Denver to be the Rocky Mountain area distributor for Monfort, limited to the HRI trade. The company thought the move would "eliminate many of the costly inefficiencies that are built into the old, haphazard methods of beef distribution."

Sales at the packing plant eclipsed $150 million in 1969. Of that, beef sales were equal to $130 million, 93 percent of which was beef and 7 percent was beef by-products. Lamb and lamb by-product sales were about $22 million.

The company had grown from just a handful of helpers to a staff of nearly 1,200, with about 200 employed at the feedlots and 800 at the packing plant. The Denver Mapelli Brothers operation had a staff of 125.

The feedlots north of Greeley, meanwhile, had grown from a few pens on 80 acres to nearly 280 pens on 480 acres, with the capability of feeding 115,000 cattle at one time and 275,000 in a year. Its two grain elevators could hold almost 1.5 million bushels. It included a grain flaking mill, a veterinary hospital, an electronic feeding ration system, a machine shop and garages, five service buildings, six residences and general office quarters.

The company also owned about 2,348 acres of irrigated land, of which about 1,517 were about six miles south of Greeley on what would become the Gilcrest feedlot. That lot would have its own elevator, grain flaker mills, silage storage facilities, scales and equipment.

Equipment used in cattle feeding was extensive. It included about 50 feed trucks, 11 hay and corn cutting machines, 13 diesel loaders and bulldozers, 10 semi-trailer trucks for hauling cattle and grain, and about 44 other vehicles. It leased, or was in the process of leasing, 90 railroad hopper cars for bringing grain to the feedlots.

Unions had also settled nicely into several aspects of the operation. The packing plant had been unionized since 1962, and the Portion Foods employees were represented by the same union. The maintenance and engineers at the plant had their own union. Also unionized were employees at the Mapelli Brothers subsidiary in Denver. The prospectus stated the company "considers its relations with employees to be good."

Also according to the company prospectus, the company owed more than $23.4 million in short-term and long-term notes when it went public, which was not at all unusual. In fact, the bulk of the short-term notes were secured by cattle in the feedlot. Cattle were purchased and that required money; beef from those cattle was sold and that allowed the loans to be paid back.

Many Colorado cattle feeders at the time operated on the same principle. In 1970 there were 120 feedlots in Colorado that were 1,000 head or larger, accounting for about 82 percent of the fed cattle marketed in the state. Banks financed about 41 percent of all feeder cattle in Colorado, with the First National Bank of Denver alone having almost $30 million in livestock loans. Throughout the company's history Warren Monfort had not been bashful about taking out loans in both expansion and ongoing feedlot operations.

The prospectus indicated the company had almost doubled its sales in just four years, from $86 million in 1965 to nearly $162 million in 1969. Its net income had gone from $1.5 million to $4.3 million. Now with expanded feedlots, packing capacity and the added marketing and provision capabilities of the Mapelli Brothers operation, many people were seeing a gold mine.

Kenny was quick to point out that cattle feeding and meat packing were very volatile and unpredictable businesses. While he encouraged people to become part of the team, he didn't make any promises or try to raise any hopes. This is an uncertain business, folks, and you're in it at your own risk.

Feeding Double

The money from the sale of stock, in addition to other loans and funds from future sales, would be used for major expansion of the company. Although there would be an increase in size at the packing plant and expected construction of a consumer products facility, the biggest expansion expense was the purchase and stocking of the Gilcrest feedlot. It was estimated that it would cost $4 million to build it and another $28 million to fill it with cattle. The Gilcrest lot wasn't contingent on the stock sale, though, as its construction had already begun.

The lot was not without its opponents. Eleven local homeowners formed a group called Operation Fresh Air which sought to encourage county commissioners to deny the company's petition to establish the feedlot. Monfort had announced the construction May 1, 1969, and immediately began to feel the heat from these homeowners, who were concerned their property values might go down as a result of their proximity to a feedlot.

Their fears were not unjustified and Kenny knew it. The Monfort family had already taken tremendous grief about the smell of their lots north of Greeley, and had tried to find a location for expansion that was as "neighborly" as possible. In a Sept. 6, 1965, speech to the Greeley Lions Club Kenny said he recognized business in town was terrible, and the feedlot odor may be one component of that.

"I realize there is a problem with feedlot odor in Greeley. I pledge all within our power to solve the problem," he said. The four-point program he promised included continued good housekeeping, spraying with "odor control" chemicals, enactment of a state sanitation law to be sure feedlots do what they promise, and funding a comprehensive study at Colorado State University to see what else could be done about it.

Starting a new feedlot, however, opened up a different can of worms. And, unfortunately for the company, there was a subdivision already started in the area near the spot selected for the Gilcrest lot called Dos Rios, which featured eight homes that had been constructed and were worth between $75,000 and $85,000. These were well-appointed homes. The median house price in Colorado at the time was $17,300. There were plans in the subdivision for about 80 homes.

Kenny said he was open to suggestions for other sites and met with the group to try to find some common ground. It didn't look promising, however. The company withdrew its petition for expansion on May 27.

This led to a tremendous backlash against the homeowners and developer. A petition signed by 6,000 people was delivered to the company asking that they reconsider their decision to withdraw. A two-page ad in the *Greeley Tribune* on June 9 featured the signatures of about a thousand of those supporters. Full-page ads in the *Tribune*, sponsored by labor unions, the Weld County Builders Association and the Colorado Cattle Feeders Association and others, asked that the expansion project go forward. Letters to the editors from local farmers and others blasted the position of the homeowners and encouraged the company to go ahead with its plans.

"Let's tell the Monforts how thankful we are and urge them to reconsider their decision," the ads said. Proponents of the new feedlot pointed out that the Eaton school district north of Greeley was able to afford excellent facilities, including a new swimming pool, as a result of having Monfort in the neighborhood paying taxes.

Kenny said that the decision to withdraw the request wasn't meant as a ploy to drum up support for its plans, but on seeing the tremendous torrent of defense for the company's position in the community, they changed their course again.

"We have been extremely gratified at the overwhelming response to our announcement two weeks ago of our expansion plans in the Greeley area," Kenny wrote. "Such an outpouring has caused us to once again reconsider our decision." The company announced that it would go forward, starting with a smaller 50,000 head feedlot at the Gilcrest location, a 50 percent increase at the packing plant featuring a night shift and the expansion of the portion foods plant.

As a concession to the Dos Rios owners the company agreed to buy the houses and land at the appraised value prior to the construction of the lot, at the option of the landowners, at any time prior to July 1, 1972. It also made similar offers to six others who owned homes or undeveloped lots in the same area. Had the offers been accepted, it would have cost the company more than $750,000. In July 1969 the Weld County Board unanimously approved the Monfort expansion plans.

School districts were not known for reducing their mill levies, but both Eaton and Gilcrest were able to do so thanks to the cattle "paying taxes" at the Monfort feedlots. In fact, the company paid $241,749 in taxes to the Eaton School District in 1971, which was 31 percent of what the district received. Overall, the company paid about $577,000 in county real estate and personal property tax for the year.

Cattle were first shipped to Gilcrest on May 1, 1970. A 50-foot wide greenbelt was planted around the entire circumference of the lot to help lower the environmental impact on surrounding countryside. By Sept. 1, 1970, the lot had reached 100,000 in population, with 238 pens that held an average of 450 head per pen.

With the addition of the Gilcrest lot, the company had essentially doubled its production of cattle for the Monfort Packing plant, allowing a night shift to be added on Sept. 14, 1970. When the night shift hit top speed the total production of the plant was 2,200 head per day, or more than 11,000 per week. This increased plant employment by 175 people.

It doubled all other aspects of the feedlot operation, as well. For instance, the company now fed about 1,800 tons of flaked corn daily to the animals in the Greeley and Gilcrest lots. That equated to about 1.3 billion pounds of corn – 25 million bushels – a year.

Another feed used at the lots was corn ensilage, or corn plants that had been chopped, stalks-and-all, and stored in huge pits. Harvesting this feed was a yearly ritual enjoyed by many local students and teachers looking for some extra money, as the process took about three weeks, usually beginning in late August and going for 24 hours a day, seven days a week. Everyone worked 12 hour shifts every day until the job was completed, allowing workers to make decent money in a short amount of time – and with limited amounts of sleep, which they apparently would make up once they got back to classes.

Warren Monfort, circa 1971

In 1974 alone nearly 15,000 acres were harvested for this feed, producing about 335,000 tons of silage. About $5 million was paid to farmers for their crops that year.

Warren's health had been declining, and he had not been as active while the company was going public. He would retire as chairman of Monfort of Colorado in 1971, after 41 years of service to the cattle feeding industry.

When The Boss retired at age 78, annual company sales were $218 million with a payroll of $20 million. The quiet, unassuming and modest man had obviously set in motion a design for a family dynasty. The cattle industry was losing the services of a tremendous pioneer, and the year before it had recognized his contributions by naming him International Cattleman of the Year at the International Cattlemen's Exposition in Las Vegas, Nevada.

Expanding Nationally

Other elements of the company also were quickly expanding. By March of 1971 there were six distributing branches in the Western U.S. under the new Monfort Food Distributing Company, which was a successor to the Mapelli Brothers Provision Co. subsidiary. The distributing company would initially have its headquarters at the Mapelli Brothers Denver office, which would become the Monfort Distributing Company Denver branch.

The company was more and more focusing on the marketing aspects of beef production, and broadening its leadership at the same time. In addition to its food distributing growth, the Monfort Portion Foods plant was beginning to experiment with products that had more of a consumer focus. As far back as 1965 Kenny had predicted a time when the company would produce products in consumer-type packages. And while Monfort would try this through the years, it would have mixed success. It was this lack of success and the costs to change it that would be partially responsible for the company's eventual sale.

Monfort Distributing was under the direction of Sonny Mapelli, who was named chairman of Monfort of Colorado in February 1972. (He had been elected vice chairman in 1971.) By March of 1972 another four distributing branches had been added, and they added another eight in 1975 with the acquisition of Menu Maker Food Service Co. The company now operated 18 branches from Honolulu, Hawaii, to Miami, Florida.

Kenny had noted in press releases and announcements that the Mapelli appointment emphasized the transition from a completely family-operated business to a public corporation. In 1971 Monfort had also added two board members from outside the family and company to further accomplish the transition. Robert F. Six, the chief executive officer of Continental Airlines, and William C. McClearn, a prominent Denver attorney, expanded the board from seven to nine members. At the same time, Kenny was looking beyond the company and outside of Greeley for people he could hire who could help the company take the next step in the corporate world. But Kenny's best friend and confidant would still play the biggest role.

A New Team

As his father was fading from the picture, Kenny was turning to another man for advice and opinions. Sonny Mapelli was born

Roland L. Mapelli in Denver on June 10, 1922. He had been nicknamed Sonny at the age of 2, when as a scheme to keep him from throwing his breakfast spoon his father Herman started singing him the song *"Sonny Boy,"* made famous by Al Jolson. The name seemed to fit so he kept it the rest of his life.

Growing up, Sonny had varied interests. An altar boy at St. Dominic Church, he played both basketball and football as a student at Regis High School. In the late 1930s he found an interest in cars and ended up racing both motorcycles and midget autos. He also won several golf tournaments dating back to the early 1960s, finally scoring a hole in one at Thunderbird Country Club in 1993 at age 70.

Bowling brought out one of his true athletic talents, however. In 1942 he came within a strike of the World's Doubles Championship, scoring an average of 226. His doubles score of 1,326 with partner Wally Mowson still stands as a Colorado record. In one 1942 bowling tournament he took 11th place out of 30,000 bowlers. And in 1953 he was in *"Ripley's Believe It or Not,"* believe it or not, for having scored 12 strikes in one game and not getting a score of 300. (He fouled on the first ball in the fifth frame.)

He was married on April 5, 1942. He had met Neoma Robinson, who went by Nomie, at a Drive-in at 38th and Federal in Denver where she worked as a carhop. They honeymooned in Cheyenne, Wyoming – at a bowling tournament. Because he was classified 1A for the military and was in line to be drafted, Sonny decided to enlist to help decide his own fate. He joined the U.S. Army Air Corps in August 1942, and spent four years in active service, many of them in England, France, Germany and Italy. He served as a staff sergeant and personal equipment officer. Sonny stayed in the Reserves until 1955, retiring as a 2nd Lieutenant.

Sonny got into the meat business the old fashioned way: He was born to it. Herman and his brother had started the family general grocery and butcher business in 1906 at 15th and Court Place in downtown Denver. They sold that original property to Bill Zechendorf, who would build a Hilton Hotel on the site. They moved the business to 1624 Market Street, where they would operate until selling to Monfort of Colorado in 1969.

When Sonny got back from World War II the newspapers were full of the news: The new Hilton was going go up on the site now occupied by the Mapelli Brothers Market. That's funny, Herman said, no one has talked to us about it. Sonny, why don't you go see what's up? So Sonny went to the real estate agent to see why no offer had been made on their property. The agent hit the roof. That's it! Your family is the toughest to do business with I've ever seen! Here's our final offer. And I mean final!

It seems that when the agent visited the shop he always came in the door nearest the produce department, managed by youngest brother Mario. Mario knew that if the property sold he wasn't needed, so when asked about the store he told the agent the property wasn't for sale. Get out!

The final offer was about twice what they had expected.

Sonny had gotten interested in politics in 1953 right after he took time off from his family operation to run the Capri Restaurant, near Broadway and Colfax. Politicians took their breaks there, and he became interested after several encouraged him to get involved. With his charm and good looks, he was a natural for public office.

Sonny served on the Denver City Council from 1955-1959, making a name for himself trying to stop I-70 from going through Rocky Mountain National Park and unsuccessfully attempting to keep Denver from selling the Denver Poor Farm.

He made an unsuccessful run for Denver mayor in 1959 with the slogan "Progress without Extravagance," losing by an average of only 10 votes per precinct in a nasty, innuendo-filled campaign. The *Denver Post* had mocked Sonny's platform to economize in city government and suggested some of his associations were shady.

He went on to serve two years in the Colorado House of Representatives, then four years in the Colorado Senate, running as a team with future governor Roy Romer, whom Kenny had known in college. It was while in the legislature that Sonny got to know the man with whom he'd spend the rest of his business career.

Sonny always rolled with the famous and prominent, both in this country and in others. In 1958 he travelled to Cuba to meet with Ruben Fulgencio Batista, just a week before Batista resigned and fled that country. In 1960 he introduced John F. Kennedy at a breakfast campaign stop in Denver. Among the people Sonny had met and associated with included politicians such as Harry Truman, Dwight Eisenhower and Gerald Ford, actors and celebrities Telly Savalas and Bob Hope, sports stars Jack Dempsey and Arnold Palmer, and Conrad Hilton. But he had never met anyone like Kenny.

Another Brother

The 1969 acquisition of the Mapelli Brothers firm brought other changes to Monfort of Colorado. Sonny Mapelli's older brother, Eugene M., was the other fixture who came over in the purchase. He was made a Monfort vice president and a member of the firm's board of directors, and was named to spearhead marketing to national accounts within the HRI trade in 1971. He had been directing the operation of the Monfort Portion Foods plant in Greeley, but found that working in a growing corporation wasn't what he wanted to do with his life. Eventually he would move to Las Vegas, purchasing the Monfort Food Distribution branch there.

Not only was Monfort becoming a major player and one of the most vertically integrated companies in the meat industry, it was becoming better known among companies in the West. For 1971 it was ranked 55th among Western corporations based on sales by *California Business*, a weekly business and financial publication, ranking ahead of such companies as Samsonite, Walt Disney Productions and Max Factor. It had been ranked 66th in the same listing the year before.

The company was also polishing its reputation for quality. In 1972, 31 years after Kenny had won a grand champion award at the National Western Stock Show, the company he now led would win both the Grand and Reserve Grand Champion awards for the fat beef steer carcass contest at that same event.

Two carloads of 15 steers each had been selected from the regular inventory at Monfort's feedlots. These steers were scheduled for processing the next day and had been chosen only three days before the show, so they were fed in the same manner as all the other cattle in the lots. It was the first time Monfort of Colorado cattle had been entered in the carcass show.

Another area expanding for Monfort in the 1970s was computers, with a Data Processing Division created in 1973. Computers were new to every company, and Monfort was large enough that they needed them – but Kenny remained unimpressed and fairly skeptical of their true value. Most of the numbers Kenny needed were in his head, he believed, and he could generate the other ones he needed when he needed them. Furthermore, computers just cost too much.

When it was created, though, the Data Processing Division had nine employees in Greeley and 14 more in the distributing branches. It consisted of an IBM System 3 at the central computer complex, and an IBM System 7 computer at the packing plant. The computers' duties included inventory, payroll and personnel data, accounts receivable, accounts payable, general ledger, financial statements and sales analysis. Today a laptop computer could probably conduct the calculations those systems supplied, but the computers in their isolated and temperature-controlled rooms were considered state-of-the-art at the time.

Another expansion at the packing plant in 1973 added more production, shipping and storage facilities as well as office space. The cost of the expansion was $2.5 million. Meanwhile, a major change for the Feedlot Division would occur in 1974, when the original North feedlots closed in favor of new pens further from Greeley to the east (see Chapter 9).

In 1973 about 40 percent of the company's meat was going to the HRI trade, about a quarter of that sold by the company's own distributing branches. Only about 4 percent of the packing plant's output was actually being processed by the company's own portion foods plant, but it was starting to become profitable and that share was expected to increase. There were 18 distributing branches by the end of the year.

The packing plant went through another expansion in 1975, a $12 million effort that included a new 7,920 square foot ground beef facility that could produce 325,000 pounds of ground beef a day; a slaughter floor modification that allowed an increase in the chain speed to 300 head per hour – an industry first; increased rendering capabilities with remodeled tallow storage tanks, installation of continuous cookers and the addition of new tallow car loading and washing facilities; improvements in the fabrication facilities and equipment, with five boning lines now able to produce 390,000 pounds of vacuum packaged beef product and 370,000 pounds of MOPAC product a day; and a new computerized, 1 million cubic feet holding freezer that could hold more than 5 million pounds of frozen patties, portion products and specialty items at -20 degrees F.

Both external and internal factors had influenced the growth of Monfort of Colorado. The company had weathered a packing plant strike in 1970, a disastrous cattle market in the early 1970s, a price freeze and consumer boycotts, high energy and grain prices, feeding supplement bans, extreme competitive pressures and other calamities, but seemed poised to become even bigger and better in the decade to come. While he had little or no control over many of these factors, Kenny was deeply affected by, and knowledgeable about, all of them. Still, he couldn't possibly have seen the storm clouds on the horizon.

Chapter 5

The Politics

While getting a packing plant up and running and helping to expand a feedlot, Kenny decided to try his hand at politics. He had very strongly held points of view when it came to many issues that affected the public and society, and believed being part of the political machine was where those views could best be expressed.

Kyle was in the sixth grade and had never seen or heard her father cry. As she walked by her parents' bedroom on Kenny's 35th birthday, she did. He was sitting in the room holding a musical figurine of John Kennedy that had been given to him by his wife Pat. When wound, the figurine, featuring Kennedy sitting in a rocking chair, would play the musical tune "Happy Days are Here Again." It seemed a particularly inappropriate song on this day. Like many other Americans, Kenny cried for a life cut way too short. JFK had been one of his heroes. November 22 would never again hold quite the same celebratory air for Kenny as the date had in the past.

Later in his life Kenny would admit that as he got older and learned some things about John Kennedy, "maybe he didn't deserve the hero category he was in, in my mind." He remained a hero to him, though, mainly because Kenny believed in issues championed by Kennedy that were coming to life in the 1960s. Especially significant to him was civil rights and the opportunities being denied to some Americans by discrimination and antiquated laws. Many of his core beliefs in this area were instilled by his parents, who were offended by what they saw as immoral and disrespectful conduct by some of their fellow citizens. They believed that all people should be treated equally.

As a good capitalist Kenny also didn't understand why some workers would be valued higher than others just because of the color of their skin or their heritage. Everyone deserved the same opportunities to make a living, and that living should be based only on what they could produce.

The West wasn't immune to racial issues – nor was Greeley. It was the sugar beet industry at the turn of the century and the subsequent influx of "stoop" laborers that created a rift in the community and caused many hard feelings. These laborers were often "illiterate" immigrants from Russia, Mexico and Japan, brought in to work in the fields and factories. They took on permanent residency and changed the complexion of the area forever.

The established citizens worked hard to rid "their" community of "undesirables," of course, and what those undesirables apparently brought with them. In 1918 a "Destruction Party" was held at Greeley City Hall to pour confiscated bootleg liquor into the gutter. And in the 1920s another element that would gain national notoriety became prominent in Greeley and the surrounding region.

The Ku Klux Klan found open arms among many in the area. Membership in the KKK at the time was between 750 and 1,000, and many of the city's employees were either members or sympathizers of the Klan, which purchased 18 acres on what was then the southwest side of town. Rallies, parades and cross-burnings were a regular occurrence.

At a major rally in 1927, Christian Evangelist Owen W. Reese said to the standing-room-only crowd that there was "a good strong Ku Klux Klan in Greeley."

Warren and Edith Monfort were having none of it. They were raising their children to treat all people with the same respect and courtesy. When it came to hiring for farm labor, they didn't discriminate against anyone because of his or her nationality, and were very tolerant of the views of others. In fact, during the war Warren had hired a Japanese-American, and at one time had hired a Mexican-American and had the audacity, his neighbors thought, to pay him as much as he was paying everyone else.

In the 1950s Kenny, now in his 20s, had a good position from which to observe what was taking place. In the South the "Jim Crow" regime was continuing, with racial segregation, voter suppression, denial of economic opportunities and private acts of violence aimed at African-Americans that were largely ignored by the American populace. Many African-Americans were moving northward, where they were still facing discrimination in housing and jobs. Just to the east of Colorado the civil rights movement was having some success, with the legal victory in *Brown v. Board of Education of Topeka, Kan.* in 1954.

In *Brown v. Board of Education* plaintiffs charged that it was unconstitutional to teach black children in separate public schools from white children. The U.S. Supreme Court ruled that "segregation of white and colored children in public schools has a detrimental effect upon the colored children." Earlier rulings that "separate but equal" standards were sufficient were deemed unconstitutional.

Even though the court ruled that segregation be phased out "with all deliberate speed," these kinds of victories provided few practical remedies. Discrimination still flourished throughout much of America.

The Civil Rights Act of 1957 pushed the ball forward, providing the first anti-discriminatory legislation since immediately after the Civil War. It was during this time the movement was starting to use direct action rather than litigation, which civil rights proponents thought moved things too slowly. Using tactics like sit-ins, bus boycotts, freedom rides and similar actions, the civil rights supporters were having more success, and with the advent of television were getting the attention of Kenny and the rest of the American public. The local and state governments had to address many of the issues, not the federal government.

One of the most widely publicized of these actions was the 1955-56 boycott of buses in Montgomery, Alabama, by the African American community after Rosa Parks, considered by some to be the "mother of the Civil Rights Movement," refused to leave her seat on a public bus to make room for a white passenger. She was arrested and convicted of disorderly conduct and violating a local ordinance. Bus revenues dropped by 80 percent after the African-American community boycotted the bus service for 381 days.

Sit-ins at lunch counters in 1960 received similar publicity, with protestors occupying seats and refusing to leave when asked. When arrested, these protestors made "jail-no-bail" pledges to bring additional attention to their cause and force the authorities to pay for space and food.

It was the success of these kinds of actions that lead to the rise of Martin Luther King and other activists, who provided supporters with the means for fighting segregation and raising funds. Non-violence was the primary tenet of the groups fighting the continuing racism they saw.

Before being elected to the presidency in 1960, John F. Kennedy had a limited understanding of the civil rights movement, admitting to his advisors that during the first months of his presidency his knowledge of the movement was "lacking." Along with his Attorney-General, however – who happened to be his brother Robert F. Kennedy – the administration was making some progress.

In fact, Dr. King said at the end of 1962 that the "administration has reached out more creatively than its predecessors to blaze new trails [in voting rights and government appointments]. Its vigorous young men have launched imaginative and bold forays and displayed a certain élan in the attention they give to civil rights issues."

After two years of relative inaction (except for Robert Kennedy's exhortations), the Kennedy administration was forced by actions of Alabama's Governor George Wallace to move decisively to make a statement about civil rights. Wallace had refused to allow two African American men to attend the University of Alabama. Kennedy had answered by federalizing the Alabama National Guard to protect the students.

> "This nation was founded by men of many nations and backgrounds. It was founded on the principle that all men are created equal, and

that the rights of every man are diminished when the rights of one man are threatened. ... It ought to be possible for American consumers of any color to receive equal service in places of public accommodation, such as hotels and restaurants and theaters and retail stores, without being forced to resort to demonstrations in the street, and it ought to be possible for citizens of any color to register and to vote in a free election without interference or fear of reprisal."

President John F. Kennedy
Televised Address to Nation
June 11, 1963

A week after making his historic speech, Kennedy submitted a Civil Rights Bill to Congress. The Democratic Party hadn't always been as progressive as it was now showing itself to be, but it was taking the right steps in Kenny's eyes. It was no doubt the party's increasingly enlightened stance on civil rights that determined how he would land politically. I am, he thought, a Democrat. If he had been forced to base his decision on their stance on the Vietnam conflict, he would have thought twice.

The conflict hadn't started overnight. President Harry Truman (a Democrat) got the country involved in 1950 by underwriting costs of France's war against the Viet Minh. The presidencies of Dwight Eisenhower (a Republican) and John F. Kennedy (a Democrat) had increased the political, economic and military commitments in the 1950s and 1960s. President Lyndon Johnson (a Democrat) took even greater steps in increasing the war.

No, Kenny was a Democrat mostly because of the party's attention to civil rights in the 1960s. He couldn't understand how people could discriminate against others because of the color of their skin, their religion or the nation of their birth. When it came to civil rights he was truly color blind and believed in equal opportunity.

In addition to civil rights, Kenny believed the Democrats better understood the need for taking care of messes in their own kitchen. He explained that "Republicans tend to overly protect their own people. ... Democrats would have helped, in fact probably led, in any purge of one of their "tainted" leaders, i.e. Lyndon Johnson. ... I would guess that the Democratic ability for internal purging, internal change is what makes me a Democrat more than any other one item."

This to Kenny meant that the Democratic Party would be more open to some of his contrarian views. To have those views carry appropriate weight, he decided to run for a seat in the Colorado legislature as a representative in 1964. His timing couldn't have been more perfect. Democrats were winning all over the West, including Weld County, which had been a Republican stronghold for years.

Warren had been against Kenny's entry into politics from the beginning, believing his political activities would take away from his efforts at the packing plant. (They would.) He had been going to Kenny more and more to discuss business issues, and thought that if Kenny got started in politics he would never come back. Even though Warren was a Democrat himself, he told feedlot employees he planned to vote against Kenny and told them to do the same. He was probably joking.

Edith was a Republican. Warren would have been but "they kept putting up people he didn't like," according to Kenny. He and Edith were actually proud of what Kenny was doing, even though not pleased by the timing.

Warren, in fact, was far from an "anti-political" man. It was just that he didn't think it was the right thing for Kenny at this time. The packing plant had only recently been paid off, and the feedlot was expanding at a rapid clip. Having passed normal retirement age Warren was trying to slow down and hand off more responsibility to Kenny. He may have thought it would have been better had Kenny waited until his own retirement before getting wrapped up in politics. But it was now or never for Kenny.

Hail the Victor

Kenny beat Arthur Anderson for the 43rd District seat in the state legislature by a vote of 4,984 to 3,700. His father was not impressed, reminding him that Republicans across the country were being beaten by Democrats. Heck, Fidel Castro would have won his race, Warren later told Kenny. Not only did Kenny carry his district, but all of the other Weld County districts were won by Democrats, as well, which was extremely unusual. In fact, that hadn't happened since 1922.

Among Kenny's concerns for the Colorado House of Representatives was the vast disparity in power among the urban and rural legislators. Forty-two of the 65 representatives at the time came from Denver, Colorado Springs or Pueblo, leaving the rest of the state for the non-urban areas. "We must be as strong as possible to maintain any balance of power," he told supporters.

He was a busy and involved member of the legislature his four years there. He served as chairman of three interim committees – Flood Disaster, Financial Institutions and Property Taxes – and was on the Interim Committee on Open Records, an advisory member of the Commission on Higher Education, a member of the Governor's Committee on Mental Health and Mental Retardation, and a member of the House Committees on Business Affairs, Natural Resources, and Health, Welfare and Institutions.

In February of 1966 he suggested he might run for governor, but instead was re-elected to the Colorado House that year, one of the few Democrats locally to survive a Republican landslide in Weld County. His leadership and experience were items cited for his success as a Democrat in a solidly Republican area of the state.

In 1967 he was asked by the U.S. Agency for International Development to participate in a study mission to Kenya, and it opened his eyes to the tremendous plight of citizens of foreign countries. Though invited as a legislator, Kenny was there really to determine why Kenya wasn't maximizing its potential in beef cattle production. He was able to see the political, economic and sociological pressures on the country, and it made him better understand the kinds of issues that become prominent in developing third world countries. "In the United States we are learning the impact of tremendous pressures when the disadvantaged start moving up the socio-economic ladder after years at the bottom. These same pressures apply to Kenya as a nation," he wrote.

The Peacenik

The Vietnam War was in full throttle in the mid-1960s, and the anti-war movement was just getting on its feet. It was most visible with "teach-ins" during the spring of 1965, with students playing a lead role in the effort. The teach-ins were actually mass demonstrations, and were at first very peaceful. When students went home in the summer of 1965 the flame flickered a bit but other demonstrations soon took their place. Hundreds of campuses across the country participated in the teach-ins, although most did not.

The campuses were having their effect by capturing the attention of Lyndon Johnson's government. The U.S. had started bombing parts of North Vietnam in 1965, and was forced to call a bombing pause from May 12 to May 17 because of the criticism it was receiving. The anti-war movement – while certainly not supported by a majority of Americans – was becoming more respectable. Several leading government officials resigned as a result of growing restiveness.

However, military efforts in Vietnam were accelerating. From 1965 to 1966 the number of air raids increased from 25,000 in 1965 to 79,000 in 1966. In 1967 it had heated up on both sides of the ocean; the war was crippling Johnson's presidency and, along with other civil unrest and moral issues facing society, was paralyzing the country.

It was at the 1966 state Democratic Convention that Kenny's Vietnam views came out in full force. As a member of the Resolutions Committee for that convention, he got involved in the fight over the resolution dealing with Vietnam. A strongly worded resolution "condemning" the country's involvement in that nation had come from Pitkin County, which includes Aspen. Lots of heated words and about six or eight hours later, a resolution was agreed on that was mildly critical of President Lyndon Johnson and called for a halt to an escalation of the conflict and a halt to the bombing of North Vietnam.

The resolution passed on a tie vote with the chairman of the Committee, Rich Gebhardt, voting to break the tie and pass the resolution. As a supporter, Kenny was asked to give one of the three speeches in favor of the "peacenik" plank. Because the issue was so volatile and Kenny was an elected official who would put his political career in jeopardy, an offer was made to Kenny that he not speak. But he said he had already made up his mind to go on.

Fears about the explosive nature of the situation were not unfounded. He nearly was booed off the stage, and a 3-minute talk ended up becoming more like 5 or 6 minutes because of all the heckling and catcalls. The resolution was not passed and Kenny lost many friends as a result of his stance. But his position on the issue was now clear to everyone.

By 1968 only a quarter of the population approved of President Johnson's handling of the war – and it wasn't only the doves who were angry. Hawks were disturbed because the country wasn't taking the aggressive actions they thought were necessary to win the war. Meanwhile, the doves were beginning to gain ground. Defections in the Democratic Party were becoming more prevalent, and it was beginning to wear on the president. He had oversold the gains in the war, and by mid-1968 his presidency was all but over. All the administration could do was to dig in for continued demonstrations, as well as anti-war disobedience that was anything but civil.

Kenny favored a single Vietnam, which could act as a strong buffer between China and the rest of Southeast Asia. The South Vietnam government was corrupt, he believed, and a phased withdrawal that forced South Vietnam to become more self-sufficient would bring about an end to the war. Critics said this would assure that talks with the North Vietnamese would be unsuccessful.

Kenny was set on taking his views higher. In November 1967, he unofficially floated a trial balloon to see what kind of support there might be for a Senate run. In a speech that month he blasted incumbent Peter Dominick and urged America to be brave enough to admit that the Vietnam War was a mistake. He said the United Nations should get in, and the United States should get out.

Truth was, he had already made up his mind he would be in the Senate race. On January 9, 1968, he announced his run for a Colorado seat in the U.S. Senate to replace Peter Dominick, who had been elected in 1962. At the top of his platform was his desire to get the United States out of Vietnam.

> If the Democrats...want a man with a fresh image, broad appeal and other earmarks of a worthy challenger, they have one in Kenneth Monfort.
> *Greeley Tribune* Editorial
> January, 1968

In his announcement he said that "every day we are in Vietnam the risk of World War III increases." He believed money spent on the war effort would be better spent domestically, and that the brain power being used on the war would be more valuable at home.

In a speech on July 30, 1968, he ripped into the U.S. war policy, saying "the new politics demands that if the establishment is in conflict with the people it must be changed. It says that past deeds, good or bad, are no criteria for party power today. It places emphasis on the solutions of today's problems – new and daring solutions."

> "I am proud of the Democratic Party's progressive and imaginative answers to past problems which our nation has faced. As a party we have

> accepted gladly the responsibilities of giving this nation political leadership for most of the past three decades."
>
> Ken Monfort
> Announcement for Senate
> January 10, 1968

In 1968 Kenny was especially disdainful of Peter Dominick's "Eastern-oriented ideas" and his interests and friendships, which he believed were more in tune with the polo playing society of Connecticut and the money manipulating group in Wall Street than they were with the farmers, ranchers, laborers, small businessmen and Bronco lovers of Colorado. "I'm not going to beat him on looks, but Dominick can be beaten because he has not truly represented Colorado," Kenny said in a Jan. 10 speech to about 100 Boulder County Democrats.

> "I make the race because I believe in America. I believe in the Democratic philosophy of government. I believe that each of us should do what we can to assure an America for our children where each has the chance to make of his or her life that which they desire. Perhaps it was said best by John F. Kennedy when he said, 'One man can make a difference and every man should try.'"
>
> Ken Monfort
> Announcement for Senate
> January 10, 1968

Kenny's biggest issue with both political parties had been their support of the Vietnam War, and he didn't hesitate to tell state and national politicians his opinion of the fiasco. In 1979 he recounted an open meeting held in 1967 by a group of about 10 Colorado Democratic legislators, several county chairmen, a national committeeman and other active Democrats who were questioning the war effort. A top aide to Vice President Hubert Humphrey joined the group, and his message was less than conciliatory.

Kenny remembered him saying, in effect, that the group had no right to question the president, and by being at the meeting they were in trouble with the president, the vice president and the National Democratic Party. They were, to put it bluntly, traitors. Kenny didn't consider himself a traitor, though, and said it demonstrated an "us vs. them" presidential mentality that was dangerous to the presidency. After that 1967 meeting he also knew that Lyndon Johnson would not serve another term as president.

Vietnam was not Kenny's only platform position. He also wanted to reform the urban racial poverty complex, and increase the opportunities for rural Americans, who he did not believe were sharing in the prosperity of America. He especially wanted to stop the exodus of young people from rural areas to urban ones. "Hope, opportunity and challenge must be built in rural America," he said.

In his speeches Kenny didn't talk like a large feedlot and packing plant owner. Nor did he sound like a member of "the establishment," as it was seen by many of the young people of the day. He meant what he said, but the incongruous nature of some of his comments gave fodder to his challengers.

> "We must stop the pollution of our streams, the pollution of our air and the pollution of our natural beauty. We must build within our towns and cities transportation systems to move people in safety and comfort. We must establish adequate parks and recreational facilities. Our mountain recreational areas must be available to all and have facilities for all."
> Ken Monfort Campaign Speech
> July 23, 1968

Like in "real life," Kenny didn't sugarcoat his speech or try to straddle fences when on the stump. In a July 30 speech he said voters were "tired of a pabulum diet of vague promises meant to alienate no one." With a strong campaign manager in fellow Greeley resident and legislator John R. P. Wheeler and a young and dedicated band of followers, Kenny ran a good, well-orchestrated campaign in the primary.

The "Monfort Girls" were a group of about 40 young women, including 16-year-old daughter Kyle, who made public appearances on his behalf. They helped draw attention to the energy in his campaign and the youth his candidacy inspired. Dressed in white skirts and white blouses, with turquoise vests and white hats, the Monfort Girls were a refreshing break from the old, dry and tired campaign speeches. Kenny's 8-year-old son Charlie also got into the act and helped emphasize the "youth" element, introducing his father to about 600 Democrats attending a July Franklin D. Roosevelt Memorial Dinner at the Greeley Elks Club.

Son Charlie helped introduce Kenny at the Greeley Elks Club

Tom Gavin, a reporter at the time with *The Denver Post*, said "McNichols hasn't matched Monfort's go-get-em corps of canny young helpers." He noted that the anti-war contingency, which was just getting off the ground, was a big help.

Gavin became friends with Kenny and saw him as an up-and-comer in political circles. In a Sept. 8, 1968, column he called him a "long loose man of 39...who looks like he could suit up for either the second male lead of a western movie or as tight end for the Green Bay Packers; a gregarious man, friendly as a Great Dane puppy, sociable as a Jaycee vice president."

At the Colorado Democratic Convention in Colorado State University's Moby Gym, Kenny inspired the crowd, winning the top slot on the primary ballot against former two-term Colorado Governor Stephen "Steve" McNichols. The final vote for the top line on the primary ballot was 1,074 for Kenny to 724 for McNichols. To Kenny, McNichols represented the "old guard" and supported positions, such as the war in Vietnam, the majority of Americans no longer held.

Kenny had a large legion of young, enthusiastic supporters

He saw 1968 as a "critical year in American politics, and it is a delight for me to be involved in it." He had been noted as being an "intelligent, progressive state legislator," and many saw him as having a good shot at getting the nod on the Democratic ticket.

Kenny was finding supporters in the usual places, such as in Northern Colorado and in rural parts of the state, as well as in some unlikely ones. During his time in the House Kenny had gotten divorced but even the car of ex-wife Pat sported a "Monfort for Senate" bumper sticker.

It was Kenny's hope that the country and the state could keep as much of the power as close to the people as possible. He thought there were perils in increasing the size and power of the federal government for that reason. "It gets away from individual initiative and incentive," he said. "The new liberal philosophy doesn't shy away from new solutions to problems. It accepts the fact that the federal government can provide direction but isn't always indispensible in solving the problem." When you centralize the decision-making in too few hands, he thought, you got away from what democracy is all about.

Many of the Democrats in the state supported Kenny in spite of, not because of, his war stance.

After Kenny announced his run for the U.S. Senate in 1968 he had many volunteers from rural areas. After all, he was a country boy himself, and supported causes that were important to people who lived outside of the cities. Not all of his views were fully known by the people who initially signed up to help him get elected.

He had recruited a volunteer campaign manager in the southwest corner of the state, an old Cortez rancher, who understood the cattle business and agriculture. He was put in charge of arranging a campaign breakfast for Kenny early in the campaign in Durango. The breakfast was to take place the morning after a speech for Jefferson-Jackson Day, an annual Democratic celebration, in Julesburg in the northeast corner of the state – more than 500 miles away.

Campaigns are like that, Kenny thought. And it was no problem, the way he drove. He would just drive all night, pushing the speed limit all the way.

He got there just in time for the breakfast, with places set for 220 people. The only trouble was there were no people at the places. Only a lonely reporter from the local paper.

It seems that after the rancher found out about Kenny's strong anti-war stance, he conveniently forgot to send out any invitations for the breakfast and didn't tell Kenny that he had failed to do so. In fact, he neglected to tell anyone at all about the event.

The sympathetic reporter found some humor and poignancy in what happened, though, so at least Kenny got a sympathetic story out of the calamity. And he did catch up on a little sleep.

Kenny drove more than 2,500 miles in his Pontiac Grand Prix in covering the state during his campaign. According to the

Greeley Tribune he was a shy but effective campaigner. "He meets people well, spreading a friendly smile and offering his large tanned hand, but he refuses to force himself upon people," the newspaper said. "Joshing with a handful of admirers in a drug store in Silt or chatting with a group of ladies at a hospitality room in Glenwood Springs is the way he likes to present himself." His speeches were more full of substance than bombast by a man "who enjoys stimulating intellectual thought."

It was a civil but tough primary campaign. McNichols came out swinging at Kenny in July of 1968, saying the election shouldn't be about "pretty faces or stilted social graces, or a high rating with Dun & Bradstreet," an obvious swipe at Kenny's affluence. He said his opponent's liberal label "belied his legislative voting record, and his reputation as a 'peace' candidate is clouded by conflicting statements," although he provided no evidence of the latter.

The balanced views Kenny presented throughout the campaign, showing an understanding of and willingness to discuss all sides of the issues, were presented as "waffling" by McNichols. He asked for "the real Ken Monfort to please stand up."

Kenny learned that you needed not only the ideas but a sophisticated campaign apparatus to be successful in politics. He had spent about $82,000 on his campaign, and had only raised about $23,000 in donations. Only two of those donations were for more than $1,000 and none was larger than $2,500. About $50,000 of what he spent was his own money.

Meanwhile, Steve McNichols had spent more than that to win the chance to take on Peter Dominick in the general election. In one of his columns in 1974 Kenny noted that it would then take $350,000 to win an election for a Senate seat, which paid $40,000 a year. That, he said, was a "damn poor return" on investment.

McNichols had shown that a good infrastructure for a campaign was necessary, and he had the mechanisms for getting to all the voters. Kenny also found out being able to reach lots of people with as little money as possible made a huge difference.

In addition, he was just a couple years too early in his views. Even though he appealed to many of the younger voters, Colorado was still a very conservative state, even in the Democratic ranks. His views on the war and other issues of the day were considered too radical by some. He lost a lot of votes on the campaign trail when he said the Chicago police and mayor overreacted considerably at the Democratic National Convention. Colorado voters disagreed. "I thought that (Chicago) convention hurt my campaign," Kenny would say later. McNichols also had the know-how, experience and name recognition.

It wasn't even close in the primary elections: Kenny lost 92,175 to 65,630. At no point during the night did it look like Kenny might pull it out. The first returns that came in were absentee ballots from Denver and a North Denver Precinct. He lost them both by about 10 to 1. He was outraced from the starting gate.

It was an awkward post-election night, as Kenny hadn't previously lost an election. McNichols told a reporter as Kenny walked away after coming over to congratulate him, "I know how he feels. I've done it and it's a long walk."

A dozen years later Kenny admitted what a difficult process losing an election is. "It is tough to concede and especially tough when you are still getting jabbed," he wrote. "But you do it and you promise to support your opponent but you really don't."

It was obvious that Kenny's camp was younger and more energetic. It was the future of the party, but the future is… well, in the future, and that didn't help Kenny overcome his disappointment. Neither did it help Kenny to see McNichols lose to Peter Dominick in the general election the next month by a nearly 3-2 margin.

After Dominick's death in 1981, Kenny thought things probably turned out as they should have. "Peter was a friend who had never done anything but be nice to me," he said. "He was scrupulously honest, highly intelligent and very articulate. … Even though a conservative, he was liberal on racial issues and individual rights. He was difficult to attack except on the Vietnam issue and, even there, he had more people on his side than I had on mine." According to Kenny, "Peter Dominick represented this state well and was in tune with the average Coloradoan at that time far better than either Steve McNichols or I would have been."

Back to the Plant

After losing the 1968 primary, Kenny focused more on the business. He told a group of Unitarians in an Oct. 12, 1970, speech that he doubted he would run for office again, and he seriously doubted that he could "be elected with the ideas that I have today." He was also very philosophical about his loss. "The voters helped me decide my future," he said in a 1987 interview for *Sunday Magazine* in the *Rocky Mountain News*. "And I think they probably made a good decision. It's probably the best thing that happened to me." He was not only philosophical about his loss, he kept a sense of humor about it, quoting another Colorado politician from the 1930s: "I thought I heard the voice of the people, but it turned out to be just a very few of my close friends."

He never let up on the Vietnam War issue, though. In a column for the *Town and Country News*, a local free weekly paper, he minced no words.

> If I were to have a word with the President today I would talk to him about the long range implications of continuing the futility of Vietnam even one more day. For I honestly believe that the long range implications will include a rebellion against the military and a rebellion against any foreign commitment... Call it isolationism if you want. Or call those who espouse it pacifists, cowards or un-American if you desire. But be awfully careful for I suspect that your neighbor, your wife, your boss, your banker or your daughter might be one of them.
>
> Ken Monfort column
> *Town and Country News*
> 1971

And he never lost the taste for politics. Early on he supported Mike Mansfield, senator from Montana, for president in 1972, even though he was garnering only about 2 percent of the Democratic support. He "soft-pedaled" that support, but said the country could do a lot worse than the former history professor. Later, when it became apparent that Mansfield had absolutely no chance of getting a second look, he changed to George McGovern, who he believed would be a better president than Richard Nixon. Actually, he believed any Democrat would be a better president than Richard Nixon.

He didn't exactly throw full support to his assistant Hank Brown's entry into the Colorado Senate race in 1972. After all, Brown was a Republican and Kenny was still a staunch Democrat, and Brown's campaign would take away from his work with the company. But when asked whether he was allowed to do it, what could Kenny say? He himself had run when his services were needed by his father. So in the end Brown ran, and Kenny considered him "the type of man that would be an excellent state legislator."

When the Watergate controversy was the rage around all the water coolers, Kenny chimed in. "I don't want to know more," he wrote. "I know how far it went. It went all the way." That didn't mean as a Democrat he thought President Nixon should be kicked out of office.

"But I don't want impeachment. I want government. I hope we get more honest government. We must have a functioning government. The Greek with the lantern is still looking while there seem to be a great number who are so free of sin that they can cast that first, that second, that hundred and fourth and that ninety eight millionth stone."

Kenny came awfully close in 1973 to throwing his hat in the ring for the 1974 governor's race. In fact, he was getting plenty of pressure from friends and business associates to give it a try. In the end, though, he didn't have it in himself to break away from business, and didn't think he could get the support he would need from his family, either.

In a four-page memo to "a very weird assortment" of friends, business associates and media contacts, he wrote he was "flattered to receive the consideration," and then went through the pros and cons of a campaign for the state's highest office.

He said he felt he "could and would win" if he ran, but wasn't sure if that was just an illusion. It hadn't, after all, "withstood the pressures of campaigning, receiving those cold hard looks and those 'who the hell do you think you are?' glances." He remembered how his last campaign had ended. That had left a bad taste in his mouth, especially as it affected the people who had campaigned hard for him and had also lost.

> I had worked very hard on (the 1968) campaign – perhaps not smartly, but very hard – as had so many of you. The issues had been great; the war in Vietnam, the problems concerning minorities, civil liberties and justice within our society and the direction within the Democratic Party. Many things have changed since that time, but today the issues within Colorado are as serious to our quality of life as they were then.
>
> Ken Monfort
Memo to Friends
May 8, 1973

Probably the biggest negative to a run for governor was the lack of support from his family. He had gotten remarried to Pat about a year after losing the senatorial primary election, and she didn't like the life of a politician's wife. His children, too, didn't think much of losing their father to politics so soon after getting him back on a regular basis. "We live in Greeley, always have and probably always will," he wrote. "My kids…do not relish the life in the 'goldfish bowl' of the executive mansion."

Though he made jokes about it and rarely displayed it openly, the one thing he had no lack of was the one thing he knew he'd need for a campaign: ego – with a sense of humor, of course. "Mine would not want for that ingredient," he wrote to his friends. "I really feel that the State of Colorado would be a better state with that one indispensible ingredient – me."

> I fear that this campaign, or other campaigns, will be waged on growth versus no-growth, development versus no-development, shale development versus no-shale development, rather than on the tough issues of where and how Colorado shall grow, where and how those who do not today possess economic freedom can gain it and where and how they will live after it is gained and how to provide energy in a world that still needs energy without forever scarring the earth that gives of its treasures.
>
> Ken Monfort
> Memo to Friends
> May 8, 1973

He hated the "idiotic parades, waving at people who wonder who the hell you are, why you are riding a horse instead of in a convertible or why you look so tired that day." He thought he might rather spend the time "watching the Knicks and Lakers on the tube" than "go to the annual 'Do-Good' Banquet." But he also thought it was time for a Democratic governor, though he acknowledged John Love had done a good job during his leadership. Kenny was ready and willing to take on the responsibility.

But he also liked the ability to shoot from the hip; to say things as a public citizen that he wouldn't be able to say as governor. He liked having the option of changing his mind, as "the whole world changes their collective minds billions of times a day," he wrote. "I love to be able to comment, get off base once in awhile and say what I damn well please."

Though he knew he would enjoy the challenge, in the end Kenny just didn't think he had the will to pull it off. "My decision is made and is not revocable under any possible foreseen set of circumstances," Kenny wrote. "I shall not run for the governorship, the United States Senate or any foreseeable office." He thought there were an abundant number of capable Senate candidates, and at least four able and "very interested" potential governor candidates. "I will enjoy watching the action from the sidelines," he wrote.

He would describe himself after that time as a "retired politician." But he never did lose his inclination or willingness to comment on what was going on in the world of politics.

In 1972 Kenny announced that he would support Senator George McGovern for president. He liked McGovern's ideas on reform, and his Vietnam stance, which was similar to his. Kenny hadn't softened at all on the war, and in his columns was letting President Nixon have it.

It was something that couldn't wait, Kenny believed. In one of his columns he said he had been patient but bluntly pleaded the war should end. "You, Richard Nixon, promised us, the American People, that we were out of Vietnam, that peace was at hand. Get us out! Now." It was this kind of public display that had earlier landed Kenny on Nixon's enemies list, one of only two Coloradoans to get the distinction.

At the end of that month Kenny reminded readers of his columns of the toll the war had taken on the country and its citizens. There were 46,000 Americans killed in the action and more than 300,000 wounded, he wrote, and it had cost the country $147 billion. Those numbers were unacceptable to Kenny.

In a February 1973 *Town and Country News* column he was philosophical about how the country should "make a peace." To do that, he wrote, "killing must become an 'out' thing – whether that killing be nation against nation or person against person. Racism too must be an 'out' thing."

It isn't known how much of his anti-war stance resulted from the fact that his only brother had been killed in World War II, although that event took an enormous toll on the Monfort family and on Kenny during a very formative part of his life. Though he firmly believed his brother gave his life to protect his country, the loss of someone so close to him had to have been a tremendous blow.

Other national news during this time period was giving Kenny a wonderful supply of political mischief on which he could comment in his columns. In October 1973, in the middle of the Watergate mess, Richard Nixon instigated the "Saturday Night Massacre." He attempted to fire Archibald Cox and was thwarted by Attorney General Elliot Richardson and Deputy Attorney General William Ruckelshaus, who both resigned. Solicitor General Robert Bork finally agreed to carry out the order to fire Cox. In his column Kenny said he supported impeachment proceedings against the president, with Gerald Ford to be named president. He would have preferred a Democratic president to take his place, but certainly understood the point of people who said it should be a Republican replacing a Republican.

Even though he considered himself a good Democrat and was proud of having been included on Nixon's enemies list, he didn't demonize him as so many people in the country at that time did. He saw him for the complex man he was. In a column published the day of Nixon's resignation speech, Kenny said he felt "compassion" for the president; that he had done evil things, but he didn't think he was an evil man.

After the resignation, Kenny wrote that Nixon bowed out "with a great deal of grace." He also praised President Gerald Ford, saying his first few days "have been great," with the president showing a great deal of "commonness." Then, after the pardon of Nixon by Ford, he said "justice can best be served with a large helping of mercy...I believe he has suffered enough." Kenny also didn't think it would be in the country's best interests to drag out the issue for years. Later he recognized that Nixon had done some good things while in office, but "he is still a tough guy to like!"

He also found other ways to demonstrate he was far from a hard-liner when it came to Democrats and Republicans. In a 1974 column he wrote that even though he considered himself a strong Democrat, he "would still feel uncomfortable with too big a Democratic majority in Congress. And, I would hate to lose from the political scene some of the good Republican office holders, national, state and local."

He was especially complimentary of the work of Henry Kissinger, Secretary of State under both Richard Nixon and Gerald Ford. He said Kissinger helped sell detente to the communists and succeeded in getting withdrawal in Vietnam. He was partially responsible for stopping a war in the Mideast and he "deserves our confidence and our thanks. I think there is far less chance my sons will face a war because of him." In 1976 he could only "wish him well and marvel at his ability and guts. ... The guy frankly deserves the support of all Americans. He needs to be praised, not condemned."

He continued to believe in many principles of the Democratic Party, though. For instance he was sympathetic to truckers during a strike in 1974. And he supported those who he thought would best carry Democratic ideals forward. He had supported Dick Lamm for governor in 1974, a politician he had gotten to know while both were serving in the legislature in the 1960s. "How will we ever know what we might be able to do if we don't elect the Dick Lamms when we can?" he asked.

In September 1976 Kenny told *Signature Magazine* he recognized "politics is an ego thing, and I think I've got a lot of that behind me." He wouldn't entertain the notion of running for a public position again – at least not publicly. Kenny never shied away from commenting on the action of others in the political field, though, no matter what their party affiliation, business relationship or friendship status.

He had no use for those who, regardless of party affiliation, would play politics with the business of politics. That was something he thought was going on in 1976, when Senator Floyd

Haskell, a Democrat, personally vetoed the appointment of Republican Don Brotzman to the federal bench. Haskell gave what Kenny thought were half-baked reasons, but Kenny knew that Haskell was just stalling so a Democratic judge could be nominated should Jimmy Carter be elected president. "It is just that simple," Kenny wrote. "Why Sen. Haskell didn't 'level' with us is disturbing to me."

Throughout his life he even supported those who didn't see eye-to-eye with him on delicate business issues. He supported Wayne Sodman, who was the union steward at the packing plant and the union's chief negotiator, for re-election as councilman in Greeley, calling him a "nice guy." Sodman had been able to walk a fine line, Kenny said, neither favoring Monfort Packing, which paid his wages, or penalizing the plant, "a possible nemesis from a union point of view."

It was this kind of bipartisan viewpoint that sometimes got Kenny in trouble with people in his own party, and raised eyebrows among those in the other. He pulled no punches when he took Colorado's Democratic Senator Gary Hart to task, for example, for blaming "middlemen and conglomerates" for rising food prices in 1974. He said Hart had "oversimplified a complex problem," and "used schlocky research." The next year he said he had "been disappointed in our Democratic Governor and pleasantly surprised by our Republican President." He also praised President Ford for proving "that a single man can turn the Presidency from an office completely without respect and credibility into the respected office it deserves to be. ... President Ford led this nation well."

On the local scene some politicians said he didn't get involved enough, and was a "residual leader" because he would stay on the sidelines and didn't get involved until his interest had been piqued. Others, however, said Kenny was not one to throw his weight around on issues or wield his power by pulling strings. He got involved when he could, though, and on things he thought were important he didn't hesitate to let his opinion be public knowledge.

For instance, in an October 1976 *Town and Country News* column he listed each of the 10 state amendments on the

November ballot, what they would do, his comments on why he thought they were good or bad and what the odds were that they would be passed. He thought voters would take sides opposite to him on some of the issues, and when they didn't he said in his Nov. 11 column that he was "honored to be among the voters of Colorado."

In a *Rocky Mountain News* interview Kenny admitted having voted for Republicans while a Democrat. He also strongly supported Democrats he thought were good for the party, the state and the country, having urged people to vote for Dick Lamm in 1974. He said, however, he couldn't remember who he voted for in the governor's race in 1978, which pitted Lamm against Ted Strickland, even though he was no fan of Strickland. This wasn't because Lamm had fallen out of favor with Kenny; it was because a former colleague and one of his favorite politicians, Hank Brown, was running on Strickland's ticket as lieutenant governor.

He was disdainful of politicians – or businessmen – who wouldn't take responsibility for their actions or gloss over them. When Bert Lance had been appointed Budget Director in President Jimmy Carter's administration in the fall of 1977, Kenny was incredulous that Lance would try to justify some of the things he did before taking the government job.

"My personal view is that most of those things (corporate jets) become the almost personal toys of the executives of big companies," he wrote. "Bert Lance helps verify that feeling. And then he tries to tell me that taking his family to a football game in that jet or going to the Mardi Gras is company business and all I can think is a male bovine. That is private use of corporate property, awfully costly corporate property. There is no way that it can be justified. And Bert Lance is wrong in doing it, wrong in trying to justify it and gives all bankers and businessmen a bad image by doing so." Kenny called for Lance's resignation in that column. Right after he turned in the column and before people had read it, Lance had.

As with Richard Nixon, Kenny was understanding and thought the American people would have been, too, had Lance – and Nixon – shown some humility and apologized. "The American people have great compassion for mistakes," he wrote. "Why our leaders don't understand this and allow us to use that compassion, I will never know."

Sure, Kenny was opinionated, especially about what the government was doing. Kenny had written many columns and articles critical of government decisions over the years, and had supported the anti-war movement and been vocal in his thoughts about where the leadership of the country had gone wrong. He drew the line, though, when it came to the way people were beginning to express themselves about their country's leaders.

He believed the president and other leaders should be respected, even if people didn't agree with their decisions. The lack of civility and common decency that he was seeing in the world around him sometimes was depressing to him. "All of a sudden it seems like everyone is out of step but me, but so be it," he wrote in a *Greeley Tribune* column in August 1990. One letter to the editor in the *Greeley Tribune* in particular had, in his opinion, gone over the line.

> I would guess that, if pinned down, (the writer) would back away from calling the president stupid; if not back down intellectually, at least do it from the standpoint of common courtesy. Obviously there is room in this world for empathy, compassion, tolerance and respect. Characterizing our own American president as 'stupid' does not fit in with what (the writer) should write. If it does, someone wasted a lot of money on education.
>
> Ken Monfort Column
> *Greeley Tribune*
> Nov. 18, 1990

He thought Ford had done a good job in handling the Nixon fiasco and stabilizing the nation, and voted for him in 1976.

Earlier in 1976, however, Kenny had supported Jimmy Carter, believing Carter supported a smaller federal government and greater individual responsibility. "I am sick and tired of the burgeoning bureaucracy," Kenny wrote. Because Carter was also a small town kind of guy who went to public schools, Kenny could "identify with the man."

Before the actual election, though, Kenny became disenchanted with Carter. Mostly it was what Kenny considered Carter's "holier than thou" attitude, and that Carter would keep telling everybody that he never lied. As was his policy, Kenny was supportive after Carter won, saying the country had to "admire the strength and determination and desire and intelligence that carried James Earl Carter from the farm in Georgia to the Naval Academy, the Nuclear Submarine fleet, the Governorship of his state and now the Presidency." He tempered that by saying "some, including myself, worry about that much determination and some, also including myself, worry about the many commitments made on the way up."

After the election Kenny thought Carter might be all right after all, following some indication that Carter would be an independent president who would try to reduce the federal government and stay away from those Kenny thought were too radical. "The Carter start has to be considered impressive," Kenny wrote. "It is obvious that so far neither Ralph Nader nor George Meany is running the show...Perhaps, just perhaps, now we are going to see the real Jimmy Carter...So far I like what I see."

The bloom soon faded, though. Too many people were promised too many things, Kenny believed, and too much of Carter the politician emerged for Kenny's tastes. "From now on I will be even more suspicious of the President's words. He does exaggerate a bit," he said in 1978. Carter's policies after taking office that led to crippling interest rates and anti-business positions also kept Kenny sliding to the other side.

His columns showed just how light a grip the Democratic Party still had on Kenny. He noted that the state Democrats needed to look to their own legislative and administrative record and "meet the problem head on" when it came to legislative losses. He had been asked whether he was still a Democrat and answered that it seemed as though "Democrats were wedded to programs that were designed to solve problems but which hadn't worked, while the Republicans were wedded to never trying to solve the problems." He said on that day he was still a Democrat. "Tomorrow? It will depend on where our two major parties head."

In June of 1978 Kenny wrote that he had probably attended his last state Democratic convention. "Frankly, it is always too hot, it is almost always too boring and it is very difficult to judge whether you make any difference," he wrote. The small pleasures of being there "hardly compensates for messing up a whole Saturday to listen to boring speeches, exaggerated parliamentary procedure and a party platform that would surely lose the election for the Democrats if anyone ever got around to reading the thing."

Among everything else that was bothering Kenny about being a Democrat was the issue of government spending. Kenny admitted he was upset with the tendency for Democratic leaders to want to spend other peoples' money. "If I'm a generous man, I want it to go where I want, not where the government wants," Kenny said in the *Rocky Mountain News* interview. Like his father, he would rather find a way to get his earnings to charitable causes through donations than give it to the IRS.

By the time a roast was held in Kenny's honor on Valentine's Day in 1978 to benefit the Weld County Democratic Party, he had probably already made up his mind he may be supporting the wrong party. The event was obviously tongue-in-cheek, with more than 600 people attending and participants poking fun at everything from Kenny's wardrobe malfunctions to his political leanings. It probably included as much irony and truth as it did humor.

He felt unworthy to be roasted, but it was a once in a lifetime affair and he couldn't "help but think just how lucky I am to have lived in Greeley, Colorado and to have known the people I have known and to have the friends that I have," he said. In addition to many high ranking state Democrats, including Dick Lamm and future Senator Gary Hart, two Republicans were on the dais: Hank

Brown and Ken Lloyd, a former state Republican chairman who had Kenny as a client in his hedging business.

In 1979 Kenny enjoyed handicapping the upcoming presidential elections in his column in *Town and Country News*. On Sept. 27 he said Ted Kennedy was the prohibitive favorite to win the Democratic nomination over incumbent Jimmy Carter, and that Ronald Reagan was an even-money bet to become the Republican nominee. He then thought Kennedy would win the popular vote but lose the general election to the Republican.

The Conversion

In Kenny's world, a liberal meant a belief in civil rights, job opportunity for minorities, taxation policies based on ability to pay plus a desire to keep wealth distributed, protection of the environment, a civilized police activity, disgust with a bad war and citizen participation in the electoral process, but not in that order. It did NOT mean that all problems could or should be solved by the bureaucracy of the federal or state governments, that the police should be relegated to ineffectiveness, that a different skin color should give you more rights, that taxation should be primarily a middle class responsibility, that environmental protection should preclude our ability to feed ourselves or provide jobs, that we should become inept and a laughingstock in world affairs or that environmental and labor leaders should become the main political forces within the nation.

Somewhere in those lists Kenny became disillusioned with the direction of the Democratic Party and decided to make a change. He didn't do it in a bashful way.

It was 1980 and he had just gone through an extremely ugly strike at the Greeley packing plant (see Chapter 10). While he said it wasn't the straw that broke the camel's back, it was certainly part of the package. Kenny resented the Democrats for being the party of big labor, falling into line whether or not the support was warranted.

But that wasn't all. He was growing more and more disenchanted with the anti-business attitude being supported by the Democratic Party. The more he tried to improve his business, the more he found the government in his way. The government, Kenny insisted, shouldn't decide everything for the individual, nor should it control everything done by a business. That's what the Democrats seemed determined to do in the 1970s, however.

A good example was meat grading conducted by the U.S. Department of Agriculture. This was a service rendered by the government but paid for by the companies that used it. Kenny thought this was a good and important service that provided benefits to both companies that bought it and citizens that relied on it for information. In the 1970s, however, President Jimmy Carter appointed a consumer activist named Carol Foreman to head the agency that provided the service. Now, instead of a company-paid service providing information for consumers you had a consumer-protecting service paid for by companies.

That small distinction made a world of difference to beef packers. Foreman, who thought the vast majority of graders were on the take from companies for whom they graded meat, forbade graders from having interaction with company people. No more free cups of coffee, no more informal discussions, no more attendance at the company Christmas parties. Instead of a friendly relationship, it became adversarial and differences of opinion became huge bureaucratic nightmares. Every little disagreement turned into paper trails, slowed production and created hard feelings.

Meat inspection was another story entirely. Because it was mandatory and paid for by the taxpayers to protect their interests by maintaining food safety, Kenny could see that the government would act in a more supervisory role in the inspection system and be more adversarial. But enemies? That seemed counterproductive to Kenny. He believed everyone should work together to produce safer beef, and was on record for having supported a strong government meat safety program.

In a 1979 column he wrote: "Let it be known that I do think it is good and necessary to have government involved in the cleanliness and wholesomeness of meat. Also, although we have had our problems with one or two meat inspectors, the vast majority do…their job of protecting the public while at the same time allowing us and helping us to produce efficiently." At one point he even suggested it might be good, from a taxpayer point of view, for meat packers to start paying for inspection, rather than have the bill picked up by citizens.

He reiterated his position on May 10, 1979, when he said that while meat inspectors are "a pain in the neck...nit-pic things...are arbitrary and capricious" and make the company "do silly things," as a result of them being there the industry had shaped up. "You better bet our plant and the whole industry is cleaner, our product is safer and the business is better run with those inspectors there," he wrote. He noted that there were about 30 inspectors in the plant.

One inspector went way too far in his job, he thought, and Kenny even took some of his conflicts with that unnamed inspector public. On Aug. 18, 1977, he wrote of a conflict that was in his view intolerable. "What does a business do when a government employee (in our case one inspector out of about 30) makes it almost impossible to operate? Requests to his supervisors have as yet been of no avail," he wrote. "I honestly believe that the actions of one man are jeopardizing our company and all the jobs associated with the company. But the appeal mechanism does not seem to work...or if so, so very slowly. The badge sported by this one individual is not used, as it should be, for sanitary meat. It is used for harassment in my opinion...If you multiply this by thousands, you can see why much of the populace is disenchanted with government and governmental employees."

In a subsequent column he referenced that tirade, saying it was unfair to single out one inspector and not mention the others who were doing a good job at what they were supposed to be doing, "assuring the public that they get clean and wholesome meat." He also apologized for not being able to "name the inspector that I believe is harming our business."

When you can't even buy a dinner for a visiting government official, Kenny thought, something is out of whack. That's what happened in 1978 when Robert Angelotti, an administrator for the Meat Grading and Meat Inspection divisions of USDA, was let go after admitting he had visited the Monfort plant with no advance notice and accepted a dinner from one Kenny Monfort. He had apparently been to other plants, and probably accepted many dinners. To Kenny the reaction to the official's conduct was preposterous. "It is just one of those things we do here in Greeley when we take visitors out to eat," he wrote. "It has just never entered my mind to ask the visitor to pick up the check or suggest to the waitress that she should split the check...It is the dumbest reason I ever heard of for a man to lose his job. I did not happen to care for the policies being pushed by Dr. Angelotti but that is no reason for him to lose his job over a technicality."

The grading and meat inspection systems were only a small part of it. The National Labor Relations Board had what Kenny saw as pro-union leanings, thanks to Jimmy Carter and the Democrats. That agency also made things difficult for business, to the point of telling business whether they could operate – or whether they could close.

Kenny began to see government not for an entity that was there for a society that was fair and worked more smoothly, but for a meddlesome body that threw wrenches into the workings of business and created more bureaucracy for everyone.

As the company was getting the Grand Island plant established in 1979, Kenny could appreciate earlier times, when growing businesses providing jobs and enhancing local economies weren't stifled by the government. Nebraska Governor Charles Thone, in announcing Monfort's re-opening of the former Swift Plant, had said the government hadn't really done anything to aid Monfort's move to Nebraska or influence the company's decision. Kenny thanked him for that. As he told a group in Grand Island in 1981, "More than help from the government, we just don't want them to screw it up."

Suddenly Kenny saw the government as a body that wasn't there to support you as a business at all. They were there to keep you in line; to hold you responsible; to make sure you didn't break the rules. Because as everyone knew that's exactly what you wanted to do. It was the sort of attitude that offended Kenny tremendously. He had his father's sense of personal and business integrity and had used it generously with his employees, customers, suppliers and others. Now, it was being assumed by the government that he was just another big business cheat.

The other key player in his conversion of parties was Sonny Mapelli, who had been a Democratic candidate for Denver mayor and served in the Colorado legislature in the 1960s as a Democrat. For Sonny it was the party's full allegiance to organized labor that definitely took him over the edge. Sonny acknowledged the party had actively supported labor for many years, and that he had been part of it.

As part of that labor/Democratic Party machine when in the legislature, Sonny said things labor wanted to hear and gave them what they wanted in order to get their support. "Sure, I went along," said Sonny in an interview with the *Rocky Mountain News* Jan. 26, 1981. "I was politically ambitious; so was (Kenny). So I voted for them 100 percent, then went to my business friends and justified it."

Sonny was in the Senate while Kenny was in the House, but their political paths did cross on some issues. Sonny had sponsored a Humane Slaughter Act in the Senate; Kenny sponsored the bill in the House. They both voted for a fair housing law and both supported a liberalized abortion bill in 1967 sponsored by future Governor Dick Lamm.

Kenny had stayed more connected in politics through the years than Sonny had. In fact, Sonny had soured on the entire political life in the late 1960s. After serving in the Colorado legislature as a representative and state senator for eight years Sonny abruptly said he'd had enough in 1968, telling his wife Nomie that politics was "the most crooked thing I've ever seen." It wasn't a Democratic or Republican issue, it was a political one.

He had been threatened, cajoled, compromised, flattered, bullied, pressured, coerced and browbeat over a variety of issues. The one that led him to finally denounce politics for good was a bill he supported to regulate billboards along the highway. After being pushed up against a wall and told by a powerful businessman that if he continued to support the bill he would face certain and significant economic consequences, he said serving just wasn't worth the aggravation.

In mid-1980 Kenny had written a column about big mistakes both parties were making in their platforms, forcing their parties into taking hard-line positions that were hard for moderates to accept. The Democrats said that all of the party's candidates on any level had to support the Equal Rights Amendment. The Republicans said their presidential nominee could only appoint anti-abortion judges if elected. "If they keep doing that I guess they'll end up forcing me into the Libertarian or some other splinter party," he said.

Both Kenny and Sonny had been Democrats their entire adult lives, so their decision to become Republicans wasn't made in haste. Kenny was actually serving on a campaign committee for Senator Gary Hart when they made up their minds to do it. He called up Hart campaign officials and offered to resign, but they said don't bother.

The bottom line was both men had just gotten fed up with practices of the Democratic Party. Their conversion resulted in a tongue-in-cheek group formed in September 1980 called "The Eat Crow Club." It was the brainchild of Kenny and Mapelli, who spent about $2,000 establishing the club as a lark to bring attention to their change of heart. The club held no meetings, charged no dues and had no officers. An official total of 86 Coloradoans decided to desert the Democratic Party in favor of the Republicans as a result, marching en masse to Greeley City Hall to make their change official and give it some publicity.

Kenny said he might have done the deed more privately, but was talked into making it more of a spectacle by Mapelli, who felt the Democrats were to blame for much of the state of the country. Mapelli was in charge of the publicity; Kenny came up with the name.

Their publicity got mixed reviews. Some Democrats were offended, although none called Kenny or Mapelli into the alley as a result. Mapelli's 82-year-old mother was actually relieved when she heard the news. She had always wanted to vote for Republicans but hadn't because her son was a Democrat.

Liking how the 1980 election turned out for his new party, Kenny took it as a vindication for his support of less government and a less arrogant government. "After all, government is meant to serve us, not to rule us," Kenny said. "The bureaucrats with which I deal have forgotten that. They start out assuming that I have done something wrong...the people, I believe, have said that they are sick and tired of it."

Kenny remained a Republican the rest of his life, although with less visibility. In 1990 he stood solidly behind his good friend Hank Brown, telling readers in a *Greeley Tribune* column that Brown was what he hoped all politicians could be. "Without getting maudlin, Hank Brown personifies my hope for this nation and its leaders," he said. "He is bright, very honest and innovative. I share his belief in limited government. We agree that government, particularly the federal government, should be part of the answer to problems, not part of the problem itself." Having already served in the U.S. House of Representatives for 10 years, Brown would go on to serve six years in the U.S. Senate.

Kenny took time out to campaign for friend and former employee Hank Brown in his run for U.S. Senate in 1990

"Hank Brown is one of my best friends, an ex-employee and one of the smartest, as well as most

> honorable, people I know. I would
> vote for him if his opponent was me."
> Ken Monfort Column
> *Greeley Tribune*
> June 13, 1990

Kenny especially liked the strong stance Brown took when it came to taxes and big government. He recognized that he wasn't in the same category as many other taxpayers, but still believed he had a right to complain about how taxes were assessed. As he said in 1974, the general feeling of the populace is that the "only equitable tax is the one the other guy pays." He still thought it was unfair to put an additional 5 percent tax on individuals making above $15,000 a year, as President Ford's Whip Inflation Now (WIN) program proposed to do.

It was in a 1976 column that Kenny admitted that tax preparation was too difficult. (He did his own taxes.) "I should be able to do it fairly easily, and I can't," he wrote. "It is a real chore, and it makes me mad." He said that he looked for deductions and took them, but recognized that others weren't able to use these "loopholes," and that "suddenly it makes very good sense to have no deductions and to have everyone pay their tax on whatever their rate is." Though he said it would cost him more in taxes, it would be worth it to have a lower rate overall.

Loopholes were a huge part of his tax hangup, and he thought some in society escaped their fair share. "Why shouldn't churches and other governmental units pay property taxes when they are protected by the same fire, police and sheriffs as we non-religious, non-governmental types?" he asked. "Or, why should Public Service pay and the 'municipals' not?"

It wasn't fair for the working class, he thought. "Tax shelters and havens that allow millionaires to pay less money in taxes than butchers is an abomination in the system," he said. "Lavishness and waste set the wrong example and must go."

It wouldn't be that much longer before the government had a tax revolt on its hands, Kenny thought. "How long are the taxpayers in this country going to allow their legislators and representatives to meet the needs of every special interest and then pay whatever the tax bill is...or the inflationary costs?" he asked. "It looks to me like it won't be too much longer."

Kenny was a supporter in 1978 of a state amendment that would tie government spending increases to the cost of living. He got into heated arguments with Democratic State Senator Jim Kadlecek, a realtor from Greeley, on the merits and drawbacks of the proposal, both in print and in person. One of Kenny's columns was titled "The Country Boy Answers the Distinguished Senator," and took nearly a page in the Sept. 14, 1978, issue of *Town and Country News* to answer pointed questions Kadlecek had asked in the paper a couple of weeks earlier. Though civil, Kenny's points were sometimes testy and it may have clouded future relations between the two men.

His support of the amendment was philosophically 180 degrees opposite of where he would have been 10 years earlier, Kenny admitted. "Ten years ago I believed that many of the problems of our society could be solved by governmental action, governmental initiative and governmental spending," he wrote in 1978. "I believed that more of our individual resources should be channeled through government for the public good. Further, I believed in the validity and rightness of governmental decision making.

"Frankly, I no longer believe those things," he said. "Precious few problems have been solved in recent (years) by new laws, by hurling more money into governmental programs and by new and expanded bureaucracy. Today, this big government philosophy is creating more problems than it is solving. Today, government rather than being the servant of the people is becoming more and more a restraint on the people."

Kenny said that when he was in the legislature he would have thought he could make decisions better than the voters, too. But "the pressures on (the legislators) are so great. They are literally besieged by this or that constituency, by this group of private interests, by that group of public employees. And they yield on this bit and that bit and all of a sudden the budget is out of hand without them even desiring it to be so." The amendment he was supporting, he said, would provide them with a tool they needed to set priorities and "be able to say no."

He lost that effort. A strong coalition of legislators, school boards, public employees and other government supported groups helped defeat the amendment, although Kenny said he hoped they didn't "think that they have been given a mandate to spend more of the public's money."

As far back as 1968, Kenny had seen the perils of big government. "It gets away from individual initiative and incentive," he said. He wanted to get decisions into as many hands as possible.

> Somewhere, sometime, somehow we have to have not only the public leadership but a public that will say that the ends do not justify the means. Our government must be so lacking in corruption that they can look each of us in the eye, say we are wrong when we are wrong, without us uttering a spontaneous snicker.
>
> Ken Monfort Column
> *Town & Country News*
> Dec. 20, 1973

That didn't always mean he voted his conscience; sometimes on local issues he voted for things he didn't believe in because he thought "other people knew better." In a 1974 column he explained that citizens paid city officials and planners to make these kinds of decisions, and they needed to trust those they hire to do a good job.

By the time the late 1970s rolled around even his militant anti-war rhetoric was beginning to soften. He said one of the reasons he had been against the Vietnam War was because it "would sap our will to get involved in more important confrontations in the years to come. That has come true." He pointed to weak posturing by President Carter in Saudi Arabia,

Iran, Afghanistan and Central Africa as evidence that the United States was "getting clobbered" in international relations. "Somewhere, somehow those who attack our embassy or flaunt our will need to be less sure of what our response will be," he wrote.

He even allowed that while any thought in 1967-68 of winning the war "appalled" him, it may have been a reasonable strategy. "Looking at the human suffering (of the boat people) today, in retrospect, it was a more feasible alternative than I gave it credit for at the time."

When it came to the U.S. Constitution, Kenny thought the less tinkering you did to it the better. He was patriotic and did believe there were some things that might not belong in the constitution but were still important. "If I could find some legal way for the non-flag burner to just kick the hell out of those who burn or desecrate the flag, I might just choose that rather than a Constitutional amendment," he wrote.

Among the issues Ken Monfort had worked on while in the Colorado legislature was abortion, but he didn't see this issue in black and white. He knew there were areas of gray in it. While he was definitely pro-choice, he admitted that there were parts of the argument for that side that he didn't care for very much.

> We will never please those who think abortion is murder. We will never please those who think abortion is a woman's prerogative any time, any place, and any how. If the shrill ones will just shut up, a workable solution may evolve.
>
> Ken Monfort Column
> *Greeley Tribune*
> July 8, 1992

Even then, though, Kenny was able to see both sides of many issues. He didn't think much of the "moral majority," which he considered overbearing. But he did believe with them that the federal government had gotten too big, with federal funding too high and often spending more on the criminals than on the victims. "But I do not agree with them that our way of life is lost if we do not pray in the public schools or if we continue to allow abortions. Neither do I believe that their particular brand of religion and my personal 'acceptance of Jesus Christ' will determine just where I spend my eternity," he said.

He wished that he could get off of the mailing lists of both the Moral Majority and public interest groups – which were really the same kind of organizations with different gospels. He didn't donate to these causes. "Surely somehow, some way or sometime both the computer systems for the 'moral majority' and the 'public interest groups' will decide that I am a deadbeat," he wrote. He welcomed that day.

A World View

When it came to international relations, Kenny believed the world couldn't be a carbon copy of America. Sometimes the country needed to look beyond the politics going on in the other country and "deal with the world as it exists." According to a 1977 column, "this implies recognition of Cuba, diplomatic relations with China, economic aid to Chile, buying chrome from Rhodesia, 'cooling' criticism of the Soviets and continued military sales to Iran. None of these sound really good to me, but the alternative of trying to run the whole world out of Washington and eventually the Pentagon is totally unacceptable."

Earlier he had written that "the American people are ready to accept other governments just because they are there. I think that we would be happier and the world would be happier if we refute that 'Eastern Establishment' and accept what is real and forget our attempts at molding others in our own image."

He went further in 1978 to ask his readers whether "we have always been so pure, will we always be so pure that we can tell every other nation in the world exactly how they should live, what their laws should be like and how their courts should function." He believed that "this nation in general and the Carter Administration in particular is taking on an awfully big job to become the moral arbiter of right and wrong throughout the world. At worse, I believe it could lead to nuclear war. ... Perhaps our President should be more a President and less of a Baptist preacher."

Despite escalating world tensions, he was against reinstatement of the draft. "I believe the next war, if there is one, will be won or lost by the time the first draftee could be drafted," he said in 1980. He wanted a stronger defense, but thought it was "foolish to waste money on registration" for a draft when there were more pressing military needs.

While he conceded most people wouldn't agree with him, he saw the country's foreign policy breaking into three simple lines: 1) We must not get involved in other peoples' wars when they really don't affect us; 2) The No. 1 criteria of our relationship with other countries is whether they are friends of the U.S. or enemies of the U.S.; and 3) We cannot afford to have countries with the petroleum and mineral resources that we must have change from friend to enemy. He said that although that sounded complicated, it was a lot simpler than the criteria being used by the state department.

By and large, he thought the way the Carter administration handled international relations was atrocious. And in the end, "we have gained only the contempt that our shabby behavior deserves."

Kenny was an American through-and-through and not ashamed of it in the least. He donated the tenderloins for President Ronald Reagan's dinner in Washington, D.C. May 21, 1986, and insisted that it was an American's duty to stand behind the country's leaders. At the same time he didn't think the government should necessarily mandate that attitude.

His father would have made the same case. Less government, but more personal responsibility to our community and to our fellow man. Is that possible? One family was doing its best to show that it is. At the same time, they were out to show that being good businessmen meant more than just making money.

Chapter 6
The Businessman

A book that made a small splash in Greeley in the 1990s was called *Meatpackers and Beef Barons: Company Town in a Global Economy*. It purported to expose the human and societal failings of capitalism through companies like Monfort of Colorado. In her Marxist diatribe author Carol Andreas, who apparently had never met Kenny Monfort (or any other meat packers or beef barons, for that matter), described how much better she thought it would be if the workers were in charge.

"Almost 150 years ago, when Karl Marx declared that socialism was the natural solution to the problems of capitalism, he was not espousing an abstract idea," she wrote. "He said that the majority of the population – the workers – would have to dictate the rules and regulations of society. ... The common yearnings of human beings, espoused from time immemorial, could then be realized: 'From each according to ability, to each according to need.'"

The interesting thing about Kenny, though, was that he could have argued the Marxist's side, or at least appreciated his or her points. And unlike many capitalists, he would have enjoyed the dialogue.

Kenny did agree, for instance, that the gulf between company leaders and their workers when it came to salaries was getting way too wide. He thought most top executives were overpaid, and told the University of Colorado Executive Club, which named him the Executive of the Year in 1987, that he was astounded when he saw how much American business leaders made. "Tremendous monetary rewards, too often with little risk, too often while serving on eight Boards of Directors, running three or four charities and sporting a 5 handicap, and I wonder how they can be worth so much," he told the group. "I for one admit to being overpaid...I do not know any answer and maybe we all are worth it…but the spread between the boss and the people that do the work is getting too big and will surely lead to trouble."

Kenny was not overpaid, however. He was always among the lowest – if not the lowest – paid chief executive officers of any Fortune 500 company. In 1972, just two years after the company went public, his salary was $52,000 a year, not a paltry sum in those times but certainly a pittance when compared to other CEOs. He said it was all he needed. Money truly didn't mean that much to him. Life was about the thrill of the triumph.

But Kenny was no Marxist or socialist. He wasn't a communist, either. He was a capitalist in the very best sense of the word. He was honest, aggressive and hard working, and welcomed people on his team that shared the vision of a successful company that made a profit, was financially stable and was able to support those who worked there.

It had been the same philosophy his father had used. Warren had never used the company as a charity. It was a business, so while he paid fair prices and wages he wasn't going to make his own rules. Kenny and Warren generally didn't pay more for cattle than they had to. They were pioneers, for heaven's sake, not mavericks.

However, when they purchased feeder cattle, they would pay immediately with checks cattle sellers knew were legitimate, in good markets or bad. When they purchased fat cattle for the packing plant they would pay on the spot for the animals, something most other packers didn't do. At times they even held onto cattle in their own feedlots for a few days to purchase fat cattle from local feeders who may have fallen on hard times.

Kenny and Warren also worked well as a team. Early on Kenny and Warren would sometimes take a "good cop/bad cop" position in meetings with their bankers. At the end of the day and with loan negotiations at an apparent standstill, Kenny would go flying off the handle and stomp out of the room. Warren would sit there calmly and talk with the bankers about possible ways they could come to a compromise. When Kenny came back into the room, they were usually able to come to an agreement.

Kenny had many business interests, but near the top was his love to sell. And it wasn't the friendly, get-to-know-you, let's have lunch kind of selling. It was the "haggling, scratching, fussing. It's what I think business should be," he told the *Greeley Tribune* in 1981. "I view it as a competitive world."

And compete he did. In just about every waking moment he was thinking about his business, how to make it better and how to get a step ahead of his competition. He didn't throw the "hate" word around a lot. But when it came to the business world and those who wanted to take his business, he could get his hands around it. He hated his competitors and he wanted their customers. He hated losing.

His business side sometimes clashed with his political side, as well as those of other local and state politicians. Having been involved in politics, he knew how the game was played. And he disliked how some used political tactics to try to gain advantage in the business world.

The year was 1970. Kenny had lost his run for the Senate in 1968, but he was still a popular figure in the Democratic Party and one of the individuals being strongly considered as a front-runner for the governor's race in 1974. Although he was disappointed in his showing in the 1968 campaign, Kenny hadn't fully eliminated any thoughts of running for governor.

Monfort of Colorado had just gone public and had begun plans to construct a new 100,000 head feedlot near Gilcrest, Colorado. The state's unions had asked for a meeting with Kenny, so he and his right-hand-man, Hank Brown, went to Denver to sit down with union leaders from the different construction trades.

We want you to construct your new Gilcrest feedlot using union labor, the union representatives said. As a good Democrat, you should want this, too. After listening to their pitch and talking it over with them, Kenny assured them the company would consider any proposals and would give serious consideration to union contracts.

No, he didn't understand, they told him. We want you to have a union contractor, regardless of the cost. And if you'll do that, we'll support your run for governor.

Even if the firm had been his alone, he wouldn't have thought twice. It wasn't, and he didn't. As the representative of a now-public company Kenny knew he had to represent those people who had invested in Monfort and make decisions that were financially sound. After he thanked the union leaders for their time, he went ahead and bid the construction out to the most competitive contractors. It was the right thing to do for the company.

As Monfort of Colorado grew to a size that got the company noticed, politicians in the state would sometimes use it in examples, or single it out for criticism. Kenny sometimes thought politicians were picking on him and his company; at other times he thought they were just not listening. In 1977 he chastised then Governor Dick Lamm for criticizing business for not being progressive enough. "If the governor wants to castigate the business community, he should be sure that he has really tried to converse with that community or with the different segments of it," he wrote. "After all, many of us think differently about different items."

National policies also had a huge impact on the company. In response to consumer pressure and increasing prices, the government had instituted price freezes in the early 1970s. Boycotts in early 1973 had hit the beef industry as prices kept rising, and Kenny had actually recommended a ceiling price on meat because the cattle market kept getting higher and higher and he thought "it was too high…Enough is enough."

The government announced in July 1973 that price freezes would be lifted on everything except beef. That was an absolute disaster for beef packers, as many cattle feeders could hold their cattle until the freeze was scheduled to be lifted and prices could go up, which was Sept. 12, 1973. With fewer cattle going to market the price for them went up during that two month period, but the price of beef couldn't. So packers were destined to be the ones forced to eat any losses. Or so the theory went.

Kenny was no fan of Richard Nixon and the feeling was mutual, as Kenny's inclusion on Nixon's enemies list proved. Nevertheless, he saw the Nixon ruling for what it was: an attempt by the president to hold down the price of beef for consumers. It was a stupid way to do it, Kenny thought, but there it was. It had the backing of law, which meant to try to circumvent the freeze was going against the spirit of what the president was trying to do.

To have the integrity to obey a law that he felt was wrongheaded and bound for disaster was costly to Monfort monetarily. Some days trucks would leave the plant that could have carried a sign that said "$10,000 in losses inside." When he had a hundred trucks in the yard, Kenny must have swallowed hard before loading them up and sending them on their way.

Meanwhile other packers were having their lawyers see what kinds of loopholes they could find in the freeze. Some just ignored the law. But it turns out there was a big loophole they could squeeze through. The freeze was only on carcasses and beef, not on live animals. So other plants would find ways to get their customers live cattle and custom slaughter the animals for them. This went on for weeks and weeks, and Kenny was the only one who would not do it, as to do so would violate the spirit of the law.

This generated some goodwill among his regular customers, who were able to purchase the meat at lower prices than his competitors. (Beef had to be rationed to those customers, and new customers could not be added because the demand was so great.) At least it did for a time. In a competitive business like commodity beef where margins are very slim, goodwill among customers often eventually fades away. When the freeze was lifted, many of Monfort's customers again went where they could get their meat for half-a-cent a pound less. After all, a buck was a buck.

Kenny's business relationships were based on trust, respect and honor. His handshake was his bond, and together with eye contact was how he struck his deals. No legal documents would make any difference in how he handled his business affairs.

> I was always taught if you play according to the rules and an agreement or a deal is made in accord with those rules, the rules shouldn't be changed in the middle or at the end of the game.
>
> Ken Monfort Column
> *Town & Country News*
> Oct. 17, 1974

The Monfort family had suffered tough times several times in the past, and bankruptcy rumors had followed. In 1954, 1963, 1974 and 1980 they had their share of financial trouble, but with the cooperation of bankers, persistence and lots of luck they always managed to stay a step ahead of what he considered "the last resort."

And that was what he considered bankruptcy: a last resort. Kenny was miffed in the early 1980s, for instance, that Wilson & Co., which had more equity than his company, was declaring bankruptcy and was going to walk away from a $53,000 bill from Monfort for beef trimmings it had purchased to use in its hot dogs. There was no honor in that. From then on with Wilson it wasn't an honor system, it was pay as you go.

> A couple of years ago in our company we had the same (financial) problem. At that time no one suggested bankruptcy. If that had been suggested I would have had a fit. I thought and still think bankruptcy is and should be the last thing done. ... Obviously, however, with some the onus is not there. With some it has become a business strategy.
>
> Ken Monfort column
> *Greeley Tribune*
> April 27, 1984

It was also about honor when communicating with your stakeholders. He didn't mince words when he was writing about the company's troubles or successes. And he wasn't going to mess around with the numbers just to make investors more comfortable. It was what it was.

That integrity and sense of ethics made it very easy for the company's legal team. They rarely had to come up with creative ways for getting out of a scrape, because there were few scrapes to get out of. They tried to conduct every transaction honestly and make every business dealing above board.

Kenny's trust in those with whom he did business was also paramount. He wouldn't waste time with people he had to keep an eye on, whether it was employees, customers or suppliers. If a contract was legally required he would put one together, but it meant no more to Kenny than the handshake or the phone call that went with it.

As with employees, if he thought mistakes were honest, he wouldn't allow the person across the table from him to take unwarranted losses. If he trusted you, there were no worries about an occasional slip-up. And if he didn't trust you, he didn't do business with you.

Kenny Lloyd had been on the Republican side in the 1960s, but Kenny trusted his judgment nonetheless. Lloyd was a commodities trader who helped the company hedge its positions in the cattle market, making sure the company took no excessive losses when it came time to process the animals.

In the commodity business things move very fast and it can be easy to cover your tracks should you make a mistake. That wasn't Lloyd's method, though, and especially not with Kenny. The truth was the only way to handle communication.

One day Kenny asked Lloyd to liquidate a significant position the company had in cattle. That meant selling futures contracts the company owned on the floor of the Chicago Mercantile Exchange in Chicago. So Lloyd instructed the broker on the floor and told him that unless he heard from him otherwise, he was to sell a certain number of contracts every half hour, to make sure they got the average for the day.

At the end of the day he found that there were a hundred contracts that hadn't closed – about a $10,000 loss. Oh, boy, Lloyd thought. This is trouble. So he called Kenny up and said, I've got to tell you, I made a mistake. I didn't get it all done. Get out of it in the morning, was all Kenny said. And nothing more was ever mentioned about it.

Kenny loved working with numbers. At one point his staff was going to the unusual length of producing daily profit and loss (P&L) statements, which they would reconcile with weekly P&Ls to see how close they were coming to goals. Rarely were they off by more than 1 or 2 percent.

Kenny didn't take unnecessary risks with the company's money. Not much, anyway. The futures market was where Kenny did his gambling – ostensibly to offset possible losses in the future. He wasn't always successful.

Futures trading is another form of competitive buying and selling, but it's buying and selling product in the future, not today. Conducted on the Chicago Mercantile Exchange (CME), it's a form of instantly connecting willing buyers and sellers coast-to-coast, who are basically expressing their opinion about what the prices on a particular commodity will be in future months. If they're right about what the prices will be, they make money; if they're wrong, they lose.

According to the CME, a futures contract is a "legally binding, standardized agreement to buy or sell a standardized commodity, specifying quantity and quality at a set price on a future date." Entering into the contract is more than a guess, but less than a science. What you're really doing is saying you know more about the direction of the market than other individuals and companies that are involved. It was a gamble to some extent, but often even if you weren't exactly right you could lock in profits – or spread out the risk – if you "hedged" properly in the futures market.

Kenny would study the markets for hours on end, trying to get a handle on supply and demand and carrying home USDA and other reports, economist newsletters and past results to see if he could determine what would be happening on the beef or cattle markets down the road. He was a member of the CME, so could conduct trading whenever he saw the need. He also relied on experts in the field to help point to potential pitfalls and opportunities.

He believed participating in the futures market was an important way to hedge the company's positions. His father, however, wasn't so sure. Futures trading for live cattle hadn't come around until 1964, so he had never even been involved in the process before then. And he didn't really trust it. Warren thought that over the long run playing the futures market would lose you as much money as it would earn you. His philosophy was to just raise the cattle to produce the best beef possible, then sell it on the market to people who appreciated its quality. In fact, it's rumored that occasionally Warren would find out what futures trades his son had made, then make the opposite ones. You can't lose money that way.

Kenny thought you could protect the value of cattle you bought by buying and selling futures contracts on those cattle. He also thought you could sell meat ahead of time at a predetermined price, then hedge that sale by buying or selling futures for that sale date.

When it came to futures trading, Kenny was a hedger and not a speculator. That was more than by definition; that was the rule. Speculators in the futures market are not allowed to own or produce the commodity they're trading in. They only buy or sell the contracts in the hope of making a profit when the prices change.

Because commodity prices can be volatile, the potential for profits are much greater than in the stock market. The potential risk for losses, of course, is equally high. Hedgers, meanwhile, are just trying to transfer the price risk on the commodities they own to other hedgers – and to the speculators, who are sometimes willing to roll the dice for what might be a big payoff.

When a decline in the price of the commodity is expected, hedgers will try to seek protection by participating in the futures market. Hedgers will also get involved if they think a futures price seems higher than a situation warrants. Finally, if a loss has to be avoided at all costs, the hedger can get protection in the market.

It sounds a little more complicated than it is. Here's a simplistic example for cattle: Determine the cost of the feeder cattle you are buying, and the costs of feeding those cattle over the prescribed number of days, including feed, labor, machinery/equipment/buildings and miscellaneous costs. Build in a profit margin to establish what you think would be a good selling price for those cattle at the end of their feeding time. Then sell a contract that represents those animals at that price and date – if you can.

If you sell at that price and the market has gone higher, you've actually lost some money that you might have made otherwise – but you've still locked in a profit. If the market has gone lower, you've essentially dodged a loss by transferring the price risk to others in the market. At any time during the contract you can buy it back at the current market price (minus margins).

You've got another decision to make, too. If you find the right price but believe the market is going to go higher still, you might want to wait for a better opportunity to make more money. If you're wrong… At any rate, good hedging is dependent on estimating properly, which includes getting the right price for what you think your animals are going to cost plus what you consider to be a fair profit.

There was no better estimator than Kenny. He knew his business and his industry frontward and backward. He would pore over business and government reports, markets, everything he could get his hands on. He was thorough and meticulous and determined to get it right. Sometimes, he got it wrong.

Because they had their own packing plant and feedlots, it was different at Monfort. Both the plant and the feedlots were responsible for showing their own profit or loss. While the principal of hedging was the same, sometimes they would need to determine if they wanted to "deliver" on their contracts instead of slaughtering the animals. And that's when it became complicated. With trucking, shrink and other costs of delivery as well as grading costs – along with lost opportunity at the Monfort packing plant and the need of that plant to have animals to process – it would rarely make sense to deliver on a contract. Sometimes, though, they did.

The company had been challenged once on the way it used the futures market and LIFO accounting to reduce the amount of taxes it paid. In using the futures market in 1968 Kenny had made a $32,738 gain, but used it to reduce the company's ending cattle inventory by a like amount instead of treating it as an individual item of income. The IRS said it was income, and assessed the company for taxes due. The company paid and sued for a refund.

In 1977 the Court of Appeals for the 10th Circuit finally agreed with Monfort, saying there was nothing in the regulations that kept the company from accounting for its hedging gains the way it did. Monfort had adequately established that hedging was a crucial part of its overall operation that directly and exclusively related to cost control. Kenny had testified in the suit that the company never participated as a speculator and that "he would be fired if he ever participated in cattle futures as an investor or speculator."

Kenny didn't always guess right when it came to the futures market and would sometimes go too far in hedging positions. And he occasionally got frustrated with his abilities to consistently guess right about what was going to happen. In fact, in a Jan. 7, 1974, memo to his leadership team he resigned from his position as futures trader for the company because of costly decisions he had made. "In the spirit of (losing sports teams), if the coach doesn't win he either quits or gets fired," he wrote in the memo. "This one quits. (Only so far as the futures business goes.)"

He appointed Sam Addoms to take up oversight of the futures operations – or lack thereof. "This will not pertain to hedging of outside purchases at the Packing Plant. I would like to become a member of the advisory committee, although I see no reason why anyone would listen to me." He said he was "out of tune with the market and think that I must be replaced." It's not known how long that hiatus lasted.

Luck was sometimes involved in making good futures trades and it was also crucial to having success in business, Kenny believed. He said luck was a huge problem solver. Kenny had known hard workers who weren't successful, and slackers who were.

Still, he believed in the Thomas Jefferson adage that "I'm a great believer in luck, and I find the harder I work the more I have of it." Often his work habits were such that they could leave little time for socializing and family, and what work he couldn't finish at the office he often took home with him. Work weeks that exceeded 100 hours were not uncommon.

Whether Kenny actually slept was a subject for debate. He was always there when people got there in the morning, and there when they left at night. And often he was wearing the same clothes. (More about that in Chapter 8.)

Kenny's briefcase was truly unique. He would take an empty copy paper box and place it beside his desk, throwing everything that didn't require immediate attention into it. At the end of the day the box went home with him, coming back empty the next morning to be filled up again.

He liked to say he wasn't a planner. In a 1986 *Greeley Tribune* interview he said he had "no idea what the company will look like five years from now. ... I do spend a lot of hours (working). But I don't always get a lot done because I'm not very organized." He had told others he "never had any big goals. I always sort of just did what made sense at the time." And, after being named a recipient of the Bravo! 2000 Lifetime Achievement Award, he said "I never had great plans. I got where I did by luck, timing and hard work. I've gotten up early in the morning."

There's no question his timing, like the timing of his father, was good. He also worked hard and put in long hours. It was because of his actions that he was lucky, however. Furthermore, some of his actions belied his expressed sentiments about planning. Many of his associates remember Mondays when he would come into the office after a weekend spent at home with company records and a yellow tablet. He would throw his meticulous company projections on the conference table, give each of the executives a few minutes to look them over, and tell them what needed to be done. He did his homework and wasn't a spur-of-the-moment kind of leader.

He might not have called it planning, but he had great vision for the future and how things would work out not only for him but for the cattle and meat industry and for society in general.

Crystal Ball

In 1969 he made predictions to the Oregon Cattlemen's Association that were eerie in their accuracy of the future. For instance, he told the group that "the fear of fat in diets may well signify a lowering of our grade standards, and we shall certainly see an end to conformation as a factor in determining the grade of meat." Conformation was eliminated as a factor in quality grade standards in 1975.

Other problems with government grading were costing the company a lot of money. In 1970 Monfort was putting steers into the feedlots that weighed in the upper 800 pound range and putting about 300 pounds on them. More than 83 percent of these animals graded Choice, about 6 percent Prime and only 11 percent didn't qualify for the top two quality grades. By 1974 the company was buying younger cattle that weighed about 100 pounds less and putting 375 pounds on them. In that year, however, only 63 percent graded Choice. Because the antiquated grading system was partially dependent on maturity, the company was losing about $50 a head on many of its animals.

Kenny got impatient with the government's actions on grading changes and in 1974 decided to see if customers would be willing to accept a product with Monfort's own specifications. Called Monfort Gold, if the product had been graded by the government it would have fit into the USDA Choice and Prime categories with a cutability of Yield Grade 1 or 2, which delineate the leanest, highest yielding cattle. The company believed Monfort Gold would be a premium brand name product, more merchandisable than the existing Choice, which at the time contained too much fat, Kenny believed. By 1975 about half of the cattle coming out of the Monfort feedlots qualified for the Monfort Gold label.

Finally in 1987 the USDA changed the name of the "Good" grade to "Select," reflecting society's perceptions and desire for less fat on their beef cuts. In addition, the USDA had previously required carcasses that had been graded for quality also be graded for yield. They now "uncoupled" the grades, meaning carcasses with excess fat could be trimmed on the slaughter floor and still be graded for quality without requiring a yield grade.

Kenny also told the Oregon group that consumerism would be much more prevalent in the future. "In this time of affluence, consumer demands for clean, wholesome and honest product will take precedence over cheapness, slipshod sanitation and artificial additives. Bacteria counts will become as familiar a term (to packers) as yield grading…the clean and honest packer will profit at the expense of those who can't or won't comply." While consumers don't yet monitor bacteria counts, packers – and government agencies – do. Cleanliness and wholesomeness are becoming more uniform across the industry and are an expectation of consumers.

In addition, he predicted packaging would improve. "I believe that in 1980 we still will be handling the vast bulk of our beef in fresh (unfrozen) form, but the packaging will be such that its shelf life will be measured in months, not days." In the late 1970s Monfort scientists were among the first to come up with packaging that gave beef a shelf life of 100 days, allowing greater international sales and improving marketing worldwide. In Japan tests had shown that shelf life for Monfort's package was equal to 180 days – or about six months.

Among Kenny's favorite speeches to groups was one that spoke right to where he thought the company was headed. People called it "the box speech." For this speech, which was usually made to a cattlemen's group, Kenny would bring along one of the beef boxes from the packing plant and tell the group, "Your cattle need to fit into this box." His point couldn't have been more clear:

As cattlemen, you need to think more like marketers and less like cowboys.

The animals had to be raised so primal cuts fit into the boxes being used by packers. Otherwise, they were of less value. He always got an excellent reaction to his box speech because no one could argue with it. He was speaking as the customer, after all. Their animals would need to fit into that box.

Though his company was huge, there came a point Kenny thought quantity should give way to quality – at least as far as the industry was concerned. He told a group of newspaper farm editors in December of 1977 that "cattlemen must reduce production to be profitable. It's very simple – we can sell 110 pounds of beef (per capita) for more total dollars than we can get for marketing 128 pounds, like we did last year. That's a lesson that we have to learn throughout agriculture."

His knack with numbers was legendary. He had a calculator for a mind and could remember figures he had given an employee a week earlier. It was amazing to watch him in meetings with his yellow pad and pencil. Others knew not to question figures he had derived or calculations he made. He was invariably right.

While it isn't known quite how he did it, some believe it might have had its origin back in the 1930s when he had rheumatic fever and spent nearly a year in bed, often in a darkened room (See Chapter 8). During those times his mother would have him do calculations and multiplication tables in his head to keep his mind occupied. It helped him picture the numbers without actually seeing them.

Kenny was on the Board of Affiliated Bankshares of Colorado, of which the Greeley National Bank was a part. Clark Weaver, who had been staff attorney for Monfort of Colorado in the 1970s, had gone on to work for Intrawest Financial Corporation and was involved in a merger that involved the two banks. Weaver knew what others working at Intrawest probably didn't: The casual dress and easy manner of the tall businessman participating in the negotiations could be deceiving.

In fact, when the discussions around the table turned to interest rates on a certain facet of the transaction, calculators were furiously busy at every seat except where Kenny was sitting, where nothing was stirring but his mind. Off the top of his head he had the interest rate calculated before the others got all of the numbers entered. No one underestimated him after that.

It helped that Kenny came prepared to these meetings. He always did his homework and listened intently. But his decisions, once he made them, were quick and decisive. He didn't waste time thinking about "what might have been." He was too busy dealing with what was.

Kenny was not only quick with the numbers, he didn't hoard the information. He was generous with his time and knowledge.

When the dairy industry believed it was getting too many cows in the 1980s, it convinced the government there should be a "dairy buyout" to encourage some dairymen to get out of the business. One of the problems with this idea was that the dairy cows had to go somewhere. That "somewhere" was the beef market. And that meant increasing beef supplies, which meant decreased beef prices. That didn't please Kenny at all.

Another problem, though, was there were not enough packing plants to take care of the extra cows. As one of the small dairymen taking the government up on the offer, Bob Fillinger was selected by the Mountain Empire Dairymen's Association to visit with Kenny Monfort to see if his company's plant could help take up the slack. His was the largest packing plant in the region, and perhaps it would make economic sense for them to play a part.

Fillinger walked into a haze of smoke and sat in the chair opposite Kenny. Two cigarettes were going in an ash tray already filled with butts. Kenny lit another, then pulled out some papers from his drawer and spread them out on his desk. His handwritten costs and calculations made it clear he not only had a good understanding of the situation, he also had a well-researched and thoughtful prediction for what would happen in the future. And he was right.

No, he couldn't be part of helping slaughter the dairy cows. But he had good, solid business reasons for his decision. You can't argue with that.

Kenny hated losing, and he was no fan of inefficiency, either. He thought insurance companies were among the biggest inefficiencies in society.

You were in business, right? That meant taking risks, right? Kenny thought most insurance was a waste of money and that companies in the business of taking risks – as all companies should be – need to be willing to absorb some of the risks associated with that business.

Kenny moved more and more of his business to self-insurance. That meant health insurance for his people and other insurance for other risks that he might face. He hired a risk manager, Lucille "Lucky" Gallagher, to make sure all of the risks associated with what the company was doing were covered. And he expected everyone else on his staff to minimize risks so that he wouldn't have to worry so much about it.

Kenny also didn't have much use for public relations people; he was his own PR guy. He was upfront, congenial and quotable and most reporters loved him. His views were always appreciated, but not always used.

Young reporter Lynn Heinze had written what he thought was a pretty good article. He had done due diligence and interviewed those who knew the most about the topic, which in this case was the cattle industry. It was the early 1970s, and it could certainly be a complicated subject.

He sent his story to his editor at the Greeley Tribune, John Dugan, who called Heinze to his desk and said those words no reporter wants to hear: We may have a problem. Off they marched to the publisher's office. Mildred Hansen was the daughter of an early editor and publisher of the Tribune, Charles Hansen, and ran the paper with an iron hand. What she said was law.

Dugan showed her the article and Heinze held his breath. She looked up, gave him a steely stare and said matter-of-factly:

We don't quote Monforts in this paper. By her attitude she made it clear that no explanation was necessary, and none was forthcoming. Heinze knew that from then on, while he could call Kenny for background and Kenny would be happy to oblige, he would need to get his quotes from someone else.

It isn't clear why Hansen had a problem with Kenny – or with the Monforts, for that matter. One of the issues may have been that Kenny and Hank Brown were columnists for the only competition the *Tribune* had at the time, the upstart *Town & Country News*, which was capturing some of the advertising dollars Hansen may have thought should be theirs. The *Tribune* also carried the title the *Greeley Republican*; with Kenny on board and Colorado Senator Jim Kadlacek also contributing material the *Town and Country News* may have leaned a little more to the left. It didn't really matter; later the *Tribune* would buy out the *Town and Country News*.

Kenny believed wholeheartedly in freedom of the press, but at times it bugged the heck out of him. "Those who are governing are protective of their own position," he wrote in one of his early columns in *Town and Country News*. "Obviously, they do not wish to be exposed or to rock the boat. The press, the radio station and the TV should have no such constraints. It should be their job to question, to 'rock the boat'."

Kenny had a generally good relationship with the media, but there were times he regretted his open style.

> I was interviewed by Channel 9 once. Because we knew it would be a hatchet job we taped it and compared it with what Channel 9 ran. I, of course, didn't like it, wanted to sue, etc., but our lawyer (not my wife this time) told me it would cost more than we could get and then probably any decision in our favor would be overturned. So I was chicken, and

> now I simply don't believe anything that Ward Lucas says or does.
>
> Ken Monfort Column
> *Greeley Tribune*
> August, 1990

The 1984 interview had two elements that incensed Kenny: innuendo and an attack on Kenny's integrity and the integrity of the products he sold. Lucas suggested that because Kenny had been a friend of the U.S. Attorney General for Colorado, a blind eye was turned toward some possibly spoiled product sold by the company. Despite detailed and reasonable explanations, Lucas ran with the piece with only cursory mention of them.

Kenny was incensed at the suggestion, and didn't mince words when he told his shareholders about it in the 1984 Annual Report. "KUSA, a Denver (television) station, aired a purported investigative report on me and our Company," he wrote. "The report was full of errors and half truths. We were advised by counsel that our case would be good should we sue the station and the reporter for slander. However, we decided not to spend the money and the effort but I am not sure that was a good decision. Eventually, we in business who try very hard to produce excellent products must take a stand against this type of shoddy journalism."

Branching Out

By the 1970s Kenny was putting more and more of his attention on what was happening outside of this country's borders. The company was a major supplier to Japan's Expo 70, sending about 500,000 of its choicest steaks to the event. Monfort was a perfect supplier to a country like Japan, which valued the personal touch and wanted products it could associate with an individual – especially one with Kenny's personality. Because it was his family name on the box rather than just letters or a clever label, Japanese buyers felt confident they could trust the quality and wholesomeness of the product. When they met Kenny, who to them was the quintessential "Marlboro Man," they were even more inclined to be good customers.

Among the people who were crucial to making the Japanese market work for the company was Seigi Horiuchi, who had many contacts in Japan and had been the Monfort liaison to Japan for some time. Kenny credited Horiuchi for helping Monfort become one of the leading meat suppliers in Japan. By 1988 Monfort sales to Japan had reached $100 million a year.

Meanwhile, France had become the leading purchaser of Monfort beef livers. Other countries purchased by-products that were not valuable in the United States. Kenny was even more sure the international market was the wave of the future.

When Kenny served as chairman of the American Meat Institute (AMI) in 1988, among the issues he paid particular attention to was an increased Japanese market for U.S. beef. He told *Meat Industry* Magazine in September 1988 that he thought he "earned every bit of what I got paid," which, of course, was nothing. Others helped by his efforts to open up that important market would argue with that appraisal.

In the 1970s and 1980s the company was also making strides in the European market. Torben Lenzberg of Denmark had seen a *Fortune Magazine* article on Monfort in January 1973 and become enamored with the company, even more so when he met Kenny and saw his "warm humor and charm, coupled with intense hard work." He began working with Kenny to bring beef to Denmark. When he said he couldn't buy more because credit wasn't easy to come by in Denmark, Kenny suggested Lenzberg pay for the product once it was sold. Kenny's trust in people went all the way across the Atlantic.

Kenny's son Charlie would continue the international emphasis into Europe when he became head of Monfort's international division in the early 1980s. In the late 1980s the EU banned beef from cattle raised using growth hormones, however, and sales to European countries came to an abrupt halt.

During Kenny's tenure at AMI – which, by the way, may have been the only time he carried a briefcase – he also helped promote the streamlined inspection system, which put more of the responsibility for keeping beef defect-free on the companies producing it. Companies, he said, "should be responsible for presenting a clean, defect-free carcass, and USDA should be responsible for checking for the possibility of microbial contamination, rather than looking at every carcass to see if there's a defect," he told *Meat Industry*. "In the past I think we relied on USDA to be a quality control program for us…the program makes us a better processor."

Not everyone saw it that way. The meat inspectors union believed it would reduce the wholesomeness of the product. "That's understandable," said Kenny. "These people are concerned about their jobs."

In the late 1970s, though, Kenny had taken his company to the next level when it came to food safety by preventing problems, rather than just finding them. He hired Rod Bowling, a Ph.D. from Colorado State University, to oversee a food safety program that was exceptional in the industry. He spared no expense in funding Bowling's programs and supporting his solutions to problems he identified. Bowling also acted as Kenny's own "contrarian" to challenge accepted notions in the industry and ways of doing things.

Later Kenny was appointed by the U.S. Secretary of Agriculture to serve on the Cattlemen's Beef Promotion and Research Board, which had been established in 1986. The Board helped the USDA oversee a new $1-per-head assessment on cattle for use in beef research, education and promotion programs. Cattlemen would pay the fee when their animals were sold.

Kenny was generally no big fan of generic promotion programs. He compared them to "seeding clouds. When you run out of water you have to do something…" But because his company was feeding hundreds of thousands of cattle a year and paying the industry's $1-a-head fee on these animals, he was a natural choice.

Kenny had never before participated in voluntary assessment programs for these kinds of efforts. Still, he did believe the state and national beef promotion organizations were on the right track, spending money on education and information programs that helped consumers understand the benefits of including beef in the diet. But this new mandatory program was more like a tax, and despite its good intentions everyone knew how Kenny felt about taxes.

It could be argued that it would have been unusual had Kenny not been successful. He had a computer for a mind, did his homework, worked long hours, played fair and took the right chances. There's one more ingredient Kenny knew he needed, though: The right people to work for his company.

Chapter 7
The Help

Employees always knew where they stood with Kenny. He was blunt and direct, and his expectations were clear. He spelled things out, and after a decision had been made everyone knew the marching orders.

Yet he listened. Really listened. Not like some bosses, with one ear and the mind working on what the mouth was going to say next. He wanted ideas, opinions, comments on how things could be done better. It didn't matter what part of the company the employee worked for or where in the hierarchy he or she stood. He honestly wanted to know what they thought.

From the earliest days Monfort employees knew they were part of a larger family. While Kenny was the boss he was also one of them and worked just as hard as – most of the time harder than – they did.

His approaches to employee management and relations weren't gathered in business school; they were learned from his father, who had many of the same strategies with a much smaller workforce. Future Monfort President Sam Addoms would call it a "spiderweb management philosophy," where all of the trails led right back to the center. Warren would exhibit it by keeping a close eye on everything going on in the feedlots. His son would do the same, but from a slightly greater distance.

Standing a foot from the wall the handwritten sign was unavoidable.

> *Please do not throw cigarette butts into the urinal. The janitor does not like to clean them up – would you?*
>
> *Ken*

Another sign over a different urinal was more to the point.

Don't throw your cigarette butts in my urinal and I won't come piss in your ashtray.

Ken

A highly paid assistant with a half dozen memos couldn't have been more effective. There were no cigarette butts in the urinals.

Weekly meetings were not conducted like democracies. Yes, Kenny solicited suggestions. But only one vote counted. After that vote had been cast the direction was set and the staff was expected to fill their roles. It was never "let's have another meeting about this," or "let me think on this for a few days." Procrastination and postponements were for losers, and Kenny was no loser. Here's the plan: Let's just do it.

Open, honest and spirited dialog would be encouraged. Insubordination was not tolerated. Sometimes a general consensus would be reached and Kenny would do just the opposite. Was it to be contrary or did he already know what he wanted to do? It didn't matter. He would just flash his crooked grin, and the charge was set. Everyone knew not to question the decision.

Occasionally Kenny would throw a friendly pop quiz at his managers during a meeting, which seemingly had nothing to do with work. The quiz most often took the form of a verbal math question dealing, for example, with trains, times, speeds and destinations.

Staff wasn't allowed to use calculators to come up with the answers to these voluntary quizzes. Some managers thought they were just meant to be fun ways to take their minds off pressing business problems. Others knew, however, they were more likely intended to see how well different individuals could watch the numbers, and who would be the best to keep an eye on the bottom line.

An open door policy was more than just a slogan at the company. And it wouldn't have mattered anyway: Kenny was often not in his office. He floated through the offices, cigarette and coffee cup in hand, to visit with his managers and staff about what was going on and problems they might be facing. He would also take frequent trips through the plant to see how things were operating and talk with the supervisors about any issues that had come up.

It was similar to what his father did at the feedlots. Employees didn't view it in a way that said "the boss is watching; be careful." They knew the connection meant the work was appreciated and not forgotten. Unlike his father, though, Kenny was less quick to offer praise to people he thought were doing good jobs. That was expected, and they should know that he knew.

Kenny rarely swore at his employees, and if he did the employee knew it was deserved. More often he would use his index finger in the face of the worker – the employee was sure it looked more like a log – to get his point across. Anger passed in minutes, and then was forgotten. In a day it was as if it had never happened. Twenty-four hours in the meat business is a lifetime.

One day during the Nixon price freeze in 1973 Ike Kelley got a call from A&P wanting a shipment of two loads of beef chucks and ribs – 80,000 pounds – in New Orleans. Monfort had never before shipped to New Orleans.

It was Kelley's account, but he knew he had better check it with Kenny. Because of the price freeze beef was highly valued and few loads were being diverted. Kenny said if he could he would, but he couldn't. The answer was no.

About five minutes later Kelley gets an angry call and summons to Kenny's office. Two truckloads of beef were at the docks in New Orleans. He had made a mistake and authorized shipment of the loads two days before. Oops.

Kenny gave Kelley the kind of look only a stern father could give. What did you do? Kenny asked. Kelley could say nothing. Don't worry, Kenny told him. We'll get through this. Though the shipments were a financial success, there was a principal here

Kenny didn't want Kelley to forget. He learned that lesson. They both knew this kind of thing would never happen again.

In the late 1970s a job efficiency study was conducted to determine if there were ways of doing business that were more organized. Despite its good intentions, most employees found the company conducting the study to be less than helpful. Job description? Well, it was whatever Kenny told you to do. Kenny liked it that way and had always felt free to move individuals as he saw fit to positions he thought were better suited to that person. An efficiency expert wouldn't let you do that.

In his eyes it was all for the good of the company. If an employee had good intentions and wanted what was best for Monfort, he was behind that person 100 percent. If there were ulterior motives or someone was trying to take advantage of someone else – internally or externally – Kenny would have none of it.

Working on Saturday was frequently expected. Employees knew Kenny would be there. In fact, he would be the one bringing donuts for the workers who would join him. It was your "bonus" for coming in when it wasn't actually required. He wouldn't keep a list of those who were there... at least not a written one. But having delivered the donuts, he knew.

Productive people were highly valued. If you were making the company money, you were more important than if you were on an administrative or support staff. He wouldn't come out and say so directly, but people understood. That was one of the reasons he wanted a small management team.

It wasn't a "leaders" and "followers" idea, it was a "tellers" and "doers" concept. People who were "doers" made money for the company. That's why if it needed doing, Kenny wasn't above doing it himself. A man who had grown up near feedlots, he knew the value of hard work and appreciated how hard others worked, too. He wanted people under him who had that same understanding. A willingness to do whatever was necessary was an attitude that was shared by Kenny and the employees he would keep around him.

The truck needed loading and the luggers (plant workers who carried carcass quarters into the trucks) were refusing to load it. Perhaps their shift was over; perhaps the pay for this duty wasn't adequate. The details of the issue are lost to history. Salesman Joe Meilinger saw that the truck of beef arm chucks he had sold wasn't getting loaded, and it needed to leave. He decided to take the matter into his own hands.

He and fellow salesman Bobby Parris threw on hats and frocks and went down to load the truck themselves. One of the union workers saw what they were starting to do and told Meilinger that if he continued to load the truck they would meet later in the parking lot, and he'd be damn sorry for doing it. This truck needs loading, Meilinger responded. He would just have to see him later outside.

After the truck was about half loaded the union workers relented and finished loading the truck, and Meilinger and Parris went back to the office to finish up their regular work. Kenny was in the offices at the time and had been aware of the conflict. While he hadn't jumped into the fray, he approved of the way it was resolved. That's the way he would have handled it. If there was something that needed doing, and if the company would benefit, he would just do it.

Kenny's attitude toward raises was similar to his father's. If someone deserves a raise, we'll give it to him. If he asks for one, maybe he doesn't really deserve it.

Most everyone on staff knew about the "Rocky Mountain Discount," though few knew it by that term. When raise time came around, Kenny would take the employee near the West-facing windows, put his arm around the person and say, "Look at that. Do you think you'd get this kind of view in Dakota City, Nebraska?" Someone thinking about going to the headquarters of IBP would have to think about how much living near the mountains added to the value of their Monfort employment.

Pay for packing house workers was good in the beginning because that's what the job in packing houses paid. Companies in Chicago and elsewhere were paying people about the same and

Monfort was more modern and efficient, so the company could compete with them. When the union came in during the early 1960s, Kenny was unconcerned. Unions were just a part of the meat packing industry. If the other companies had them, so would he.

Employees would be promoted from within, but Kenny also went out of his way to hire people he knew and trusted or people he thought would be good candidates for specific positions, thereby surrounding himself with extremely capable and loyal managers. He did this regardless of age, political affiliation, cattle business experience or personal beliefs. These people helped to strengthen the company in their own ways, and some would go on to have successful careers in other endeavors.

Nepotism? No problem. When you were hired, you were part of the family. If good employees had a brother, sister or other relative or friend they thought would be a good worker, often they were hired. But they wouldn't be kept around if they couldn't pull their weight. That went for the Monfort family, too. If you were employed, you would contribute to the extent of your position.

Both a frugal and generous person, Kenny had a way of demonstrating by his actions how he expected others to care for each other – as well as the company's money.

As the company's vice president for corporate development, Hank Brown was appointed to help phase in international operations for Monfort. He and Kenny had just finished a visit to Australia to work out a joint marketing arrangement with an Australian firm. It was around 1974, and the trip had been long and hard – about 16 hours on the flight over, alone. For employees of Monfort all traveling, even international, was done in coach. You don't get there any sooner in first class. Not much, anyway.

Now they were on the trip back and it looked to be another long and uncomfortable ride. Kenny was upgraded to first class because of the number of flights he had previously taken. At least one of them would travel in comfort.

About an hour into the flight Kenny came back to where Brown was sitting and suggested that he go try out his seat. No, Brown said, that's your seat. But Kenny insisted and was sincere, so Brown went up to the front of the plane, sat in the seat and reflected on Kenny's generosity and tolerance.

Tolerance. The fact that Kenny had hired him in the first place was a testament to his tolerance. Brown had worked on the campaign staff of Republican Peter Dominick in 1968 while Kenny was running in the Democratic primary for Dominick's U.S. Senate seat. And they hadn't even been close to seeing eye-to-eye on the Vietnam War issue. But given all that, Kenny had hired him in 1969 and made him his assistant, promoting him along the way. It was a classy thing to do, Brown thought. With that he stretched out and promptly fell asleep.

He woke with a start and looked at his watch. They were about an hour away from landing. He had been asleep for hours. Surely Kenny was stewing back in the coach cabin, wondering why Brown had hogged the first class seat. He sheepishly walked back to where he originally had been sitting. He didn't know how he would explain himself to Kenny.

Brown is no small man. As a sophomore at the University of Colorado in the late 1950s he had been a top wrestler in the heavyweight division, and was no smaller in 1974. But Kenny was nearly 6'5" and well over 200 pounds. There he was, scrunched up in Brown's coach seat, fast asleep. He had to have been a contortionist to fit into the coach seat for that long. Rather than wake Brown up, he had traveled the whole trip in a tiny ball that Houdini would have found uncomfortable. What kind of a boss is that, Brown wondered?

Probably one of the reasons Kenny paid himself so little was to keep the overall wage scale at the company low. How could someone ask for that kind of money if even he wasn't making that much? No one should make more than the president of the company.

Loyalty to the company was important and it worked both ways. Loyalty to the company was the same as loyalty to Kenny.

And Kenny was loyal to those who stuck by him. Sometimes employees who left the company – especially if they went to competitors – were not mentioned again, having disowned the family and chosen to share their talents with others. Kenny did have it in his heart to forgive, however, and accepted back those who may have strayed. As long as they saw the errors of their ways, these wayward sheep could find their way back to the fold.

Doug Carey had worked for the company since he graduated from high school, starting work 30 days short of his 18th birthday in 1962. In those days the company had some of the best paying jobs around and he felt fortunate to land one of them.

Carey worked many jobs, eventually working his way up into sales and becoming a member of the Monfort sales team. He was generally satisfied where he was. It was just that darn salary issue, with grasses greener all over the country that was of any concern whatsoever.

One of his Florida customers had been after Carey for some time to go to work for him. No, Carey kept telling him, I appreciate the offer but I'm happy here. I hope it won't affect our relationship. But the customer kept offering Carey more and more money, and eventually he knew he had to do what was best for his family and his career.

So he did the hardest thing he had ever done in his life: He wrote out his resignation letter and gave it to his supervisor, Joe Meilinger, and to Kenny. Are you sure this is what you want? Kenny asked. At this point in my career I think it is. Then I wish you the very best.

An employment contract was supposed to be provided by his new company and signed prior to starting, but because it was the year-end that company wasn't able to provide it. No problem, Carey thought, I trust them. The only work environment he'd ever known had been Monfort, and if the shoe had been on the other foot there would have been no question. If Kenny had said he was going to do something, it would get done. Carey assumed that was the way the business world operated, and his new company would come through.

Three weeks later there was still no contract. Almost there, the new boss said. Because his family had not yet moved, Carey was scheduled to fly back to Colorado at the end of the following week. He said he wanted a contract in his hand before he got on the plane. Absolutely, was the reply.

On the plane Carey decided to peruse the contract and he couldn't believe his eyes. Half of the things they had agreed to verbally weren't in the contract and the other half had been twisted around. He was furious. Upon landing he tried calling Florida and couldn't reach his boss. He tried all weekend; no luck.

You know, Carey told his wife, if he's going to screw me now he's going to screw me every step of the way. I'm flying back and driving home. We'll find something else to do.

He sheepishly called Meilinger and asked for a letter of recommendation. Of course, Meilinger said, what happened? After Carey explained he asked if he could pick up the letter at Meilinger's house, as he was too embarrassed to go to the plant and get it. Sure, Meilinger said, I'll call you when I get it done.

Fifteen minutes later Carey's phone rings. It's Kenny. What are you doing? he asked. Right now I'm sitting here licking my wounds, Carey answered, explaining what had happened. So what are you doing at 5 o'clock? I'm not doing anything, Kenny, I'm just looking for a job. Well, you come by the plant at 5 and have a cup of coffee with me.

They called it a leave of absence. Carey started back with Monfort the next Monday, taking ribbing from his fellow salesmen – and from Kenny – but feeling tremendously fortunate to work for such a forgiving man.

It didn't matter what color you were, or what religion, or what sex. If you had the best interests of the company at heart, Kenny was on your side and would stand behind the decisions you made.

Lucky Gallagher had only been on the job as Monfort of Colorado risk manager for a short time when she knew things had to change. There were a lot of holes in the insurance coverage the company had and it was very vulnerable should disaster strike. So she contacted the insurance company and laid out what needed to be done to better protect the company.

For example, the company didn't have off-site power interruption coverage. So if something happened elsewhere that kept the plants from processing, they weren't protected. They needed that protection right away.

The insurance company dragged its feet while Gallagher stewed. It shouldn't be that difficult, she thought, there are lots of companies that write this kind of insurance. Sure enough, one night several months later she got a call at midnight from the company engineer saying that a tornado had hit the Grand Island plant. When she found out that the insurance company hadn't gotten the coverage they were supposedly working on, she was livid.

Her first action was to fire the insurance company. She had documented the company's failings, so she wasn't worried about the consequences, despite the fact that the company had been hired long before her.

Her second was to get a new broker, who discovered a loophole. They were able to show that the tornado struck the plant before it struck the off-site power, meaning the on-site coverage was in effect. It saved the company millions of dollars.

Kenny backed Gallagher on her actions. The original insurance company, whose principals went way back with the family, called Kenny to ask for a meeting. He put them on hold and got on the phone with Gallagher, asking when she was available. When they showed up in his office, she was sitting there.

It was an uncomfortable moment. This must have been a very emotional decision, they said, something that was made by a female who just wasn't acting rationally. Kenny listened patiently, then told the insurance company representatives it would have been easier for Gallagher to sit back and collect a paycheck to work with a long-standing company than to find a new broker because she thought it was the best for the company. Why didn't you just fix the problems initially?

It got even more awkward. So what do we need to do to get the business back, Kenny? Kenny turned to Gallagher. The first priority is to take care of the business, and the ball was already rolling the other way. The meeting was over.

Working with the unions was a different story (see also Chapters 4 and 10). In 1969 the company signed a new labor contract with Local 641 of the Amalgamated Meat Cutters and Butcher Workmen's union for its new portion control plant. The next year, though, trouble was brewing for the packing plant.

The same union local had the contract for the packing plant, and it was up for renewal in 1970. The company was already feeling the heat from some of its competitors.

To the surprise of no one, the issue in 1970 was wages. The average weekly pay of the employees was $157 a week based on hourly wages of $4.22 an hour. In negotiations just before the strike was called Nov. 1 the union had asked for an immediate 21 cent-an-hour increase, which was less of an increase than other major packers had recently accepted across the country. Kenny had offered a 45 cent-an-hour increase, but the increase for the first year would be 15 cents an hour. After a 56 day strike, and with the help of a federal mediator, the union settled on a 20 cent-an-hour increase over each year of a 3-year contract.

The strike was testy at times, but Kenny and both company and union officials expressed their satisfaction at how well the strike was conducted. In a 1971 company newsletter he wrote that the strike was "peaceful and just for both sides," but that it had disastrous effects on production down the line because cattle purchases had been adjusted due to the strike. He wrote that he hoped "we shall all remember these problems some three years from now" when a new labor agreement was negotiated.

Certainly that work stoppage was nowhere near as nasty as the strike that would be called in 1979.

> We must continue our concentration on efficiency if we are to make up for the $1 to $3 an hour cheaper labor at

> IBP, Missouri, American and National. And we must concentrate even more on our quality control to compete with the highly-skilled, personalized type butcher work done in New York.
>
> Ken Comments
> Company Newsletter
> June/July 1971

Kenny looked at himself as not just the lead manager, but the conduit between management and labor. In late 1971 he became frustrated at what he saw as substandard execution by both the managers leading his teams and by the workers on the lines. The performance of the company in the previous year had suffered, and he blamed not only himself but his managers and the line workers.

The seven-week strike in 1970 had certainly been one of the culprits for reduced company profits. Other strikes by rail workers and longshoremen also had an impact. In the company newsletter Kenny wrote that "we had far too many 'errors,' 'miscues' and 'turnovers.' A substantial number of these were of my own doing. Many others were attributable to our other management people."

He also pointed out, though, that productivity at the packing plant was down. And that, he said, had much to do with how hard the line workers were working. "Attitude is, as much as anything, the main answer. Simply, give a damn. Work for the common good. If you get paid for eight hours of work – work eight hours. Expect others to do the same."

> I would guess that my philosophy of management and employee relations is indeed considered corny by many. I just do not believe in the "diametrically opposed" best interests of management and labor. If our earnings are good, benefits and pay to

employees will be better, whether negotiated by the unions or granted by the company. If earnings on investment were to remain at this year's 1.7 percent, only a third of what they could be if that investment was in a bank savings account, jobs, not just profit sharings, are in jeopardy. I believe that we are all working for the same goals.

Ken Comments
Company Newsletter
October/November 1971

Among the items that irked Kenny about labor contracts was the cost of living adjustments. He believed they didn't adequately reflect the true increased costs, because people made modifications to their consumption of items used by the government to figure the adjustments. People drove less or drove more economical cars when gas prices got too high, for instance, or reduced their consumption of bacon if the price of it went up.

That would inevitably lead to problems with employee relations, he thought. "We honestly believe that by blithely accepting cost of living increases plus other wage increases and fringe-type improvements, we run the risk of pricing ourselves out of the market," he wrote in the fall 1975 company newsletter.

Far from being facilitators for working with employees, unions were becoming impediments to Kenny's employee relationships. If the employees were working for the company, they deserved loyalty. If they were working for the union, they didn't.

Non-union people had no such confusion or displaced loyalties. They knew you could get a paycheck anywhere. As has been said by other institutions, this was more than just a job. This truly was an adventure.

Chapter 8
The Man

It's hard to identify and separate all of the factors that forged Kenny's colorful personality, quirky traits, innate intelligence and moral character. His early life, of course, had something to do with it and was shaped by his family – especially his mother and father.

He was the baby of the family, having been born nearly seven years after his brother and eight years after his sister. But unlike some youngest children Kenny wasn't given free rein. Warren and Edith to a great extent retained the high expectations they had set for their two older children.

His mother had a huge influence, and not always a psychological or emotional one. Early in Kenny's life his mother, on the advice of their doctor, decided that his two pinky hammer toes had to go. So off they came. He never indicated whether having only four toes on each foot caused him to ever lose his balance, or was one of the reasons for his occasional lack of coordination in sports he played. It is known, though, that shoes are made for people with five toes on each foot, and wearing shoes was often uncomfortable for him.

In the late 1930s Kenny contracted rheumatic fever and was confined to bed for many months. It was traumatic for Kenny and his parents, as there wasn't a lot of knowledge at the time on how to deal with it. Caused by an infection that damages the heart valves – something that would play a role in Kenny's health later – the disease was tricky for parents and health care workers alike. Edith cared for Kenny at home, as parents often did with children who contracted the disease. There was just not that much else they could do.

He spent most of his time resting in bed. His mother made sure the treatment went beyond the cure, especially since the disease is active not only during the acute stage but during the convalescent stage, too. But she did try to make his life as normal as possible in other ways, taking him to the 1939 World's Fair in

San Francisco and carting him to the different exhibits in a wheelchair.

One of the beliefs of the day was that it was best to keep the children quiet and still, and to do that you should keep the room dark. Kenny spent many quiet days in his darkened room, and tried to keep his mind active by reciting multiplication tables and doing mathematical calculations in his head. This may have led to his uncannily analytical mind and ability with numbers as an adult. He usually trusted his own calculations in his head, on one of his yellow legal tablets or even on a napkin before he trusted numbers spit out of a computer or calculator. And he was usually right.

As he grew into an adult Kenny's true personality emerged. At 6-foot-4½-inches and 220 pounds, Kenny could command attention in a room just by walking into it. With penetrating blue eyes and a gravelly deep voice caused partly by years of smoking he had even more potential for a menacing mien. Instead Kenny chose to use a quick wit, captivating charm and self-deprecating humor to make people feel comfortable around him. He was quick to flash his gap-toothed smile and brought others into conversations with surprising ease.

He ambled rather than walked, his size 14 shoes – almost always loafers or other kinds of slip-ons – carrying him around in an easy and sometimes circuitous manner. He had a face that was weathered but gentle, and when he began to talk his mouth would work itself into a crooked grin, with his lips going sideways before the first words came out of his mouth.

That isn't to say Kenny was always care-free and happy-go-lucky. He could be stern when he wanted to be, and employees knew not to cross him or make mistakes too often – especially ones they'd made before. When he got angry his lower lip would quiver, and you'd know you had gone over the line. He could be forgiving, but never forgot.

Kenny was about as down-to-earth as you could get; an anti-snob, if you will. He had time for everyone and didn't look down on anyone. He listened in a way that made you feel important and respected. He was just Kenny.

Mike Croot's father had worked for Swift in Grand Island, Nebraska, for four decades before Monfort of Colorado purchased the plant in 1979. The Croot family just sort of came with the facility.

Even with his big, white loafers, Kenny was an imposing figure. When introduced, all Croot could think to say was, nice to meet you, Mr. Monfort. You know, I wish you would call me Kenny, Mike. Mr. Monfort makes me feel old.

Later in a visit to the Greeley corporate offices their paths would cross again. Hello, Mike. Hello, Mr. Monfort. Silence. We're never going to break your habit of calling me Mr. Monfort, are we, Mike? No sir, I don't think we are. Kenny just shook his head.

As he matured and took more of a leadership position in the company it was always Ken or Kenny, not Mr. Monfort. He thought it sounded too much like his father. Few ever called Warren Monfort anything other than Mr. Monfort or Boss; Kenny would prefer to let his father retain those titles.

He liked simple meals, almost always featuring beef. It was cheeseburgers for lunch and steak for dinner, medium rare. He enjoyed french fries with his cheeseburgers, and would put butter on each fry before putting it in his mouth. Sometimes he would put butter on his cheeseburger, too.

His favorite steaks were ribeyes, which he preferred over the more expensive tenderloins. "A lot of people think tenderness is the main thing, and they'll buy a tenderloin, which I think has lousy flavor," he told *Meat Industry* Magazine in July 1983.

He was never without a cigarette or a cup of coffee. At one point he was probably smoking three packs of cigarettes a day and his coffee consumption would have been calculated by the gallon rather than the cup. He could absentmindedly have three cigarettes going at the same time and would chew around the edges of his Styrofoam coffee cups. Much of the time the empty cups would be tossed into the back seat of his car.

Kenny had tried to quit smoking "30 or 60 times," he once said. Associate Sonny Mapelli had been a smoker and once he quit he tried doggedly to get Kenny to join him. And Kenny wanted to, but the addiction and his enjoyment of the act were just too strong.

His cigarette of choice was Kent if he was looking for a strong cigarette and Merit if he wanted a medium smoke. Earlier he had smoked Old Golds, too. But what he really smoked was whatever his employees were smoking at the time, because he would bum cigarettes rather than buy them.

Rudy Schlotthauer had worked at the packing plant since it opened in May 1960 and ended up running the rendering department before going into sales. He smoked the same kind of cigarettes as Kenny and knew he'd be by in the morning. So he would put his pack near the edge of the desk in preparation. Sure enough, here came Kenny, who would sit down and throw a foot up on Rudy's desk. He would take a cigarette from the pack on the desk and put it in is pocket, take another and put it behind his ear, then take a third and light it up. Then in the afternoon he'd repeat the process.

At various times others in the Monfort offices who smoked were essential players in similar kinds of rotations. Although Kenny often smoked several packs of cigarettes a day, he paid for only a small fraction of them. But he paid for the habit in other ways.

Some employees would buy cartons of cigarettes and put them in their desk drawers, knowing packs would be missing within a day. Others would hand Kenny half-finished packs, or find other ways of making sure he was supplied with his nicotine fix.

It wasn't usually possible for Kenny to buy cigarettes because until the mid-1980s, when his wife Myra made sure he had cash in his pockets, he rarely carried a dime. And he never carried any credit cards. He was always broke and borrowing money from his employees. Occasionally he would go to Judy Schlotthauer (Rudy's wife), who ran the Monfort Credit Union, borrow some money and tell her to get it back from his secretary at the end of the week or the end of the month. And she did. But usually, when it came time to get lunch or to purchase small things he needed, he had to rely on the kindness of employees and friends.

The habit of going around without any money wasn't without its dangers. Occasionally, Kenny would even have to rely on the kindness of strangers.

Bob Fillinger had just finished filling his pickup with gas at the new gas station on 35th Avenue near the Highway 34 Bypass. Greeley was growing, and this station on the south side of town was one of the few places to stop if you were getting low on gas. While at the counter getting ready to pay he noticed a nasty confrontation on the opposite side of the pay counter. There, Kenny Monfort was explaining why he couldn't pay for the fuel he had just put into his car.

It wasn't that he couldn't pay, exactly. It was just that he couldn't pay right then, he explained to the cashiers. And everyone in town knew who Kenny Monfort was, didn't they? They knew he was good for it, didn't they? Kenny was very apologetic, but the cashiers weren't having any of it, and were rude and condescending to Kenny and his obvious predicament. Kenny was sheepish about the situation he'd put himself into and probably didn't even have a dime to call his office to have someone run out with the cash.

Fillinger's sister Charlene worked for Kenny, so he introduced himself and asked if he could pay for Kenny's gas. Kenny thanked him profusely. When Fillinger got home several hours later a young girl was waiting in his yard with the money and a thank you card from Kenny. He's kept both ever since.

That was another challenge for Kenny. He was always running out of gas. Always. He had his own mathematical formula that showed, he said, you should travel as far as you could near empty before filling up. No one but Kenny really understood it, though. It was exasperating for his team, but brought smiles to a lot of faces.

Kenny walked a lot in those days, and not because he was on a health kick. Rudy Schlotthauer looked out the window one day and saw Kenny was walking again, carrying his trusty cardboard box that doubled as his briefcase. Hey, Rudy, I ran out of gas down the road a ways. Can you go get the car and fill it up for me?

That same afternoon Rudy made the commitment that he would take Kenny's car to get it filled with gas at the feedlot a couple times a week. Check the oil, too, because he never had time to check the oil. And clean it out, because the back was always filled with his Styrofoam coffee cups. After all Kenny had done for him he felt it was the least he could do.

His friend and former legislative colleague Rich Gebhardt said Kenny had it all figured out. He believed the fewer times you stopped for gas, the less time you wasted. (Kenny didn't calculate, of course, the time he spent hiking to gas stations after he had run out.) Everyone got it, though. He just didn't like to stop for gas.

The Monfort family was on vacation in Yellowstone Park. A huge sign before they entered the park said: Stop here and get your gas. No gas past this point. Ah, they're just trying to get our money, Kenny said, and traveled on. Sure enough, they ran out of gas. The only thing that saved the family was a nearby work crew that allowed Kenny to buy gas from them to get back out.

His cars? There are a thousand stories about them. If you wanted to know which car was his you would look for the messiest one in the parking lot. It's an understatement to say he didn't take care of them. The only value he saw in cars was as a way to get him from one place to another. He usually preferred yellow American cars, if he could get one. But you just never knew.

Eddie Baker was the head meat buyer at A&P Tea Co., the huge Eastern supermarket chain that was a key customer for Monfort of Colorado. One day Kenny went to the airport in Denver to pick up Baker, driving an old green and black Datsun station wagon. Baker, a huge man, barely fit into the front seat, even with the seat pushed all the way back.

It was an uncomfortable ride all the way back to Greeley, with one stop when a sign beckoned: cheap gas. You know, Baker told Kenny, there are only two CEOs anywhere that drive Datsuns. You and the president of Datsun.

It was probably the only Datsun he ever owned, and he was probably then on an energy, economy or ecology kick. But it must have suited him at the time. He believed cars were meant to go as fast as the gas pedal would allow, and that if it had four wheels and went forward it was an all-terrain vehicle.

Speed limits meant little to Kenny. It was said that one of the reasons he enjoyed being in the legislature was to get the license plate tag that would permit him to skirt those kinds of small issues. *Greeley Tribune* reporter Marcus Newton remembered one 1968 drive to Briggsdale with Kenny in his late model car, out of alignment, driving about 80 miles an hour as Kenny smoked and chatted away. "That drive to Briggsdale scared the daylights out of me," he recounted in a column.

There were four of them piled in Kenny's 2-door Pontiac coupe. It wasn't a long way to go; across town, at most. When they reached their destination, local businessman Don Herdman got out and said, Kenny, you're the only person I know who has a vehicle where you have to wipe your feet when you get out of the car.

Kenny wasn't cheap, but he did know the value of a dollar. He knew how hard those dollars could be to come by sometimes, and where they originated. So he wasn't above trying to make one go as far as it could.

Kenny, Sonny and a few of the sales people were taking some customers to lunch. When the subject of location came up, Kenny knew just where they should go: The Red Steer just north of the corporate offices.

After lunch Kenny pulls out a coupon that he had cut out of the newspaper that morning. He politely asked the waitress, can I use this 2 for 1 coupon with this group?

Kenny and his parents were far apart when it came to issues like smoking and drinking. His parents did neither; he did both. He didn't drink in their presence and hid his smoking habit from them for as long as possible. Warren and Edith apparently indulged in few vices that would be considered unhealthy.

In addition to smoking, Kenny enjoyed the occasional scotch – before dinner, of course. Or maybe with dinner. Or socially. Chivas Regal if he could get it, less costly scotch if he couldn't. In his early years he enjoyed partying and having a good time, and that usually meant both alcohol and cigarettes.

Kenny was a regular emcee at the annual Ducks Unlimited banquet and always took a great deal of pleasure in doing it. Naturally these events included drinks, and one year Kenny probably had a scotch or two too many at the event.

He was in his yellow Buick following salesmen Joe Meilinger and Bobby Parris, who had gone to the event in Parris's car. They came to a red stoplight and Kenny smacks right into the back of them.

This was before the increased focus on drinking and driving, but there were still stiff penalties for the offense. They got out of their cars and started inspecting the damage. After a short period of silence Kenny finally said, is that a company car? Yes, it is. Oh, hell, Kenny said. Get in the car and let's get out of here.

Kenny enjoyed personal freedoms and was incensed that the government would want to take them away. Safety regulations were one of his bugaboos. "If we follow all of these safety kicks to their logical conclusion, booze is out, cigarettes are out, coffee is out, butter is out, fat is out, and on and on," he wrote in his March 17, 1977, *Town and Country News* column. "Please slow down on the laws. Please slow down on the regulations. Please leave some freedom to us individuals rather than mandating your collective brilliance upon all of us who aren't that brilliant. Let us have a few things that are just flat 'bad' for us left to enjoy."

A Fashion Statement

No book on Kenny – no mention of him – would be complete without some reference to Kenny's manner of dress. As one acquaintance put it, Kenny "took casual to a whole new level. He got dressed because he needed to be clothed to be out in public." That's not to say he was a bum; he wasn't. He was always clean and clean-shaven with hair combed and cut to an appropriate length. Yet, there was something about what he chose to wear.

It was 1973 and salesman Joe Meilinger had been working for Monfort of Colorado for only a couple of weeks. Kenny had hired Meilinger, who was from a long string of butchers back East, from A&P Tea Co., the huge Eastern supermarket chain. Kenny put up him and his family – wife and four children – at one of the inexpensive motels on 9th Street in Greeley while they looked for a house. It was the cheapest lodging around.

Joe and his family had gone to Kenny's house one morning to meet Pat. Kenny came into the room and asked Pat, where's my shirt? I put it in the laundry, she said. Dammit! I wanted that shirt, he replied. So he went into the laundry basket, pulled it out and put it on to go to work. Pat looked at Joe. He just insists on wearing the same shirt every day, whether it's clean or not.

It wouldn't be unusual for Kenny to wear the same shirt for several days, causing employees to do a double-take. You know, they would think, he was at that desk wearing that shirt when we left last night... When he found clothing he liked, he stuck with it.

Bill Bragg had helped construct the Kuner feedlot in the early 1970s, and when they were finished he interviewed with Kenny for a job and got it. On the Monday after Christmas he came in with a new shirt, a stylish western number in heavy cream with a wrinkle on the inside elbow. Lo and behold, Kenny came in that day wearing the same shirt! They had a laugh about it, and

Bragg knew Kenny liked the shirt because he came in wearing it again on Tuesday. And on Wednesday...

Kenny had a distinct dislike for ties. If the event was formal, he may show up in a turtleneck and sports coat. If giving a keynote speech it wasn't unusual for Kenny to show up wearing a short-sleeved shirt and slacks. He believed that what he said was vastly more important than the way he looked, so he put a lot more time into thinking about what he was going to say than in deciding what he was going to wear. Those in his audiences wouldn't believe that he was worth millions, until they heard what he had to share.

Early in the public company's existence, sometime in the 1970s, Kenny, Sonny and company financial officer Don Mueller were in Chicago looking at a business they were thinking of buying. After touring the plant they went to the owner's club for dinner.

Kenny was wearing his usual formal attire: A turtleneck with a sports coat. Trouble was, this club was very particular. They required ties for service. Kenny looked around. That was no problem. There must be a tie around here somewhere. Did they have one he could borrow? Of course, sir, and they produced a tie. Kenny proceeded to put the tie on over his turtleneck and walked in to be served dinner. And he was.

Kenny liked to call the shots and that could sometimes work to the discomfort of others. And he didn't let little things stand in his way.

Kenny called Bill Webster and asked if he would be going to Fort Collins to attend an organization's CSU luncheon at the student center. Yes, Kenny, I'll come by and pick you up. No, Bill, just get over here. I'll drive.

So Bill went to the feedlot, where Kenny said, let's take my car. They didn't get two miles down the road when Kenny said, my gosh, we don't have any gas. So they headed back to the feedlot where they could fill up the tank.

They were really going to be late now and Kenny was in a huge hurry. After filling the car he must have removed the nozzle too quickly, as it belched back and drenched Kenny's pants with gasoline. Oh, Ken, we'll have to go to the house to get some clean clothes, Bill said. No, get in the car, we've got to go. So hop in the car they did, speeding down the road.

Kenny was a heavy smoker at the time and that, along with the gasoline fumes on Kenny's pants and the lead foot Kenny had at the wheel, worried Webster. He just knew they were going to get blown up. Kenny, you wouldn't mind if I opened the window would you? Kenny just smiled.

When they got to the luncheon people were already eating so Kenny and Bill found their seats, sat down and started to eat. Soon the lady sitting next to Kenny looked up and said, I smell gasoline; where's it coming from? Kenny looked around. Gosh, I don't know. They ate their lunch and enjoyed the rest of the program.

A lot of people would have aborted that mission early. But he wasn't going to be sidetracked by a lack of time or a little gasoline on the pants. As Webster describes him, Kenny was just an old shoe kind of guy.

Another person who calls him an old shoe kind of guy is his ex-wife Pat. She knew he couldn't care less about the way he dressed, but still tried to make him more presentable in public.

Kenny was headed to a business trip to Florida, and Pat was determined to make sure he had appropriate clothes that matched. So she took the time to put matching threads on matching clothes. She spent a great deal of time making sure he knew which ties went with which shirts and slacks. Did he appreciate it? He called Pat from Florida and his only remark was: You smart aleck.

Kenny himself admitted that he would "never make the best dressed list." And many people tried to dress him up, sometimes successfully, other times less so.

Their future in business depended on this 1981 meeting with bankers in New York. If they didn't secure some capital soon, they would have to take drastic measures in the day-to-day operation, and they were running out of options.

Sonny knew how important first impressions with bankers were. They needed to at least look like they could pay the money back. He was worried that Kenny, being Kenny, would mess it up by not portraying the right image for a billion dollar company CEO. He sized up Kenny as they rode up in the elevator. Looking good. He had taken the time earlier to go out and get a new suit, and this one looked nice on Kenny, or at least as nice as a suit on Kenny could look. White shirt, business tie, black shoes. Yes, they might just pull this off after all.

As they made their introductions and sat down on the chairs in the office, Kenny crossed his legs and Sonny winced. White socks.

Kenny liked the casual approach at work. None of his employees were expected to wear ties, but sometimes the casual look wasn't appropriate. And he expected his employees to know the difference.

Kenny's son Charlie had been working in sales at Monfort for a couple of weeks. This day he was wearing a pair of favorite green Chuck Taylor tennis shoes, which at the moment were propped up on the desk as he talked on the phone to his girlfriend. It was a casual place, after all. No formalities here.

But at the very least the timing was bad. Kenny was bringing some Safeway customers through on a tour of the offices and instead of seeing green he saw red. This is my son Charlie, he told the customers, and in one swift motion he not-so-gently swept Charlie's tennis shoes onto the floor. And he was just on his way home to change his clothes.

That night Kenny had a talk with Charlie about respect for the work environment, especially when customers are around. It was a good lesson. And Charlie never saw that pair of green *tennis shoes again, although he has a suspicion of what happened to them.*

When it came to dress, Kenny made many interesting first impressions. But those impressions were never permanent.

Al Yates met Kenny when Yates was interviewing with the State Board of Agriculture for the job of president of Colorado State University. Kenny was on the Board at the time, and was one of the leading proponents of bringing Yates in for the interview. He had been the provost at Washington State University for nine years and this was definitely a step up.

Before the first formal meeting Yates had visited with four other members of the Board who were Colorado heavyweights and gotten a good impression of the Board's style and demeanor. Of course, meeting Kenny was a whole different experience and threw all of the other first impressions right out of the window.

He was sitting at the other end of the table; plaid pants, white shoes, white belt, and a pastel colored sports jacket. Yates was initially taken back a bit, but he would learn that the dress belied the man. It was soon apparent by the actions of the other people on the Board that this was a very significant person, indeed. There was a lot of deference to him, and Yates knew he had better pay attention.

When Kenny talked people listened, and he carried a lot of weight. And the weight he carried was not because of any financial resources he might command. It was a result of his intellect, his personality and the depth of his thinking. He was a man that Yates would soon learn was wise, accomplished and embraced a set of values that everyone should aspire to.

Practicing his Beliefs

In Kenny's later years he would say one of his proudest accomplishments during his lifetime was helping bring Albert C. Yates to CSU. Chair of a search committee at CSU in 1988 to identify a new president, Kenny had gathered the names of many solid candidates, including Yates. He had been a magna cum laude graduate of Memphis State University in 1965, with degrees in chemistry and mathematics, and had earned a doctorate in theoretical chemical physics from Indiana University at Bloomington in 1968. In 1976 he had been appointed professor of chemistry and vice president for graduate studies and research at the University of Cincinnati.

Yates obviously had the right credentials to be tapped for the CSU presidency. But CSU had never before had an African-American president. Heck, no Colorado institution of higher learning had ever had an African-American president. The population of Colorado in 1990 was about 3 million; of that about 133,000 were black. At CSU less than 2 percent of the students were black; in Fort Collins at the time about 1 percent of the population was African-American.

So believing in civil rights was one thing. Putting them into practice in a state that had never really had to display its sense of diversity at the highest levels was something else altogether.

Kenny knew Al Yates was the right person for the job. It wasn't that others saw it differently, it was just that change is hard. And there were plenty of qualified applicants. Still, Kenny and his allies prevailed and Yates was hired. He had a stellar 13-year stint with CSU and brought significant prestige and honor to the position and to the university. It wasn't because of his race, it was because of who he was. And that was Kenny's point all along.

Kenny had earlier made the same kinds of efforts in his own corporate world. Isaiah "Ike" Kelley, Jr., was the son of a sharecropper from South Carolina and lived a life of poverty in Columbus, Ohio, in his early life. He had been a star high school football player at Columbus East High School in the late 1960s and played for the CSU Rams in the late '60s and early '70s.

That's how he initially caught the attention of Kenny Monfort, who was serving as a member of Colorado State Board of Agriculture at the time. Their first meeting was in September of 1970 on a plane coming back from a pounding at Arizona State University in Tempe. Kenny and his wife Pat struck up a conversation with Kelley. They got to laughing and visiting about all sorts of topics, helping ease the painful memory of that day's beating. After landing, though, Ike quickly forgot about the friendly couple on the plane.

Later Kenny would invite Kelley to go to work for him. Although Kelley didn't know the difference between a hoof and a moo, Kenny took him under his wing and taught him the ropes. The relationship was more than that of a boss and employee, however. Kenny looked after Kelley, a single black man in a mostly white community.

In the late 1960s Greeley was far from integrated. It was mostly white, with a strong Mexican-American community. African-Americans were rare in town.

Kelley was comfortable around Kenny and his family. Kenny and Pat would have him over for dinner, and Kelley could drop by anytime just to socialize. Kenny would drop by Kelley's place sometimes, too, just to say hi. Ike was part of an extended family that was casual and fun to be around.

Kelley was one of the employees who could also inspire Kenny's social conscience. Asked to be the Greeley chair for the United Negro College Fund, Kelley had expressed to Kenny how important this cause was. Could he help? Kenny not only gave Ike time to work on the cause but agreed to host a fundraiser luncheon for the fund. Kenny gave his share. They raised about $25,000, then Kenny picked up the tab for the luncheon, too.

Kenny was about as far from a bigot or racist as you could get. He believed everyone should be given equal opportunity and held to equal standards. And he was unflinching in his support for integration. "I believe in integrated schooling," he said in a *Town and Country News* column in 1971. "I believe the best schooling also relates to the neighborhood concept. Therefore, it follows that I believe in integrated housing. I believe in an integrated community. Integrated racially, socially, and economically."

His sense of right and wrong was deeply ingrained, and he never hesitated to let people know what his sense of it was. In his Dec. 20, 1973, *Town and Country News* column he wrote about businessmen who cheat, cities burned in riots, soldiers who desert and self-righteous people who proclaim that 'legal or not, the validity of our cause justifies the means we use.' "Have we lost completely our sense of right and wrong, our sense of the rights of other people, our sense of live and let live?" he asked.

He criticized welfare programs, but didn't believe those programs were about race. In one column he said he hoped "welfare recipients (could) find good jobs and break the welfare cycle, whether they be brown, black or white."

He was for equality, but against quotas. He called it "social tinkering," and said it hurt as many people as it helped. "And still they wonder why many of us are sick and tired of too much government and too many social tinkerers." He hoped that new President Ronald Reagan would appoint some qualified minorities – but only because of qualifications, not because of race. "When we get to that point, the battle will be won."

Kenny took aim in 1983 at a newspaper in Brighton that catered to rural Americans and whose editor at the time ran material that was blatantly anti-Semitic, anti-big business or anti-government. Kenny said that he found the newspaper "very offensive...I have a problem in how to deal with this kind of garbage." He didn't want to censor the editor, and didn't believe in laws telling the editor what to carry or write. So he thought the best thing to do would be to "bring to light what the newspaper is and reports. I have faith that an enlightened public may well get (the editor) to tone down a little." He also thought it "ridiculous" for businesses to advertise in publications like that. Kenny being Kenny, however, admitted that "I may be wrong."

Prejudices against certain Americans weren't disappearing fast enough for Kenny. In the mid-1960s he resigned the Elks Lodge after having no success in getting the "Whites Only" clause lifted. Though local officials agreed with him, the national organization kept the clause until the early 1970s. He argued with the local country club when his sales manager, who was Jewish, was denied membership.

Kenny didn't consider himself sexist, either, and supported women's call for equal rights. Still, he thought men and women weren't created equally in a physical sense, and they shouldn't necessarily do the same jobs. "I didn't think being a butcher was women's work because there's so much heavy labor," he told *The Denver Post*.

It was a matter of common sense, he believed. He pointed to a case at American Cynamid, a big chemical company, where OSHA would not let pregnant women work in one department because of a danger to unborn children. Therefore, only sterilized women could work in that department. Some of the women who had the operation to work there complained, but what was the company supposed to do? "Somewhere along the line the 'equality' movement is going to have to recognize the same facts that American Cynamid recognized," he wrote. "There are differences between men and women."

In the 1960s when the company opened its fabrication department Kenny said the workers "will be men except for 5 to 10 women in the office." No outcries were heard then, but "when we hired our first 8 or 10 women butchers in the 1970s we had pickets from the other butchers' wives," he told *The Denver Post*. Obviously some women supported his views, but for other reasons.

He said in 1974 he believed military academies should be male, and that telephone operators and stewardesses should be female. This obviously brought a strong denunciation from the National Organization for Women, which responded with a strong rebuke.

He did believe, though, that society was going a little too far in protecting the sensibilities of women and others. "Maybe I got a little more 'thick hided' than some as I grew up in a town/city where every odor was blamed on me, my dad or our company," he wrote. "It would help if some others got just a little 'thick hided' so that some of us could continue to write, not just apologize for what we wrote."

> My parents taught me many things. Unfortunately, keeping my mouth shut was not among their teachings.
> Ken Monfort column
> *Town and Country News*
> February 23, 1977

Kenny enjoyed a ribald joke as much as the next guy, but only in the right company. He admitted that he didn't like "off-color" language in either plays or movies. "What used to be saved for a temper tantrum, a tough sale or buy of cattle or meat or just the boys talking is now presented proudly for us on the stage," he wrote. "They call it realism. But is it?"

A firm believer in capital punishment, Kenny thought it was lousy that society sometimes put more focus on those who committed the crimes and gave them more favorable publicity than it did to those who went about their jobs and stayed within the law. "What type of society do we have that makes a cause out of a murderer (Gary Gilmore) who asks to be executed?," he wrote in his Dec. 2, 1976, *Town and Country News* column. "He killed. The valid state law in Utah says that he should die for his action. Let the law prevail. ... And let some of the energy and hysteria that is now wasted on that no-good be spent on those who do not kill, who do not become the dregs of society. And, for God's sake, let the press write about someone who accomplishes something rather than destroys."

Lawbreakers were nothing to be celebrated or protected, either, Kenny believed. When four Denver policemen shot what Kenny called "a couple of hoods," there was an outcry from many, but Kenny thought they did right. "Somewhere we have to determine what is right behavior and what is wrong and those who ignore the law may well suffer consequences more serious than they might deserve," he said.

He wasn't much of a religious man, and allowed for others to display their beliefs as they saw fit. He either believed Jesus was the Son of God or the greatest philosopher and politician of mankind. He "accomplished more in his thirty some years than any other who ever walked this earth," he wrote. "He had answers. ... Jesus Christ was a doer. He ministered to the sick. He had a trade. He provided food and nourishment to others. He was an activist, for he cleaned out the corruption of the temple."

Jesus was a simple man, though, Kenny said; a man who did not travel more than 30 miles from his place of birth. "There is no 'one' way, no 'right' way. It's a combination. A combination of personal interests – and a hope that our life makes a difference to others."

At one time Kenny had shared his religious views with teenagers as a Sunday School teacher at the Congregational Church. His suggestion to students that they feel free to question conventional wisdom and beliefs wasn't appreciated by the church establishment, however, and they removed him from that role.

His Business

Had he not been the son of Warren Monfort, who knows if Kenny would have chosen to get into the cattle business? There were certainly other pursuits that held his interest. If he had not seen the need to get involved in a packing operation to support the feedlot, however, it's highly doubtful Kenny would have decided to become a meat packer.

He was an animal lover and gentle soul who spoke out against war and killing in general. He was not a hunter and would not have hunted merely for sport. Kenny recognized what a messy and violent business meat packing was. But he was helping to feed millions of people with his work, and that made a difference. Kenny was running a meat production facility, not a slaughterhouse.

He was unashamed of that work and believed he was providing services to his employees, the community and to society as a whole. In 1975 he was approached by famous filmmaker Frederick Wiseman, who wanted to do a documentary on the Monfort operation. Wiseman's many documentaries were shot in black and white without narration; the camera simply followed what was happening and let what was going on tell its own story.

Kenny's executives advised him not to do it. First was the disruption to the production process. There just isn't that much room in a packing plant and film crews can be notoriously intrusive and demanding. Second, it was a dangerous place for them to be. Third, and at least as important, it was a potential public relations disaster. Despite the fact the film wouldn't be in color, a packing plant is a bloody, sometimes chaotic and often unpleasant setting. A film could leave a lasting negative impression on viewers about what was taking place in the plant.

Kenny was adamant, though, that what was being done in the plant should be no secret to anybody. He approved the project. When the finished film was screened for company executives, there was silence around the room. Kenny was the first to speak. He wasn't disappointed. The film accurately portrayed the hectic, dangerous and difficult operation of a meat company. No apologies were necessary, and none should be offered.

Oscar and Felix

Bill Webster answered the phone. Hello, Bill, this is Sonny. We're in a pickle. We're having a luncheon and need a speaker. Can you make it? Sure, Sonny, where and when do you need me? It's today, Bill. At the Red Steer. Noon.

I'll be there. Bill shows up and looks for the group and there sit Kenny and Sonny – by themselves. So glad you could make it, Bill. You're the speaker.

Many people got the "you're the speaker" invitation, and many fell for it – once. But it was rarely a group of people they were speaking to, and it wasn't a speech. It was usually just Sonny and Kenny, meeting for lunch, something they did almost every business day.

They were truly the odd couple. Sonny was Felix to Kenny's Oscar. He and Kenny were as different as night and day in many ways. But in other ways they were just the same. And throughout most of their adult lives they were as close as friends could be, almost like brothers.

Dark and handsome with black wavy hair and a charming smile, Sonny was suave and looked good in a nice suit. He was always one of the sharpest dressed in a crowd. With an easy smile and a soft, deep and mellifluous voice, he exuded both confidence and class and would use his charm to his advantage in both business and social settings.

His cars – usually black and luxurious – were always contemporary and meticulously maintained. He liked the finer things in life and didn't see why he shouldn't have them, since he and his family had worked hard to earn them through the years.

Sonny was on hand when Kenny was named Citizen of the West in 1991

His best friend, though, was just the opposite. Kenny was often disheveled, hated wearing ties, drove old beat-up cars, never carried any money and appeared to care not the least for the finer things in life. Sonny thought it was criminal that Kenny had lots of money, because in Sonny's mind he obviously didn't know how to use it.

When Kenny was considering a run for Colorado governor in 1973, Sonny had asked him what he would do once he got into office. He would drive his own car, Kenny said, not be driven around by a chauffer in a limousine. And he wouldn't live in the governor's mansion, but live at home and commute to Denver. Then why do you want to be governor? Sonny had asked him.

Sonny was a gregarious man who would meet people easily, while Kenny was more guarded in his relationships. So what did Sonny see in him?

Like in a good marriage, they complemented each other. They saw eye-to-eye on business issues, could complete each other's sentences, made each other laugh and basically enjoyed each other's company. They ate lunch together practically every business day for nearly 25 years, and never tired of it. Those who joined them often were amazed at the camaraderie the two demonstrated, and the ease with which they could banter and discuss an enormous array of topics.

Kenny most often played the straight man to Sonny's comedian, but they did it so well you sometimes didn't know which was which. It didn't seem to be an act, but if it was they played it to perfection and performed it in a way that didn't exclude others. They welcomed many people into their special "circle," and made everyone feel as though they, too, were part of this long, fast friendship. It was a rare gift of inclusion that served them both well.

His Family Life

Kenny's marriage to Pat ended in 1966 after nearly 17 years, but that divorce was unsuccessful. "I didn't like being divorced. It didn't work," he told friends. He was considered handsome and eligible after the split, and had his share of dates. But his hectic schedule – politics, business, the kids – didn't really allow for much serious and lasting contact with the opposite sex.

So he remarried Pat in February 1970. When he applied for his new marriage license, Kenny laughingly asked the clerk at the courthouse if he could get a discount since he'd been there before. He and Pat got remarried at the first Unitarian Church in Denver and went to Florida for a "second honeymoon."

Getting back together seemed a natural thing to do. Until their divorce Pat had been the one who would do most of the nurturing of the children, Kyle, Dick, Kaye and Charlie. Her willingness to hold down the home fort allowed Kenny to dabble in politics and spend a tremendous amount of time on business interests. Pat was a dedicated mother and loyal wife who didn't question her role in the family.

It wasn't that Kenny wasn't a devoted father. He was, however, a product of his generation. Fathers in those days, especially very busy fathers, didn't dote on their children. With a heavy business schedule and a burgeoning political career, Kenny was often the absent parent.

But he was an attentive dad who played football with his sons (Kenny was always the quarterback), sat and watched television with his youngest daughter or talked social issues, books and politics with his oldest. He listened to their problems and shared experiences that helped them establish their own images of right and wrong.

Charlie was only a youngster, so he really couldn't know what it meant. All he knew was that his father was angry. What was the big deal? It was only some lines on paper. Some decorations for the cars he was drawing, images he had seen in books and on the television.

To Kenny, though, a swastika was the embodiment of something evil and painful. He carefully explained to his young son the reasons a swastika was more than just a decoration. It wasn't until he was older that Charlie got the full story of why this image was of such importance to his father, and the pain it could inflict. It was no wonder that Volkswagens were never found in the Monfort garage.

Kenny's second marriage to Pat wouldn't last, either. They had different expectations of their relationship and although Pat admired Kenny for his generosity, unpretentiousness and great sense of humor, their union was coming apart by the early 1980s.

About that time Kenny got better acquainted with the company attorney, Myra Ellins. Born on Independence Day in 1938, Ellins had been hired by Monfort in June 1976 as a staff attorney. She had served an internship for the company while going to the University of Colorado in 1974, then after graduation had been admitted to the Colorado Bar Association before working as a clerk for the Court of Appeals. She then joined Monfort as associate general counsel. She was appointed assistant corporate secretary and general counsel in 1979. Myra was particularly adept at labor law – something that was becoming increasingly important to the company.

Myra, too, had been in a marriage that was less than stable. In the early 1980s she and Kenny were being thrown together for business under trying circumstances. They were married Sept. 23, 1982, two weeks after the marriage of Kenny's youngest daughter Kaye and very shortly after his second divorce from Pat.

"Ken was the only man I'd ever admit was smarter than I am, so I married him," Myra Monfort said. He would always playfully introduce her to others as his current wife, and jokingly say that he married her to cut company legal expenses. They were married in a simple ceremony in a gazebo in Myra's backyard in Lafayette, Colorado.

Probably Kenny's biggest demonstration of anti-bigotry could be found in the fact he married Myra, who was not only Jewish but was raised in Brooklyn and schooled on the East Coast. Her religion would have been easier for Kenny to accept than would her ties to the Eastern Establishment.

His Households

Throughout Kenny's life pets were part of his households. He had always been a dog person. When he was young it was a St. Bernard dog named Sarge. As he got bigger, his dogs got smaller. In the 1970s it was Jo (short for Josephine), a Dachsund mix, as well as Mack, a mutt he had picked up at the animal shelter, and B.B. (short for Bridget Bardot) a poodle. Later he would get B.B. 2, another poodle he would have for 18 years. The tall Kenny would lovingly carry B.B. 2 around the house in his arms, a humorous sight to family, employees and friends.

Kenny, Myra and B.B. 2

In his free time – and if you read his columns you'd think there was a lot of it, which there wasn't – he would occasionally go water skiing with the family or go hiking. He climbed Longs Peak nine times. Occasionally Kenny would also go snow skiing, but that was more for the rest of the family; he wasn't into it much. He tried camping once. Only once.

In addition he enjoyed going to the movies for an escape (*"Doctor Zhivago," "Rocky"* and *"The Sting"* were among his favorites). And he loved the Denver Broncos. He was particularly excited when they made the playoffs in 1977, going on to the Super Bowl in January 1978. He regularly made comments on the team's progress in his *Town and Country News* columns.

On vacation, when he wasn't dreaming up new ideas for improving the company, he would walk on a beach, play cards or enjoy a game of touch football with the kids. Kenny and Pat had a vacation home in Newport, California, for awhile, and he did seem to be a little more relaxed there. But it was still hard to get away from work.

Most of all, though, he would read. A voracious reader, he devoured daily and weekly newspapers, news magazines and everything by James Michener, who had taught Kenny's brother Dick in Sunday School in 1937 or 1938 when he had lived in Greeley. "I'm a Michener nut," Kenny once wrote. "I like his books – I read them all. I tremendously admire the research that goes into his efforts and he tells good, good stories."

Chapter 9
The Conscience

President Richard Nixon's enemies list wasn't the only list Kenny made. Both he and Sonny Mapelli were "targeted" by Lyn "Squeaky" Fromme and her International People's Court of Retribution, a make-believe organization she and her friends used to intimidate executives they believed were polluting the environment.

It didn't generate much publicity, especially in comparison to her undying allegiance to her good friend Charles Manson or her subsequent attempt on the life of President Gerald Ford. It made for great drama, however, and she may be in prison today describing how much havoc she created in her attempts to protect and advance our society.

Pollution was a challenge for Monfort of Colorado. The "love/hate" relationship between the company and the community, in fact, really played out most dramatically when it came to environmental issues. Of course the smell was a problem, as was the potential water pollution. But on the other side you would also have to consider the employment, the residual economic benefits and the taxes being generated. It was complex, but in fact Kenny did recognize the societal challenges associated with his various businesses.

In his "Ken's Comments" to employees in December 1969, he allowed that "Cattle in feedlots do emit an odor and this problem is intensified in wet weather," and that "next to steel mills and certain chemical factories, packing plants are probably the most notorious polluters of water in the land."

Furthermore, he noted, "in our production processes, large amounts of non-animal refuse (boxes, bags, etc.) occur, and these are hard to get rid of," and that "questions of sanitation continue to worry the public."

Pollution was a huge issue and regularly in Kenny's thoughts. He and his father were determined to help reduce the problems their firm had helped create. It happened in every division of the company.

In 1967 members of a Greeley Odor Control Committee were pleased, for example, at the company's efforts to control the smell from the lots. The Committee had been formed in March 1966 to monitor progress on promises the company had made to alleviate, as much as possible, the odor problem. They termed the efforts "impressive" and "commendable" after looking at the various methods the company was using to keep odors from wafting over the city.

Among those efforts were 52 "aerosol micro-atomizers," mounted 20 feet high at 26 different points across the width of the lots. These units emitted mists of odor absorbing gases. Water sprinkler systems were in place to keep dust down during dry periods. And, most important, a strict housecleaning effort had been in place for decades to remove manure, level pens for proper drainage and replace dirt where necessary.

In 1970 the company highlighted its environmental awareness and efforts in a company newsletter. Monfort had instituted greenbelts around the feedlots, tree windbreaks along the edges, thermal foggers to control insects, holding ponds for water runoff and recycling, and cyclone dust collectors for the elevators and milling facilities. It had tried everything it knew to reduce pollution and eliminate the smell, or at least keep it from traveling past the feedlot's edges. They even enlisted the services of Colorado State University in searching for methods to fix the problem. They had gone so far as to test whether asphalt or cement pens would help keep things cleaner, but they found pens on hard surfaces just became a sloppy mess when it rained or snowed, and even when it didn't.

After the well-thought-out and careful construction of the Gilcrest lot in 1969 and 1970, Kenny saw how the haphazard, go-as-you-grow construction of the Greeley lot wasn't conducive to outstanding pollution control. The Gilcrest lot was further away from the city, and it had a sandy soil that was much more appropriate for feedlots than was the fertile soil under the Greeley lot. The new facility was giving him ideas on other more drastic ways of improving relations with neighbors.

> Construction of (the Gilcrest feedlot) as a unit, with the best of grade, runoff, detention and drainage provides us with capabilities that just do not exist in Greeley. In the next three or four years we will be looking at results, watching the growth of Greeley and analyzing the possibilities of relocation. It would be expensive and could not be accomplished in the near term; but just an eventual possibility.
>
> Ken Comments
> Company Newsletter
> December 1969

A Lot of Scents

Without doubt the most significant step he took in recognition of the company's environmental concerns had to do with his understanding of the problems associated with the original feedlot north of Greeley. That realization led to relocating the firm's feedlots to a more environmentally appropriate site about 15 miles east of town starting in 1974. It was an enormous move, and one taken long before any legal or environmental actions could be even contemplated against the company.

As both the feedlots and the city of Greeley grew, the Monfort family knew a problem was brewing. Prevailing winds from the north made it inevitable that odors from the feedlot would find their way into town just a couple of miles to the south. Visitors standing in the observation tower on the north end of the lot could easily see houses in the city just past the river south of the pens.

Though only one of many feedlots in the area, the Monfort lot was the biggest and one of the closest. Therefore it took the brunt of the criticism. Warren had sometimes been awakened with late night phone calls from individuals in the city wanting to know if the smell was keeping him awake, too. His farmer's nose was

The city of Greeley (top) was getting too close

accustomed to the cattle smells, but he knew that people who grew up in the city didn't have the same farm sensibilities.

Warren didn't totally support the move, but he reluctantly agreed that it was necessary. He had built those pens, and they had been good to him. But the will of the people was certainly going to be done.

Doing away with the feedlot entirely wasn't an option for many reasons. In September 1965, Kenny reminded fellow Greeley citizens at a Lion's Club meeting that the city was dependent on cattle feeding and related industries, but recognized the impact feedlot odors could have on it. He presented a four-point program that included continued and accelerated efforts at good housekeeping, spraying with odor control chemicals, enactment of a state sanitation law to be sure that Monfort and all other feedlots do what they say they'll do, and funding for a comprehensive study at Colorado State University to see what else could be done about it. But with all of the odor controls they tried, Kenny and Warren knew they would eventually have to take more drastic actions.

Moved isn't really the right word for it. You don't move a feedlot. What you do is close it and open another one in a different location. That's what they announced they would do in April 1972, a move that was estimated at that time would cost about $5 million. Kenny said in a news release the strategy "well may be one of the largest voluntary expenditures yet by a major company in this region purely for environmental reasons."

Costs to relocate ended up being closer to about $7 million, and it received no subsidies or other consideration from the communities involved. In fact, in addition to the cost there was more than one negative impact on the company as the result of Kenny's decision to unilaterally make the move.

First was the distance to the packing plant. The original lot was less than a mile north of the plant and that made for an easy and relatively bruise-free trip. While 12 miles isn't that far by packing plant standards, it was 12 times more than what it was before.

Another issue was what would become of the land. Because the city was moving in the feedlot's direction, Kenny sought rezoning for the land. There were 2,000 prime acres of land there, and he thought it would make a nice site for a housing development or other residential or commercial use. He proposed it to the city of Greeley, and city leaders said they'd think about it. They thought about it, and thought about it, and years went by. Meanwhile, Kenny went forward with his plans to open a new feedlot east of town.

After all of the cattle had been removed from the north lot, the city finally said it had thought about it enough, and no, the property should permanently remain agricultural land. Why hadn't Kenny waited to move the feedlot until the city had made its decision? That's what some of his advisors had recommended he do. But he had told them the move wasn't contingent on what the city said, anyway. Still, it would have been respectful of city leaders to trust Kenny and tell the company what they had obviously already decided. It appeared they were holding their cards until Kenny had laid his last one down.

The new feedlot, located near a small community called Kuner about 16 miles east of Greeley, began getting cattle shipments in January 1974. (Interestingly, the fictional town in Michener's book *Centennial* was supposedly located about where the feedlot sat.) The new lot was a mile long and a half-mile wide, situated right alongside U.S. Highway 34. People would drive by pen after pen, amazed at the seemingly endless number of cattle. To satisfy those wanting to know more about this monstrous operation – and those just mildly curious about it – the company built a visitor's center above the offices near the center of the feedlot, with an observation deck and glass window to the computerized feeding system. People came from all over the world to view one of the world's largest cattle feedlots.

Buffer strips had been purchased all around the feedlot to assure that neighbors didn't get too close, and state-of-the-art environmental elements were built into the design of the feedlot. Sprinkler systems helped keep the dust down, while a lagoon caught runoff before it had a chance to get to waterways. The company had been careful to work with the county on zoning to make sure neighbors wouldn't again encroach and become an issue.

There were three 60,000 ton silage pits for corn ensilage and a 120,000 bushel capacity grain elevator with the ability to process about 200,000 pounds of grain a day. Each of the pens held between 300 and 400 head of cattle, and there was a computerized batching system for assuring that each pen of cattle received exactly the right feed ration. Rather than a heated water system to assure it would not freeze, water worked on a continuous flow system. Compared to the original feedlot north of Greeley, it was far more advanced and in a better location.

By September 4, 1974, the old north lot was empty. As cattle moved out of that lot to the packing plant, new feeder cattle went to Kuner. The Kuner lot was officially finished on Nov. 13, 1975, and the north lot had reverted to cornfields by May 14, 1976.

For relocating its feedlots the company was named the winner of the 1975 Environment Awards Program for U.S. Companies. Sponsored yearly by *The Environment Monthly Magazine*, the award recognized those companies that "make environmental excellence a basic condition in the pursuit of corporate goals."

Packing Problems

Significant attention was also being put on the packing plant, which wasn't as old as the original feedlot but had significant pollution issues of its own. For the packing plant, an odorless continuous rendering system was installed, along with a $500,000 trash incinerator that met the standards of the Los Angeles Air Pollution Control district, the most stringent standards in the United States.

For the first five years of its existence sewage from the packing plant went directly into the Cache la Poudre River. "As a beginner in the business I finally realized this is why all packing plants had been located on rivers," Kenny said in a 1970 newsletter. Then in 1965 the city began treating sewage so pollution didn't occur. When the company wanted to significantly increase its size in 1970, another idea emerged: a new sewage treatment plant for Monfort Packing. Getting Greeley to go along with the company's idea was another story.

The company had asked the city to act as owner of the plant, which would remove it from the tax rolls. While it wouldn't cost the city a nickel, Greeley's managers balked at the idea of issuing the necessary bonds.

In December 1971 the city proposed increasing the Monfort sewage treatment charges from $60,000 to $180,000 a year. This reflected, they said, the company's actual percentage of the city's costs for treatment at the city-owned sewage plant. They settled for something in the $130,000 a year range, but the discussions on the increase were far from amicable. To Kenny it proved that Americans – especially American businesses – were getting fed up with the arrogant way the government sometimes operated.

By 1970 the company had invested about $1 million on air and water pollution control equipment and was spending about $750,000 a year to maintain it. But even though he was on board with most environmentalists, there was no denying that Kenny's business meant that he would get more and more pressure on environmental issues.

> No longer is it legal, or acceptable, to dump raw sewage in the river, least of all the Poudre. No longer is it acceptable to own and operate a feedlot as near a community as is ours north of Greeley, especially upwind – no matter what it does for the economy, no matter how hard we try good housekeeping and no matter how many friends we have.
>
> Ken Comments
> Company Newsletter
> March/April 1972

The company had gotten its hand slapped hard for a Jan. 26, 1972, incident that allowed liquid beef fat to flow from the plant through a storm sewer to the Cache la Poudre River. The EPA called it "vast quantities," while the company attorney called it about two bushels that acted like an oil slick and covered a large area of water.

The fine the company received was OK with Kenny; the accident was not. He had worked hard to improve his company's reputation when it came to pollution, and this incident took those efforts two steps back. He said in the company newsletter that the company wasn't trying to pollute. And, "if we goof, we deserve a penalty. Nothing tightens up procedures as much as a fine, a conviction or bad publicity. ... Our procedures have now been tightened."

As a result of the spill Kenny put the corporate attorney, Clark Weaver, in charge of a newly-created job of policing the company's total environmental posture. His authority in that regard, Kenny said, was "absolute. ... I request, I plead and I demand that all listen, help and comply with his questions and decisions."

Even though his company faced some of the biggest challenges from an environmental standpoint, from his earliest days Kenny and his father had demonstrated a huge sense of corporate responsibility and tried many things to minimize the company's impact on the environment. Manure seemed to be one of the firm's biggest challenges, and one that seemed to be ever-present.

Using it as a natural fertilizer on the crop fields surrounding the feedlots made sense and that had been done for years. But they wanted to know if there were other possible uses for it. At one time in the early 1970s the company investigated the possibility of mixing manure with glass or sand to make tile. With society's increasing energy needs, capturing the methane gas from manure was also explored, and they contemplated putting a methane gas plant near their Kuner feedlot. Anything was worth trying, as the cattle produced hundreds of thousands of tons of manure a year. In the end, though, recycling it back to the land as fertilizer remained the most cost-effective and logical.

A Hungry World

Kenny thought cattle feedlots had other serious consequences for our society. The less time cattle spent there the better, he believed, for more than just environmental reasons. Economics, for example; it cost more to put a pound of meat on cattle in a feedlot than it did on a pasture. If steers spent more time on the range before going to a feedlot, it was possible to get grain usage down to the point that cattle ate only 2-3 pounds of it per pound of edible meat. At the time feedlots would buy 700 pound steers and put 425 pounds on the animals. He suggested it might be better to buy 800 pound animals and put only 325 pounds on them.

The bottom line, he said, is that when only the feedlot is considered, cattle are not good converters of grain to meat. Alive they convert at a rate of about 1 pound of gain to 9 pounds of grain.

When you factor only the carcass, it converts to 1 pound of carcass weight to 14 pounds of grain. And when it gets to what's consumed, it's about 20 pounds of grain to 1 pound of edible meat.

> "God didn't give us the right to eat steak any more than He gave us the right to drive 8-mile per gallon automobiles. The era of red meat on every dinner table and a porterhouse on every barbecue is over. Beef prices will soar and beef consumption will plummet in the coming years."
> Ken Monfort Interview
> *Signature* Magazine
> September, 1976

Kenny went on to tell the magazine that he was concerned about world population, and he believed that just as television made the violence of Vietnam unpopular it would "make any large scale famine equally grim." He said livestock should only be fed grain that's available, and they were last on the list. "It's obvious that humans come first," he said.

"We have a responsibility for not letting other people starve to death," he said. "If we decide to say the hell with everyone else, we'd better spend a lot more money on defense."

In the mid-1970s beef was having a field day with consumers. Per capita consumption hit its zenith in 1976, topping 95 pounds per person (retail weight equivalency). In the March 2, 1975, issue of *Empire Magazine* Kenny said that consumption "will drop dramatically in future years," and that in the future beef would become a luxury item. Today Americans eat about 65 pounds of beef a year per capita.

In addition, grading standards in the 1970s encouraged overfeeding of animals, and 36,000 acres then needed for corn production could be freed up if standards were modified to reward less fatty meat. Those government standards have been changing in an attempt to reward meat with less fat.

Among the problems he saw at the time was the fact that individuals could use cattle feeding as a tax shelter. This harmed both the people who were actually trying to make a living from it and the environment, he thought.

Keeping it Real

In his heart, Kenny was a full supporter of the organic movement. He thought humans hadn't "taken adequate care of the natural resources of our planet. We have over-cropped and leeched our soils. We have allowed it to be washed away and wasted fertility. Lazy farming has brought too much dependence on commercial fertilizers and herbicides. Ignoring nature's ecological balance has brought too much dependence upon insecticides and drugs."

But he was also a realist. He knew that the population was increasing dramatically, and the alternative to using drugs, additives and chemicals was "mass starvation. We could not begin to feed the citizens of our own nation without these scientific advances, let alone continue to aid mightily in the feeding of the world. So, we cannot go back…Science and research have almost become dirty words. But without them, disaster would result."

When it came to using science in cattle feeding, Kenny was all for it and refused to allow emotion to sway his opinions about what was right. (See Chapter 8.) For instance, he began adding Aureomycin (chlortetracycline) to feeds in the mid 1960s because it reduced liver abscesses in the cattle. He found that adding the drug returned $2.72 for every dollar invested in it, and caused no apparent problems.

The same good/bad approach was taken when he thought about environmentalism. He thought the "environmental movement is a must," he wrote. "We must control our destiny." At the same time, he felt for the Wyoming sheep rancher trying to protect his day-old lambs from predator wolves. "A man stealing for his hungry family is at least due sympathy. But a rancher protecting his crop, in this case baby lambs, from predators is a mean man. Obviously we have some interesting double standards." At the very least, he believed, "we must be careful not to go overboard and forget that there are those still worried about jobs, housing and tonight's meal."

Finding Jobs

Kenny believed giving good jobs to people was an important responsibility for someone in his position. In fact, he thought it was more helpful than almost anything he could do. It not only gave people an opportunity to make a living, it helped strengthen the economy and provided the foundation for a successful community and a prosperous, balanced society. He believed it was of more consequence than either charity or government.

In 1970 Monfort of Colorado participated with the U.S. Department of Labor and the National Alliance of Businessmen in a nationwide effort to hire and train disadvantaged jobless persons. The long-term goal of the "JOBS" program was to place 614,000 persons in training by June 1971. The company was the first company in Colorado outside of Denver to contract with the program, agreeing to hire and train 60 persons during a six-month period. The government would provide funds for some of the training.

The people in the JOBS 70 program averaged a fifth grade education, had nine people in their family, had been unemployed for 15 weeks out of the year, and earned $1.52 an hour wages when they did work, for an annual wage of $1,300. These were local folks, many of whom were field workers. Some were migrant workers who were too poor to even buy a car to follow the crops. Others had prison records. The state penitentiary regularly contacted the company about convicts who were about to be paroled.

Kenny said the company wasn't using the program for public relations or social motives. He knew if the company trained local people turnover would be less, and they wouldn't have to raid other companies for employees. It was the company's policy to hire whoever was available and whoever the managers thought could do the job. That would still be the case.

They did discover, though, that there was less turnover among Hispanics than there was among Anglos. The Mexican-

Americans were closer to their families and many owned their own homes. They were an important part of the workforce and the community, Kenny believed.

The company didn't have to go to extra pains to hire more Hispanics, but Monfort did have some trouble in another area, Kenny told Mountain Bell for one of its 1971 brochures. "We did make a conscious effort…to see that a proportional share of our supervisors were Mexican-American," he said. "This took special effort, not because of ability, but because of expectations. Most Chicanos who worked here didn't expect to become supervisors, and, for that reason, didn't show the leadership qualities they could have. Now that a goodly number of them have been promoted, it's no longer a problem."

Some viewpoints Kenny expressed had prescient application to what would go on at the company in the 21st century. Kenny was offended when lawmakers said his company and others who hired illegal immigrants at cheap wages should be penalized. People were hired for their ability to do the job, not their citizenship, he said. Furthermore, they were paid the same wages as everyone else.

"What should we do in your infinite wisdom? Require birth certificates?" he asked. "And if so, require them of all or just those who might be Mexican citizens? What sort of policy can we adopt to keep you happy and not chastising the business community because you have not come up with a governmental solution of stopping the illegal flow across the Rio Grande?"

Energy Crisis Continued

As they are today, energy issues were on the minds of many people in the 1970s. Kenny was frustrated by the lack of attention to reducing American dependence on foreign oil and finding alternative sources, while using the ones we have in this country. In his Nov. 18, 1977, *Town and Country News* column he called it a "national disgrace" that just a few years after an oil embargo the country was in worse shape than it had been. "We are importing an ever increasing amount of oil, an ever increasing amount of our energy needs."

He minced no words about what needed to take place. "We flat just got to get off our duff and solve some of the problems," he wrote. "We have to start using our coal, start conserving our fuel and get with all these alternative sources...Surely we can figure out how to mine the coal and leave the land in some acceptable form...Surely there is no excuse for the inaction of the Administration and the Legislative branch of the nation, our state or any other state."

Overall, Kenny leaned on what he considered his Democratic principles when it came to issues like world hunger, the environment, fair hiring and energy conservation. Some others in the cattle and meat industry considered him too radical in these areas, but he was comfortable with his stances and could argue them logically and forcefully with anyone.

He would find, though, that a huge Democratic issue would be an impediment to his plans for expansion and success. If he had taken off each of his company shoes, he would have noticed two major Achilles heels: size and unions.

Chapter 10
The Roller Coaster: 1975-1987

> *Commodity: A good or service whose wide availability typically leads to smaller profit margins and diminishes the importance of factors (as brand name) other than price.*
>
> Merriam Webster
> On-Line Dictionary

It's great to be a legend among your peers and within your own community. It's quite a different challenge to redefine your industry. While the landscape is changing, beef is still by and large a commodity.

On several levels it would have benefited Monfort to have become a brand name, and the name had become more well-known than most in the beef industry. And the company in fact had explored the possibility of expanding further in that direction several times. But as the company discovered, creating a branded identity with consumers is extremely expensive. For a company with limited resources it made little practical sense.

The fact that they were producing a commodity was the reason for their low profit margins, as other meat packing plants had found out before them. And low profit margins essentially led to many of the problems the company found itself facing beginning in the 1970s – including its labor unrest. It all had to do with the new kind of competition the company was up against.

In the early 1900s the beef packing industry was controlled by what was then called the Big Five packers – Swift, Armour, Morris, Cudahy and Wilson. These five companies slaughtered about 82 percent of the cattle intended for interstate commerce, and 95 percent of fresh beef. They operated out of the terminal markets – Chicago, Omaha and Kansas City were the primary ones – with cattlemen shipping their cattle to the stockyards in these communities to be marketed and processed.

It was a difficult and dirty business in more ways than one. In addition to the obvious mess of slaughtering animals, packers of the day would use every means possible to successfully crush worker dissent and keep order in their plants. Beginning in 1935, when Congress passed the Wagner Act declaring a national policy that encouraged collective bargaining, the major plants began featuring more union activity, and the workers began finding more success in gaining solidarity.

In 1941 the United Packinghouse Workers of America, a union that was part of the Congress of Industrial Organizations (CIO), was established. In 1948 they conducted a nationwide strike against the major meatpacking companies. The strike had a key result; the companies found it advantageous to "follow the leader," similar to what the automobile industry did with General Motors in establishing contracts with its employees.

It was under this umbrella that Monfort would settle as it established its relationship with the union and its packing plant workers in the early 1960s. The basic labor contracts were established by either Armour, Swift or Wilson, and when those contracts were settled the other plants, like Monfort, fell into line. Kenny at the time had no problem with this. He believed the company could compete with these giants by providing better productivity for its labor dollar. There was just one problem: A new set of players was coming on the scene, and these companies wanted to play by their own set of rules.

The most prominent of these new players had gotten its start at the same time Monfort established its packing operation in Greeley. Iowa Beef Packers, Inc., officially began in 1960 under the direction of A.D. Anderson and Currier J. Holman, two meat industry veterans. They had one packing plant in Denison, Iowa. Anderson and Holman believed that not only was the way beef processed in those days antiquated, but the way people were paid for processing it was old-fashioned as well.

Their vision in one sense was similar to the vision of the Monforts: Bring the packing operations closer to the source of the cattle, thereby improving the efficiencies and economies of production. It made little sense to them that the cattle needed to be shipped to high cost and dated processing facilities, which were located near unneeded stockyards with superfluous middlemen. Use your own buyers to go out to local producers and acquire your fat cattle. Hire local farm boys to work in your highly mechanized, union-less plants at lower wages. From the beginning, Iowa Beef Packers would focus on efficiency and productivity while at the same time lowering labor costs.

It worked, for a time. The company was able to keep national unions out of its plants as it grew quickly and extensively. In just a few years Iowa Beef Packers had become the largest in the industry. And as it grew other older, more established beef packing companies, with their outmoded facilities and cumbersome labor contracts, were getting out of the business.

Even though Iowa Beef Packers had succeeded in keeping national unions out of the plants, that didn't mean there was no labor strife. In 1965 workers at two of its Iowa plants walked out over issues related to their right to strike, and the conflict got ugly before Iowa's governor stepped in to stop it. With the company's entry into fabrication and the boxed beef market in 1967, things began to get even nastier.

In 1969 the Amalgamated Meat Cutters and Butcher Workmen Union had seen enough jobs flowing to plants near the cattle. The union believed those jobs belonged to its members. So it stepped in to help organize workers at the Iowa Beef Packers plants. By now there were eight IBP plants in the Midwest.

The 1969 strike by 1,200 workers at the Dakota City, Nebraska, plant to gain a first-ever national contract brought the operation to 50 percent capacity and lasted for nine months. Before it was over on April 13, 1970, one worker would lose his life and many people were injured. There would be 56 bombings, more than 20 shootings, death threats, many tires slashed and extensive property damage. Iowa Beef Packers, meanwhile, would be accused of slandering a union official and failing to bargain in good faith. They would finally settle on an increase of 20 cents-an-hour over the wage first offered by the company.

> I have mixed emotions. On one hand, [I applaud] the Union trying to get comparable wages for employees in Nebraska and Iowa to what they get in Greeley, and, on the other hand, (I'm) worried about inflation and pricing ourselves out of the market.
> Ken Comments
> Company Newsletter
> November 1969

Back in 1969 Kenny was happy with how employee relations at his plant were going. He got great comments from plant visitors about how hard the people worked, as well as about their overall efficiency. Kenny said there was both respect and pride within the company ranks. "It seems so simple and maybe a little corny," he wrote. "Good pay for good work. Everyone profits. Management is not interested in cheating a little on the pay, not interested in being 'cute,' not interested in contracts way under the national rate and not interested in the 'hard line.' Our employees are not interested in a slow down or in inferior work. This is a combination that has worked to everyone's benefit."

As long as the playing fields were level, Kenny didn't have a problem with unions. When the union first became established in the Greeley plant, he didn't challenge it because all other packers lived basically by the same rules. But with new competitors like IBP, that was changing. Taking a very tough stance, Iowa Beef Packers was standing up to unions and saying that things were different as long as they were around.

The Competition

Deep down, though, Kenny must have seen it coming. On August 1, 1966, the Swift plant in Denver closed its doors. There were many reasons for the closing, including a failure to modernize, inefficient operations and poor community relations. But among the leading causes was "atrocious" labor relations, with low productivity, featherbedding and long and frequent work stoppages. Kenny tried to give his employees a heads up.

"We cannot afford to become soft and complacent," he wrote to employees in a May 1966 newsletter. "You who do the actual work in the plant must... see that we remain competitive with increases in your productivity. It no longer is enough to do as well as in years past for there is always someone doing better. No contract can guarantee a job. It can only guarantee pay and benefits if that job exists."

"Someone doing better," or Iowa Beef, had already been aggressive in every aspect of its operations, including its relationship with its workers. While the company paid lip service to improved employee relations, they made it well known that they weren't then and would never be a union-friendly shop. Their philosophy was, why should we pay Chicago wages in Dakota City, Nebraska? And, why should we pay skilled butcher rates to someone who only has to learn to trim tenderloins?

The company would have union problems again in 1972, when its contract with workers came up for renegotiation. This strike in Dakota City would last 27 weeks, and the workers gained significant wage increases through arbitration. Another violent strike in 1977 would last 14 months and involve 1,800 workers, with the company bringing in strikebreakers to keep the plant working.

In all, Iowa Beef had strikes that stopped operations for 28 months over a period of 13 years. During that time, Monfort had one 56-day strike over wages in 1970. Clearly, the folks in Dakota City were playing hardball in the labor market.

Kenny detested the company and wanted to beat them at every turn. It wasn't just because of what Iowa Beef was doing on labor issues. He believed they were playing fast and loose with ethics and the laws – something the government would substantiate in the 1970s.

It came out that during the 1969-70 strike that one of the company's founders, Holman, was anxious to save his company by getting into the New York City beef market, which was, to his chagrin, controlled by the union. He made a $1 million surcharge deal with a broker with organized crime ties, who ended up paying off union officials and supermarket executives with the money to get IBP beef into the market. Holman was indicted on bribery charges in 1973.

The judge was lenient, however, saying Holman had been taken advantage of by a crooked meat marketing environment in New York, and that the company was obviously destitute when the company made the deals. That hand-slap made Kenny Monfort pretty mad, as the company probably made $10 million on the deal only to pay a $7,000 fine. "It is enough to discourage those who want to remain honest," Kenny said.

And IBP wasn't destitute for long, either. By 1974 it had grown to be the world's largest beef producer, larger than its five largest competitors put together. After it tried to name one of the relatives of a key figure in the New York bribery case to a high level company position in 1975, the *Wall Street Journal* claimed the company attracted "criminals, gangland figures, civil wrongdoers...and people engaged in vicious beatings, shootings and firebombings."

The USDA got into the act in the late 1970s, investigating whether the company was using practices to drive other packers – like Monfort – out of business. It dropped its investigation in 1979, apparently comfortable in the belief that IBP was merely a very aggressive and hard-nosed competitor. Nevertheless, it had found that IBP had violated the Robinson-Patman Act between 1971 and 1975 by giving discounts to customers who bought large quantities of beef, and the company was convicted in 1981 by a Brooklyn jury for giving $10,000 price breaks to a New York supermarket chain from 1970 to 1974.

If it had just been labor and legal issues, it may have been more manageable. But while this was going on the company was getting huge. It changed its name to Iowa Beef Processors when the company started fabricating most of its product, then shortened it to IBP when it began processing pork in the early 1980s. Then, to top it off, in 1981 IBP was acquired by Occidental Petroleum

Corporation, the huge energy conglomerate, giving it deep pockets and capabilities that others with less capital to work with didn't have. Over the next six years the company would add 8,000 employees and four additional locations to further solidify its world dominance in meat production.

Processing about 1.6 million head of cattle a year, IBP at the time was selling about eight times the amount of boxed beef as Monfort. Monfort was actually now the third largest, behind a company called MBPXL (formerly Missouri Beef Processors, the company would be acquired by Cargill in 1979 and change its name to Excel), which sold 610,000 head.

When it all got started in 1960, the size discrepancy wasn't there. But it was into this changing and fast-expanding environment Monfort was thrown as it began to grow. No one could beat Kenny Monfort's competitiveness, and no one could match his decency and sense of fair play. He wasn't about to roll over and play dead. But he wasn't going to do what he considered unethical to stay in the game, either. He believed, as his father did, that if you played by the rules and treated people right, things would work out in the end.

That stance would be seriously tested several times. The plant workers, many of whom were friends of Kenny's, were very loyal through the 1960s, but believed the slight increase offered in 1970 was not helping them keep up with inflation. (See Chapter 4.) Their 56-day strike was civil but conveyed a message: Our pay will be negotiated, not dictated.

With the rapidly growing and increasingly unionized employee base, and with a new corporate board of directors and stockholders he must report to, Kenny knew what had to be done. Talent from outside the company needed to be brought in.

New Leadership

Sam Addoms started with the company on April Fool's Day, 1972. He had caught Kenny's attention back in the mid-60s when he was with the Continental Illinois National Bank and Trust of Chicago, where he had been the vice president for national development in charge of major Western U.S. accounts, including

Monfort. In trying to explore other ways of structuring loans for the company he had come up with a system based on trade acceptance financing, which was used in international banking and could do something that meant a great deal to Kenny: save the firm boatloads of money.

It was an inspired move. Like most feedlots and packing operations, Ken and Warren Monfort relied heavily on loans to run their facilities. They generally paid prime plus three-quarters of a percent or similar rates for their loans, which was standard at the time. Addoms, however, wondered why they couldn't use trade acceptance, which came under the Federal Reserve Act of 1913 and was used to finance the storage of fungible commodities, such as grain or cattle. Trade acceptances could be sold for under prime, which was great for the bank. They then could attach a commission on it and sell it to the company for only slightly over prime. When you're borrowing millions at a pop, a half a percentage point can mean quite a bit of cash in your pocket.

Addoms was an up-and-coming star at the bank, having graduated from Wesleyan University of Middletown, Conn., in 1961. At the age of 32 he had become the bank's youngest vice president. When Don Mueller, Monfort's chief financial officer, left to take a similar job at Spencer Foods in Iowa in 1971, Kenny called Addoms and asked if he wouldn't mind becoming his finance guy. But Addoms was already a finance guy. That wouldn't entice him to leave his position in Chicago. If he was going to leave, he wanted to run something.

That's fine, said Kenny. If you'll join me, I'll let you run something.

His first responsibility was turning around a Portion Foods plant, which with the help of Wayne Harrison he did. It was then on to the Transportation Division, and eventually responsibility for the packing plant and feedlots were also put under his control. With the exception of the distributing and marketing functions, the company was more and more reporting to Addoms.

The Transportation Division is a good example of how the company grew under Addoms. In March 1976, under his direction, the trucking operation was completely converted into a successful component of the Monfort team. A fleet of 60 tractors and 170 refrigerated trailers became part of Monfort Transportation Co., which set up shop at the old feedlots north of Greeley, with its own maintenance shops and offices.

Monfort hired drivers for new White Freightliner tractors hauling Timpte trailers to join a team of owner-operators in taking the product to the Northeast, mainly Boston and New York. It was probably the best publicity the company would get.

Sometimes called "circus wagons," trucks that carried Monfort meat were known in the 1970s for their colorful Monfort of Colorado script on the trailers. Also well-known on the road were the drivers, who stopped at nothing to get the product through. In CB radio lingo the left lane of the highway had in fact gotten its own name – the Monfort Lane – because of the aggressive, non-stop and speedy truckers hauling the meat. Monfort trucks were ubiquitous; they hauled about 5 million pounds of product on 125 weekly runs, with the company's drivers hauling meat some 250,000 miles a week.

Seeing the success with which Addoms was running the assignments he had been given, Kenny thought perhaps this was his chance to take a step back and further increase the "outsider" influence in the corporation. He had suggested as much in a *Denver Post* March 10, 1974, interview when he said he felt "very strongly that a company of our size should not be run by the same person too long." Although he said he had "no political aspirations," he wanted to do other things – maybe teach or write. In mid-December 1975, he approached Sam Addoms and suggested he might like to be president of the company.

> I hold the school of thought that in any one job, someone is apt to use up most of his or her good ideas in a rather brief period of time and that after that time he or she is more apt to know what cannot be done rather than what can be done. Add to this the fact that the administration of modern

corporations such as ours is very complex and may well demand more than the cattle-feeding, start-a-packing-plant, entrepreneurial-type training I have had, and you can see that it is undoubtedly time, corporately, to make the change.

Ken Monfort
Letter to Employees
Company Newsletter, 1976

It sounded strange to Addoms, but Kenny insisted that it could be run like a partnership. Addoms agreed to give it a try.

It couldn't have been more awkward or unusual. In fact, it was probably doomed to fail. The boss would become the employee, who would still be the boss. But Kenny always did have a contrarian philosophy. Just because it had never been done didn't mean it couldn't work.

They sat down one afternoon to discuss if this might succeed. Addoms had his doubts. But Kenny told him everyone liked the idea but him; that if he didn't want to do it Kenny would just go out and find someone else who would. Turning the reigns over to someone else at this stage of the game wasn't appealing to Addoms.

So they agreed they would run the company like it was a two-person partnership. Addoms said he would become the president of the corporation and as long as there was agreement between the two of them he would stay, and if there was disagreement, he'd leave. Not to worry, said Kenny. If we disagree, I'll leave. Addoms laughed.

In 1976 Addoms became the president and CEO of the company, and Senior Vice President Kenny Monfort reported to him. Until, that is, they got to the Board meetings, when Addoms reported to the Chairman of the Board, Sonny Mapelli, who essentially reported to the majority shareholder and Vice

Chairman – Kenny Monfort. Although strange, that system worked for three-and-a-half of Addoms's remaining four years with the company.

By July 1976 the company had grown to nearly 2,400 employees and its yearly sales were $386 million. By 1978 they had increased to $451 million. While the company had reported a 72 cent/share loss in fiscal year 1976, it had shown profits of 37 cents and 39 cents per share in 1977 and 1978, respectively. Obviously, things were headed in the right direction.

> If the job is big and if it is tough and if the pressures are great, something like 10 or 15 years is long enough. The day-to-day grind and the day-to-day decisions do take their toll. The ideas and even the vision of the future get used up if one is a mere mortal. It becomes far too easy to defend past decisions rather than making the new tough decisions that must be made, and there comes a time for a change.
>
> Ken Monfort column
> *Greeley Tribune*
> March 2, 1983

Things were looking up, albeit briefly. In late 1978 Kenny was still optimistic that both the economy and the government were on the right course. He said he saw "a government responding better to the wishes of the people than I have seen in recent years. I see an understanding of, and a desire to deal with, the economic problems of the nation all through the population. I see a movement away from the burdensome and ridiculous governmental regulations and red tape that have deteriorated our ability to do business and our way of life. ... But maybe I have always been too optimistic."

The first real difference of opinion between Addoms and Kenny occurred in 1978, when Kenny wanted to make Oakley,

Kansas, the site of a new packing facility that could process up to 1,500 head of cattle a day. Addoms didn't think the proposed site was the best for a new plant, nor did he think it was the best use of the company's capital. Nevertheless, Kenny bought the land and made the announcement in August 1978. After further discussion, Kenny decided Addoms was right.

Instead, Addoms helped engineer a $46.5 million expansion beginning in 1978 with the purchase of a 21,000 square foot facility in Jacksonville, Florida, from Armour & Co., which produced ground beef patties and portion control meats. He also completed a company image revamp, changing the company logo to broaden its appeal, remove references to Colorado and make it more contemporary.

Then in 1979 the company purchased the former Swift packing plant in Grand Island, Nebraska. That plant, dedicated August 25, 1979, would serve two purposes; it would help increase production capabilities and provide the company with a production facility should workers at the Greeley plant go on strike Nov. 1.

Approval to purchase the Grand Island plant was not a foregone conclusion. It had to be approved by the Grand Island City Council, and those individuals weren't falling all over themselves in support of welcoming this Colorado company. Kenny, Addoms and associates Dean Davis and Jay Boeddeker and others flew to Grand Island for the council meeting, at which Kenny and Addoms were scheduled to speak.

The voting was to be done through a lighting system, where a green light meant approval and a red light meant a no vote. Kenny leaned over to Boeddeker and said if all of those lights go green, we've got it made. They went green.

Later that night they were celebrating in the hotel bar and Kenny was ecstatic. The drinks are on me, he yelled. Addoms just smiled. The drinks were always on Kenny.

Addoms went on vacation in July, knowing that in Greeley labor negotiations would begin in earnest when he got back. While he was away Kenny took actions Addoms viewed as insubordinate. He believed Kenny's actions resulted in the company going from a slight profit for the year to a loss.

It was a disappointment for Addoms, who had shown slow but steady progress in building the company's profits. He went to talk about the situation with Kenny. You know, Addoms jokingly told Kenny the employee, a worker could probably be fired for something like this. Kenny the board vice chairman and major stockholder believed he was doing what was best for the company, and disagreed.

It was at this point Addoms knew the "partnership" was strained and nearing its conclusion. He went home and told his wife Cathy that when the labor agreement was completed, the Monfort/Addoms relationship would be finished, as well. They were moving on.

Labor Headaches

Labor unrest in many industries was getting underway in the late 1970s across the country. But the problems for Monfort went way deeper than that. Interest rates were about 22 percent before the strike and the company was not in compliance with some of its loans. The economy was terrible. The cattle market was terrible. Things were just going downhill for the company.

Monfort in Greeley was getting eaten alive by its major competitors when it came to wage rates. The packers near the terminal markets they had been competing with in the 1960s were getting out of the cattle slaughtering business, and the new ones were obviously more aggressive when it came to labor. IBP had about a $3,000 per employee advantage on the lines, and that was enormous for a commodity-producing plant with small margins. The per-animal slaughter costs in Greeley on its yearly production of 600,000 animals was about $30; IBP's cost was about $20. About half of those costs were attributable to labor.

Kenny was stepping forward and talking publicly about labor issues and how the company intended to address them. He gave an interview to the *Greeley Tribune* July 31, 1979, in which he said it would be a new day for labor negotiations. No longer would they follow the big packers – which were getting out of the business, anyway. They would need to follow tougher competition now in the beef industry.

"We who are in the situation cannot long exist," he told the Colorado Meat Dealers Association in June 1979. "It is an impossible situation." Labor costs at the Greeley plant were about $6-$7 million higher than their competition.

There was a line that needed to be drawn and Kenny was not bashful about drawing it. If the union wanted to negotiate, it would basically be talking to itself. The company, which was now the state's third largest, would take a hard line because the structure of a new agreement would need to lead to a profitable plant. It had lost money at the plant in each of the previous four years – $7 million in all – and at one point considered selling the facility, moving all of the production to Grand Island. In the end, though, they thought selling the Greeley plant was the easy way out. Their decision was to craft a proposal to the union they thought was difficult but fair, and one that would keep them in business.

The situation itself was a reversal of fortunes, and of positions. Monfort in the past had been willing to live with whatever terms had been negotiated with its competitors, which over time had become the "Big 3" packers (Swift, Armour and Wilson). In 1979 the company's principle competitor – IBP, whose employees were represented by the same union – was paying significantly lower wages. Now one of the industry leaders when it came to wages, Monfort saw that its competition wasn't taking the same road Monfort had when it came into the business.

Monfort wanted a "standstill" agreement with its union workers to allow its competitors to catch up to the Monfort wages and make the company more competitive. Union members resent paying union dues when they're standing still, however. Furthermore, unions have trouble attracting new members if they're not moving forward aggressively.

The workers at the Grand Island plant were also represented by a union, but not by the UFCW. They had organized under the National Maritime Union, which was representing workers at a few other plants in the local area. UFCW saw this as a "sweetheart" deal that kept them out of the plant, and in fact Monfort didn't fight that union and had no anti-union campaign whatsoever to keep the Maritime Union out. Whatever it was, initially it kept labor peace among the workers and allowed the company to get its production started.

UFCW Local 641's contract in Greeley was set to expire at midnight on Oct. 31, 1979. Talks, such as they were, had been going on since August. Union officials called company offers "shallow and bordering on the line of poor-faith bargaining." From Oct. 13 to Oct. 31 only two negotiating sessions were scheduled, and on Oct. 13 the 900 union members at the plant voted unanimously to strike if an agreement wasn't reached. Senior Vice President Kenny Monfort still held out some hope for a resolution.

The company's "bottom line" offer came on Oct. 30. Except for a few minor adjustments the last, best and final offer the company provided was essentially the one they had been presenting all along. It was the only one they believed they could live with.

The company's bulldog on negotiations was none other than Gene Meakins, who had been Kenny's editor in college at CSU and been in his wedding party. Meakins had joined the company in 1969 after spending 10 years with United Press International in Denver and several years with the American Institute for Free Labor Development (AIFLD). The group was created by the AFL-CIO as its international arm in the Western Hemisphere to attempt to develop trade unions in Latin America, but received U.S. government support and was thought to have strong Central Intelligence Agency ties.

In addition to working with the firm's labor staff to handle labor relations, Meakins served as the company's public relations staff with media and the public. A wiry and taciturn man with steely grey eyes, he was a good point man for an impossible position. Meakins preferred to do the negotiating behind closed doors, but Greeley is a small community and city leaders and others wanted to know what was happening. Meakins said as little as possible.

Finally, in an Oct. 29 full-page ad in the *Greeley Tribune* the company put all of its cards on the table. The ad was in the form of a letter to employees, just in case their union bargaining committee had failed to fill them in adequately. It also laid out for the community what the company was paying its employees.

After some background the company said its offer included pay rates from $7.98 to $9.18; three weeks vacation after eight years; 10 paid holidays, including the employee's birthday; company-paid medical, dental, optical, prescription drug and major medical insurance for the employee and family; company-paid life insurance policy of $10,000 per employee; company-paid 90-day disability plan; company-paid profit sharing plan; company-paid 15 minute rest period.

The company proposed to take away plant sanitation work from the union to be conducted by an outside contractor and pay new union employees at a lower rate. But most of these new employees would go into a second shift, which would increase production at the plant. The letter noted that with a second production shift there would be more union jobs. The letter was signed by Samuel D. Addoms, President, who in the letter said many of the company losses were "caused by the present wage, benefit and work rule costs which exceed the wage, benefit and work rule costs of our profitable competitors."

The union was not amused. In comments to the *Greeley Tribune*, union representative John Urban called Addoms's comments "palpably phony." He also didn't believe the packing plant labor contract was bringing the company down. "The company's contention that its labor costs are higher than its competitors' is nonsense," he said. "Its labor costs are lower because of its efficient, hard-working employees."

The union couldn't have made its position more clear. "Monfort wants to return to the industrial dark ages of starvation wages and destructive working conditions. This is the way Monfort rewards the people who have enabled it to build a vast and wealthy commercial empire. We shall not surrender to Monfort's selfish demands."

Urban pointed out that some of the offers the company made actually represented cutbacks, as one of the rest periods was eliminated and health and disability benefits were reduced.

Furthermore, new workers wouldn't get the same pay and would be deprived of dental and eye care benefits. He said the union had filed a complaint with the National Labor Relations Board, saying the company didn't come into the bargaining session in good faith.

In a prepared statement Urban stated the union's case: "We have all known for a long time that the Monfort company is ruthless in the treatment of its employees – that it does not pay fair wages or provide decent working conditions. Now, we also learn that the Monfort company is completely dishonest."

The union was clearly gearing up for a strike, as was the company. Management employees were informed they would work in the plant to help fulfill contracts for products should union workers walk out. Union workers were meeting to discuss strategy, filing the necessary picket permits and preparing picket signs.

Before a strike would even get off the ground the union and company exchanged NLRB charges, each saying the other side wasn't following the rules of engagement. The union said Monfort was bargaining in bad faith. Meanwhile Monfort said the union was not only bargaining in bad faith, it was restraining and coercing employees, refusing to work (through walkouts, or "wildcat strikes"), participating in incidents that damaged company equipment, and had been unwilling to face economic reality.

Although every attempt had been made to broaden the leadership in the corporation and negotiate as a company, everyone knew who pulled the strings. Kenny Monfort still owned most of the shares and while he was taking a low profile at this point, he was highly involved in the company and couldn't become invisible. One of the union members revealed his recognition of Kenny's role, when he was quoted as saying "we were expecting Monfort of Colorado to forget the lessons of the past and go ahead and behave in a callous and inappropriate way. It reflects *his* attitude about the people of Greeley and the butchers in particular." (emphasis added.)

Kenny was concerned with the possible upcoming work stoppage, but it was the employee disloyalty and insolence that really got his goat. Sheep slaughter workers on Oct. 29 conducted a wildcat strike, using the time to confront Kenny about conditions and the lack of a contract. While he always had an open door policy and would have been happy to talk with the workers in off hours, he was furious they would shut the line down to make their case. When the workers left the building, he instructed company engineers to rip out all of the sheep slaughter equipment. The operation had been losing money for a long time anyway. That would be the last of sheep slaughter at the Greeley plant – ever.

The federal mediator who had been involved in bringing the two sides together to resolve the 1970 strike was also called into this one, but had been unable to bring any resolution to the impending conflict. Fred Lusk had not been involved in any of the negotiating sessions, and said no such sessions with him had been scheduled.

At midnight Nov. 1, 1979, the strike officially began, although because of a contract clause no picketing started until the next day. It was a fairly peaceful start to the work stoppage, but the company might have been happy to have the workers out of the plant. Later it would be revealed that pre-strike sabotage, such as ball bearings dropped into the ground beef grinder, had caused more than $100,000 in damage to plant equipment. Because it couldn't be determined who was responsible, no one was fired.

The strike itself wouldn't remain calm and orderly. The company would beef up security, hiring uniformed off-duty sheriff's deputies for $10 an hour to not only patrol the plant but to guard the company's Kuner and Gilcrest feedlots. (Later they would agree not to wear their uniforms while conducting this work.) More than 40 deputies signed up for the duty.

Pickets officially went up Nov. 2, with 24 workers on the line at any one time. They picketed in 4-hour shifts, filling the line 24 hours a day. Each member was required to picket one shift a week. Union spokesperson Steve Thomas again told the Greeley Tribune the union doubted the company's claims of impoverishment, and said the company didn't "care one iota about the people who have built the company to the point it is today." The union also wanted nothing to do with the two-tier wage system, saying it would drive a wedge between new and old employees.

The Christmas season had not yet started, but the city's retailers were concerned. The community had yet to feel the full brunt of the strike. Payroll at the plant was $270,000 a week, and restaurant owners and others knew you couldn't take that kind of money out of the economy and not be affected. Sales taxes alone would amount to $8,000 a week, diminishing the level of services that could be provided by the city. Strike benefits were only $45 a week, rising to $55 the third week, and that didn't come close to the average $319 a week base pay before the strike.

Strikers, along with their spouses, were determined to stick it out. One wife told the *Greeley Tribune* that they were "ready to lose everything we've got." Union spokesperson Thomas said the members were "prepared to stay off work for as long as it takes."

Strike incidents were minor the first week, with a few scratched cars here, a few bumped picketers there. Those on the picket lines were slow to move out of the way and they let those crossing the line hear about it, but they generally acted peacefully. Things heated up the next week, though, as three picketers were arrested for throwing rocks at one of the company's closed circuit television cameras. Later six others were arrested when they were seen dropping nails on a roadway leading into the plant. The men were released after each posting $50 bail.

The union had complained to the city paper that the sheriff's office was not objective, as many of the deputies were being paid to work on their off hours in security for the company. Several incidents of taunting and inappropriate action by the department were claimed by union members – denied by sheriff and deputies – after the arrests. "That's the most incompetent sheriff's department I've ever seen," the union spokesperson said.

After another eight arrests of picketers at the plant the sheriff withdrew off-duty Monfort security entirely, telling Kenny he had to find other ways to keep his plant safe. He cited a possible conflict of interest, as well as threatened legal action against the department by the union. Though Sheriff Harold Andrews said he thought his staff had acted appropriately, he "must remove any element of doubt that has been created through criticism of off-duty employment."

One of the arrests was for criminal extortion, felony criminal mischief and disorderly conduct when a picketer threatened to kill a company security guard. With all of those arrested in their 20s, none was old enough to have worked at the plant during the 1970 strike, let alone when the plant was started nearly 20 years before. The union's Thomas said the arrests demonstrated "the continuing pattern of harassment by the sheriff's department," and it planned a march Nov. 18 at the sheriff's office to protest its actions.

Reactions by the community to the strike were decidedly mixed. Some believed the perceived impact on the community's economic well-being was overblown, as only about 1½ percent of the community were plant workers. Although no polls were taken, the company and workers seemed to be evenly supported. Ultimately, most people just wanted things to get back to normal.

After nearly four weeks – and following a huge storm that left 8 inches of snow on the ground to make picketing difficult – the union decided its story needed to be better told in the community. In an interview in the *Greeley Tribune* six members said that if there were financial problems at the plant, management bungling had to be a key reason. Furthermore, they asserted, because of the company's vertical integration, shenanigans were probably taking place with the books. Although Kenny wasn't talking, neither of these charges could have made him very happy.

Even though cattle were heading to the Grand Island plant, that facility was still not fully operational. After a month Monfort needed to find a new outlet for cattle finishing at their feedlots, so it purchased a plant in Denver owned by Flavorland Industries, a subsidiary of Foxley & Co. The plant could process between 900 and 950 head per day, compared to the Greeley plant's 2,400 head/day capability, and had a workforce of 250. The sales price was estimated to be $2 million.

Union officials tried to put a good face on the purchase, saying it showed the company wasn't as broke as it said it was, but the company's increased production capabilities couldn't have helped force Monfort's hand. With the Grand Island plant quickly getting up to speed, the strike could have gone on indefinitely without affecting the other aspects of the company's business.

At the height of the strike the FBI approached Kenny to alert him they had uncovered information that a contract had been put out on his life. An FBI informant in Cincinnati had tipped them to this mafia contract. The police chief's response was to encourage Kenny to take the matter seriously and to learn to shoot a pistol, and to assign a squad car to follow him until the strike was over. Police protection was provided to Kenny for nearly half a year.

No attempt on his life was ever made and it may have just been union posturing. Kenny owned the company and it certainly would have been counterproductive to have him killed. Still, Kenny did buy and learn to shoot a gun. He was never comfortable with it, however, and asked others to carry it for him at times. And the only thing that came out of having the firearm was that it forced him to drive under the speed limit for a couple of months.

The union negotiators also used more subtle threats. Entering meetings they would inquire about the company representative's neighborhood and family, calling each family member by name and mentioning the ages of the children. They would also happen to mention the schools those children attended. It was their way of saying we know where you live, we know where your family is and it's easy to reach out to you and your loved ones.

> "I believe it goes without saying that I would rather not have the UFCW (in Grand Island). They certainly were not helpful in Greeley to us or to the employees they represented, and the head of their Packing House Division has vowed to me a 'fight to the death.' I frankly do not wish a death fight with a 2 million member union but I guess I have no choice."
>
> Ken Monfort
> Grand Island Speech
> March, 1981

It was apparent that the union wanted to personalize this strike. It wasn't just about the contract. It was about winning and losing, and the union doesn't like to lose. It was also about Kenny Monfort. That reality wore heavily on him.

Kenny was in a foul mood, and those around him in the sales office certainly understood. Like them he had just driven through a throng of striking employees who were yelling expletives and cursing Kenny's heritage and existence. It was late 1979, and the workers had been on strike since Nov. 1. As the weather worsened, so did tempers on both sides of the conflict.

The strikers had done their best to impede Kenny's entrance to the plant, but by slowly moving forward he was able to enter the parking lot, where he was greeted by more hateful shouts from outside the plant gates. How dare he keep them from their jobs, and from doing those jobs at pay rates they deserved?

He stomped up the outside steps and stormed through the office doors. His ears were red and his lips quivering. It will be a cold day in hell before they keep me from walking into my own plant, he declared to all within earshot.

A security firm from Omaha was hired, and it passed along intelligence it discovered about which company people were going to die and who was going to get blown up. Police followed key company employees everywhere. Christmas parties attended by the Monforts were strange affairs that year, with police officers sitting in the hallways and keeping a close eye on any unusual or suspicious movements.

Finally, on Dec. 6 the international union called for resumption of talks and the company agreed to meet Dec. 7. It was the first talks since Oct. 27. It lasted less than half an hour and accomplished nothing. After a month the lack of logic in a drawn-out strike had to have been going through the minds of strikers. The longer they stayed out, the more they would need to earn to make up for the money lost by being on strike. It wasn't looking good for either side, and tensions were high all around.

In January 1980 the company said it was going to reopen the plant on Jan. 14, with or without the union. They started taking applications, and it soon became apparent just how well paid many in the area believed the workers were. Even at the lower wage scale, about 1,800 people started lining up as early as 6 a.m., shivering in long lines to apply for positions at the plant.

Five union members took umbrage at these "stinking scabs" trying to take "their" jobs, and heckled them as they stood in line. Most taking applications were unperturbed, though, and showed little sympathy for the plight of the union members. Even at $6 an hour the wages were much higher than most in the community. The majority couldn't understand why people making $7.98 to $9.18 an hour would give those jobs away.

Seeing the huge demand for jobs, union members again thought their message was going unheard. In another interview with *Greeley Tribune* reporters Jan. 7, union members tried to put the wage issue in perspective, saying the reason they got paid so much and had such good benefits was because of the union. "Monfort did not give us these benefits; the union bargained for them in past contracts," a union member said.

A slap in the face would have been less insulting to Kenny. He and his family had provided good jobs to thousands of people through the years, and paid fair wages with good benefits – without unions. He already was feeling betrayed by people his company had provided jobs for. Now Kenny saw a belief by some union members that he and his father couldn't be fair to the people they employed.

On Jan. 11 the union took a vote and decided to end the 73-day strike, going back to work without a contract. It took the company by surprise, to say the least, and it wasn't ready for this action. When the plant doors opened Jan. 14 the only thing waiting for workers was a letter stating they'd be called back when the plant was operational, sometime later in the week. The company was apparently expecting hundreds of unskilled workers needing training. Instead it got 900 trained workers ready to process beef.

It was an unusual move, but strikers were worried jobs they previously did would be permanently given to new employees who wanted them. They believed the move placed control back on their side. They could walk out again if an agreement couldn't be reached. According to the company the terms of their employment reverted to the Oct. 27 offer which froze their wages and slightly reduced some of their fringe benefits.

Now the people who were nervous were the replacement workers who had been hired by the company. Some had left other employment to start to work for Monfort Jan. 14. Others had turned down jobs in favor of the ones they thought they had at Monfort. A few thought they might have been pawns used to get the union workers to come back to work.

Kenny calmed their fears, however, at a Jan. 13 meeting at which he said they all would be hired regardless of what the strikers did. Most would be put into positions at other divisions of the company, at the same rate of pay, until positions at the plant opened. "We felt a definite commitment to you," Kenny told them at the meeting.

In an editorial Jan. 15 the *Greeley Tribune* lauded the union's decision to go back to work, saying it gave a brighter economic picture for the community. "The return of the workers is pleasing because members of the Monfort workforce have been a valuable part of the community for a number of years, and it will be good to see them back on the job," the editorial stated. It also asked that the company and union get back to the bargaining table. "It is to be hoped they will be able to come to terms that will make the plant profitable and provide a solid employer-employee relationship for years to come." That wasn't going to happen.

Fourteen workers were fired for strike-related incidents and told they wouldn't be welcome back to the plant. And the company strengthened security to assure that sabotage similar to what took place prior to the strike didn't recur. The union took exception, saying no one should be fired for what happened during the strike. Those things happen, it declared, and the company was just trying to single out strong union people. Management personnel believed otherwise. If employees would turn against the company to that extent during the strike, they wouldn't be model employees after.

Charges were filed by the union with the NLRB on the firing. They said the company "harassed, impeded, restrained, coerced and molested representatives of the union to prevent them from acting on behalf of the employees." All was not forgiven when the workers returned.

Despite the firings, it soon became evident there were returning union workers who were bitter enough about the company's handling of the situation to cause problems. Despite increased security various acts of sabotage were being uncovered, although company spokesperson Meakins tried to downplay it by telling the *Tribune* "things are about as normal as could be expected, given the circumstances."

It was obvious, though, that after the union workers returned many of them, with full union backing, had no intention of making the plant efficient and productive again. In her book *Meat Packers and Beef Barons*, author Carol Andreas quotes union leader Steve Thomas describing the pro-union, anti-company efforts of the workers.

"This one guy figured out how to make a drop of water fall on this 440 (electrical) box and shut the whole thing down about every hour," Thomas is quoted as saying. "It took them about a week to figure what was going on. It was an electrical thing. It was pretty slick."

It was a small percentage of workers who were determined to bring the company down at the expense of other employees who depended on their jobs. Whether the other employees were unaware of the sabotage, were aware and supported it or were afraid to report it because of what might happen to them is not known. Nevertheless, the sabotage continued, and it became evident that normal employer/employee relations would be difficult if not impossible.

> "We've got a bunch of people here now who want to work and a small number of people who are trying to mess things up. Before the strike this place was like a zoo. We were

> determined when we reopened the plant that we weren't going to let that happen again and it hasn't."
>
> Ken Monfort interview
> *Greeley Tribune*
> Feb. 1, 1980

Kenny opened up to media in late January, trying to quell concerns that high security at the plant was turning it into an "armed camp." He admitted he and the other Monfort managers were confused by the union's decision to go back to work, and that it made things difficult at the plant. It was Meakins, he said, who convinced him not to sell the plant several months before.

In fact, the union continued to charge the company with illegal tactics, saying Monfort had no right to implement its final offer and that negotiations were still open. Local 641 was particularly miffed that perceptions among the media and others was that the company had "won" the strike. The 12 charges filed by the union with NLRB addressed what the union considered to be grievances against its members.

On Feb. 1 UFCW Local 641 also took its case to the public, running an ad in the *Tribune* that put its own spin on the situation. It claimed the company was conducting "psychological warfare" with union members, and that it was "an all-out war with no holds barred." In the end, the only satisfactory conclusion would be a victory for the union. "When victory comes – and it will – we will share it with you," the ad concluded. How either the victory or the sharing would be accomplished was not described.

The union had said several times, however, that its true goal was to bring the company to its knees by any means, including putting it out of business. At the same time its workers were on the job after the strike, the national UFCW set a boycott of Monfort products, saying it would contact all of Monfort's customers to urge them not to do business with the company. "Who ever heard of a boycott when people are working?" Kenny asked in a *Tribune* interview.

Six weeks after restarting work at the plant, workers asked that negotiations resume, confronting Kenny in front of the plant demanding that the company and the union again sit down to talk. The union had not contacted the company about establishing a meeting since Dec. 7, and the workers were taking it on themselves to see if they could get the other side to get the ball rolling. The company and union, however, continued to conduct their negotiations in the newspaper.

By mid-March the layoffs were coming. Saying the company's Grand Island and Denver plants were the "most economical," Meakins hinted at the future as he said economic conditions in the industry were requiring the cutbacks. Profit margins for the plant were "really tight," he told the *Tribune*. At least this time the workers would be eligible for unemployment benefits.

A $6.8 million Monfort of Colorado loss for its second quarter spelled the beginning of the end for the Greeley plant. On Friday, March 28, the company decided to shut the plant indefinitely, making the formal announcement March 31. It would cost the approximately 1,000 employees, along with the community, more than $15 million a year. And with the 1980 economy in a funk, it was doubtful the Greeley area could absorb that many people out of work.

The union couldn't believe it. It must be a ploy to break the union. The company would sell the plant to another company, which would come in and lower all of the wages. In a truly ironic statement union representative Steve Thomas said laid off workers would get an assist when they got their profit sharing checks, which could average about $6,000 per worker.

Monfort Chairman Sonny Mapelli thought the move strengthened the company's economic health because it eliminated Monfort's "weakest economic link...without affecting our ability to continue to supply a large customer base and without a cutback in other operations." The Board overwhelmingly supported the closing of the Greeley plant at its March 28 meeting.

That signaled the end of the Sam Addoms era. He had proposed keeping the Greeley plant open at partial strength and closing the Denver plant, which was not as efficient and didn't have the same fabrication capabilities. He also thought that because property values in Denver were higher the company might get as much out of the plant as it put into it.

But the Board of Directors saw it in a different light. While Addoms didn't think it was necessarily a bad idea to close the Greeley plant, he had worked to keep it open. So it was a bad idea for him. Addoms knew it would take all of the management and Board pulling together in the same direction to make it work. He submitted his resignation April 1, exactly eight years after starting with the company.

Kenny had been leading the charge to close the Greeley plant. The economy was bad, interest rates were up, cattle numbers were down and any beef plant was going to lose money. But reports of sabotage and lack of productivity and efficiency at the plant had left him fed up, and he didn't want to deal with the union anymore. His decision, which was supported by the Board and which he would call one of the most difficult of his life, was to close the Greeley plant.

> "There is great validity to the fact that the more aggressive union people ended up on the bargaining committee as the strike progressed. As the strike got wilder, the more wilder union people assumed more responsibility. The more solid union people – who weren't agreeing with us either – eventually resigned the company and found other work."
>
> Ken Monfort Interview
> *Greeley Tribune*
> April 8, 1980

Kenny may have been kicking himself somewhat for not going ahead and selling the plant the summer before. He hadn't realized how significant the changes in labor relations had become.

In the early 1960s if the plant was having tough times and he needed to tell his workers how bad things were, all he had to do was round them up and lay it on the line. With a union as an intermediary and a government that provided that union sanctuary, those days were over. He and his management team thought they could still get the message of economic hardship through to the union members. They were wrong.

Ever the optimist, Kenny said the company was strong even after the plant was closed – and it was. Other divisions were profitable and there was a cushion as a result of the LIFO reserves (see Chapter 4). In July of 1980 those reserves were $69.1 million, which didn't help operating revenue and couldn't pay employees but did mean the inventory was worth more if the company was ever sold and provided a cushion for negotiations with banks.

> We will continue to be aggressive competitors and superb (we hope) suppliers. We continue to have a multitude of able and dedicated people. We are financially sound and plan to stay that way. Ours is a tough business but you had better believe that we plan to be a survivor, not a casualty.
>
> Ken's Comments
> Company Newsletter
> Spring 1980

He noted in his *Tribune* interview that the company had been in worse shape several times earlier in its history and persevered. "We'll make it," he said.

A Very Bad Year

When he made that statement he couldn't have foreseen two more very trying events later in the year that would weigh heavily on two of his divisions. In April of 1980 the company was found to have implanted about 80,000 cattle with diethyl stilbesterol

(DES), which had been originally banned by the Food and Drug Administration (FDA) in 1973, approved for use again in 1974, then banned again in 1979, the day Donald Kennedy resigned as head of the FDA. Company veterinarians had thought they had permission from the FDA to use up supplies on hand; they did not. They had to "dis-implant" the cattle that had been given the drug, a costly process from both a labor and public relations standpoint.

Kenny had never been a fan of DES, but not for food safety reasons. He thought all the talk about the dangers of its use in improving cattle weight gain performance was just hype. Kenny had served on an Office of Technology Assessment (OTA) committee at one time that investigated this hormone in animal feed, and one statistician had arrived at a very worst case scenario of one case of cancer per million lifetimes, and a best case scenario of one cancer per 100 trillion lifetimes at the other end. He had pointed out earlier that Iowa State nutrition researcher Wise Burroughs had shown that use of the product could increase weight gain by an average of 12 percent and reduce beef prices by about 5 percent. And it had never been found in meat, just in some beef livers at a level equivalent to – as Kenny liked to say – about one drop of vermouth in two railroad tank cars of gin, which would make a very dry martini, indeed.

Still, he thought the use of the product led to overproduction, which was not good for the industry. "I really believe that we will have a better market and that we as cattle feeders will make more money without using DES or...antibiotics," he wrote in 1979. "Prices will be higher because the supply will be less. So, frankly I am happy with the ban."

He only used it because it was effective and everyone else was using it. If he didn't use the product, he would be at an economic disadvantage to other cattle feeders who could raise their animals more efficiently. The only losers to its discontinued use, he thought, were consumers, who would have to pay higher prices for beef, and some drug companies that manufactured it.

One company official had said the FDA appeared "vindictive" in its singling out of Monfort for disregarding the ban. If so, it may have been a negative column Kenny had written about Donald Kennedy's ban on DES the day Kennedy had left his position that led them to tweak the company's nose. If government regulators saw the column, it couldn't have helped.

Then on June 3 a series of tornadoes hit Monfort's Grand Island plant, completely shutting down production for eight days. By this time Kenny's son Dick, then in his mid-20s, was working in Grand Island helping run that operation. Thankfully no one was hurt and insurance eventually covered most of the physical damage. But problems caused by the tornado would continue to be felt by the company for four months.

The plant had gotten its feet under it and was operating under full-scale production by the time the tornadoes hit, so with the closing of the Greeley plant the timing was awful. On the plus side, Kenny's reputation for fairness must have come into play as IBP – the company's biggest and fiercest competitor – purchased carcass beef from the coolers at market prices for further processing, saving Monfort and the insurance company at least $1 million.

To add to the company's misfortune, in early 1980 *Fortune Magazine* listed its top 500 companies by sales for 1979, and Monfort of Colorado came in ranked number 389. So far so good. The company had lost $177,000 for the year, which was not good, but far from disastrous. But Fortune listed the loss as $177 *million*, in a special listing right behind Chrysler and U.S. Steel. This caused a public relations nightmare, with Kenny having to answer calls from worried bankers and investors who *knew* the company was just hours away from Chapter 11, and cattle sale barn managers and other suppliers who insisted on cashier's checks for cattle and other materials.

Kenny in the 1980s

Add those unique challenges to the muddy feedlots, high interest rates and the bad market the company faced that year, and it isn't hard to see why many people would become discouraged. "Survival is not the one thing you tend to want to remember the most, but it sure counts," Kenny told *The Denver Post*.

The company had already taken the steps to go into "survival" mode because of the closing of the Greeley plant, reducing administrative and other personnel. So although the company still faced an uphill battle, Kenny was optimistic to shareholders about the prospects for the future. "Our company has had a terrible year and we still have problems," he admitted in the 1980 Annual Report. "But we survived a whole raft of non-recurring problems, and now it is time to recoup. I am convinced that in the years to come you will be proud of the company."

Those who would stick around were. In the mid-1980s the company made a huge comeback, lowering its packing plant costs to the point it was the envy of the industry and sending return on investment much higher. It would also work to accentuate positive financial periods and reduce the impact of negative ones by taking a more aggressive stance on supply and demand. The company would reduce or stop production when the market didn't reward their beef, waiting for customers to raise their offers before going back in. Though nerve-wracking, it worked to help improve the balance sheet and create a stronger company.

In 1980 the UFCW had filed a number of charges against the company with the NLRB with regard to how it handled the strike. Kenny didn't think much of the NLRB, and hardly thought it was an impartial arbiter of the situation. "I can only hope most of you realize that the NLRB does not have the best reputation for equality of treatment of labor and business," he wrote. "The courts, where these disputes will ultimately end, hopefully will be a little more impartial."

The Denver plant, meanwhile, had served its usefulness soon after the Grand Island plant became efficient. It was only operated by the company for one year, from December 1979 to December 1980, processing some 925 head per day with about half going to boxed beef. In 1981 Monfort leased the plant to Cattle King, but when that company ran afoul of the law amid unsanitary conditions charges it had to close.

Because the plant no longer fit into the company's future plans, various means of getting some value from it were discussed. After significant consideration and plenty of cajoling by Sonny Mapelli, who served on the National Western Stock Show Board of Directors, Monfort decided to donate the Denver plant to the National Western Stock Show. Valued at the time at about $4.2 million, it would be used by the show for meat judging contests and research.

Kenny would have preferred to weather this economic storm as he had in past years, with all parts intact. But the union had made that strategy impossible. His new aversion to unions wasn't overnight, though. His tolerance of unions slowly had been eroding through the years. Although initially understanding of their role and the reasons for their power, he came to view them as an impediment to both efficient and effective plant operations.

Later he became even more irate when someone from the union ranks used inflammatory and what he considered just plain wrong statements in a letter to other union members to try to keep his friend and former associate Hank Brown from getting elected to the Senate. Kenny commented in his Oct. 9, 1980, *Town and Country News* column about the letter written by Justus Drake, a union official who worked for Monfort at one time but had not been hired back because of strike related incidents. Drake had written to many union members stating the union was "now faced with a candidate for congress that is straight from the ranks of our worst enemy. Hank Brown was a Vice President at Monfort of Colorado. From personal experience in the grievance procedure, I can tell you he is no friend of the working person."

Worst enemy? No friend of the working person? Sometimes, Kenny wrote, "those who yell the loudest about being your friend may in the long run be less of a friend than those who are not so shrill and know the long-term consequences of their actions." Brown was elected handily.

Although angry about the disintegration of the union relationship, Kenny was more sad about what had taken place with the plant. "That closing and the effects of it on our community in general, and our employees in particular, are marked down in my book as my greatest failure to date," he said. "I had a number of failures in personal relationships, some political failures and those everyday type of goofups. ... But all of those type things pale in comparison to the problems that I could not solve involving our business and our plant in Greeley."

It wasn't just the union employees that were leaving Kenny frustrated: It was the union leadership. He thought the heads of the unions were leading their charges down the proverbial primrose path.

> Somehow the union leadership jobs are secure whether or not the members have work. Many members are in fact realizing that which their leadership will not, or cannot, realize and that is the fact that the enemy is not management. The enemy may well be another plant in another area, or another industry in another country.
>
> Someday there will be a new breed of labor leader who will realize what the labor leaders in Japan and Germany have known for years. That is that they and their members can only prosper if the companies and industries for which they work prosper.
>
> Ken Monfort column
> *Town & Country News*
> Sept. 10, 1981

In 1981, 56 percent of the employees at the Grand Island plant voted to be non-union. Two other unions in the running split the rest of the vote. (Kenny would later chastise the *Greeley Tribune* for burying this information.) In March of 1982 the

Greeley plant would be reopened by the company, without a union and at wage rates about half of what they had been before.

This didn't deter the union, of course. They worked to organize the workers and in June 1983 a union certification election was held at the plant. The union lost that election 396-301, but filed a complaint with the NLRB saying workers were intimidated by the company. On that issue the NLRB ruled in the union's favor, saying in 1994 the company had to pay $10.6 million, a windfall to 268 former workers and the fourth largest payment of its kind in the history of the NLRB.

Meanwhile, in 1990 the NLRB had ruled in the union's favor and called for a new union election, with Monfort appealing that decision, as well. In 1992 a federal judge ordered that Monfort hold the election and in 1994 Greeley workers voted overwhelmingly for union representation and mandatory membership through a closed shop. As Kenny was fond of saying at the end of some of his columns: And on and on.

Chapter 11
The Deal: 1987-1991

By business standards, the deal was completed in the blink of an eye. But it wasn't done without a great deal of thought.

George Doehring, a friend and fellow Greeley National Bank board member who owned an ag chemical business that had been sold to ConAgra starting in 1978, had talked to Kenny about ConAgra in the early 1980s. Around 1983 Doehring arranged for Kenny to meet Mike Harper, CEO of ConAgra, in Vail at a cattlemen's convention. That was the first time Kenny had officially met anyone from ConAgra, except for Doehring, who was then one of the three presidents of the company.

After that the three would meet at least once a year for lunch to discuss how the meat business was going. Although Kenny was well versed in what was going on at ConAgra, there were apparently no discussions about any potential future relationship between the two companies.

In the winter of 1986 and early the next year, ConAgra was looking seriously at acquiring meat packing plants in Ft. Morgan and Sterling, Colorado. In January Doehring asked Kenny to join him for lunch and told him that if there was any interest in selling, now might be the time to jump. And ConAgra might just be the suitor to consider, before it purchased other plants.

The timing was interesting. Monfort had for several years been embroiled in an action to stop deep-pocketed corporations from purchasing packing plants. The consolidations gave corporations additional resources that companies like Monfort of Colorado didn't have. Not only did it allow them to more aggressively brand and market their beef products, it helped them weather regular downturns in the market. Independent beef producers had to find additional financing during these periods.

Kenny had gone through bad cattle and beef markets, so he knew how great it would be to have a parent company to fall back on. Too many times he had to go to banks practically on his knees to get the money to keep operations going. What's more, the company had to shelve plans to become a more household name because it didn't have the funds necessary to get things off the ground. In January 1987, in fact, it had to pull some pre-cooked meat products out of test markets because of lagging sales – all because they didn't have the necessary money for advertising and other marketing strategies.

To some extent Kenny thought consolidations were the problem. No longer was it the meat companies fighting it out. Now corporations with really deep pockets were allowing the meat companies under their wings to get much stronger. Kenny wanted to reduce the power of these groups and thought his success, or lack thereof, would determine if Monfort would be able to continue being one of the major players or if it would have to maintain a mid-size role.

EXCEL, which was originally called MBPXL, had announced in June of 1983 its plans to acquire the Spencer Beef Division of Land O' Lakes. EXCEL had been purchased by Cargill, Inc. in 1979. If the sale went through, EXCEL would now have approximately a third of the beef packing market, and add to further consolidation of the industry.

At the time IBP, owned by Occidental Petroleum, was the nation's largest beef packer, with about a third of the beef packing business. EXCEL was the second largest and Spencer Beef was third. Monfort would come in a very distant fourth. The main competition would now consist of two industry giants owned by conglomerates able to use their financial muscle on the rest of the field.

"That scares the hell out of me," Kenny told the *Greeley Tribune* in early 1987. About six years earlier he had told a group of Grand Island residents in a speech that "we will be competing against very large companies. We are a peanut in comparison, but we know it and we plan to compete."

It had gotten worse, however. Kenny believed the purchase of the third largest beef company by the second largest would give EXCEL/Cargill an increased ability to pay more for cattle and, with its deep pockets, use predatory pricing to charge less than market price for its boxed beef to drive smaller companies out of business.

The sale of Spencer Foods to EXCEL had already been approved by the Justice Department, but Monfort filed suit in U.S. District Court on July 24, 1983, to keep EXCEL from making the purchase. A trial was held Oct. 5-7 of that year, and on Dec. 1, 1983, the judge ruled in Monfort's favor. The ruling was appealed to the Tenth Circuit Court of Appeals, and in April 1985 the original ruling was upheld.

EXCEL's lawyers argued that Monfort wouldn't be hurt by the purchase because it would result in fewer competitors, not more. And the primary competitor remained IBP. Furthermore, the number of plants wouldn't change, nor would the number of customers. In essence everything would remain the same, and if down the road predatory practices were proven, Monfort could then make its case. Still, Kenny believed it would be harder for smaller and regional processors to compete if the sale went through.

Kenny had been told at one time that three companies ran the world, and one of them was Cargill. He'd never win at the Supreme Court, he was told. In December 1986, the Supreme Court decided there was nothing illegal about the Spencer sale and overturned the Appeals Court. Had Kenny filed the suit as a cattle feeder and not a packer he may have had a better chance of winning the case. Nevertheless, it was at that point he saw the handwriting on the wall.

ConAgra had been in the market for beef before. In 1985 and 1986 it had made a play for IBP, which at the time was owned by Occidental Petroleum, but they couldn't come to an agreement. After the EXCEL/Spencer ruling and in thinking about Doehring's suggestion, Kenny thought it may be time to get the company its own deep-pocketed protection. The day of the big independent meat company was evidently over.

Kenny told Doehring he would think about it and call him back. Within a week he told him he'd be willing to have a meeting, but it would have to be discreet. Kenny, his son Dick, Doehring and ConAgra's Harper – like Kenny a big, tall powerful man – ended up meeting in Doehring's Greeley home. The several hour meeting didn't produce any conclusion, but Kenny said he would get back to Doehring and Harper when Kenny returned from the National Cattlemen's Association meeting in Reno, Nevada, Jan. 26-28.

The February meeting was also held at Doehring's house, with the same participants. It was at this meeting the deal was made.

The deal was done so quickly they almost didn't realize what they had done. Kenny and Harper had laid out the financial ranges they saw for the agreement and had hashed them out over several hours. When the final numbers were down on paper, Kenny told those gathered that he would take the numbers outside and visit with Dick about them. If Dick wasn't happy with it, there was no deal.

There were no questions about skeletons in closets, no concerns about accuracy of numbers, no arguments about honesty of statements. It was an unusual display of trust in the business world, but not in the world of Kenny Monfort.

Fifteen minutes later Kenny and Dick came back in and they all shook hands on it. Outside of that room, no one outside of the family knew about the agreement. It was amazingly quick.

But it was obvious that Kenny had done his homework between the meetings. Kenny knew what he wanted and it was close to what ConAgra was willing to pay. It turned out to be a good decision for both parties.

ConAgra at the time had about $5.9 billion a year in sales, which was about six times what Monfort sold. It could provide instant diversification for the company. There would now be a safety factor for the cyclical nature of the cattle industry. It was also a good deal for existing Monfort owners. The offer would instantly double the stock price to $76 a share, so value to stockholders was very attractive.

A huge factor, though, was that Monfort now had the know-how – and the capital – to conduct more branded marketing. ConAgra also owned and was buying other companies with products that were more branded in nature. These included Morton's, Armour, Banquet, Chun King and Golden Star. Monfort needed better marketing understanding and financing if they were going to get out of the commodity business, which put too much cyclical pressures on the company.

In 1982 he had told *Business Week* Magazine that he "could not care less whether our name is on the product." From an ego standpoint, that may have been true. But the company had tried (and failed) several times to distance itself from the commodity herd. They believed it was a way to get away from haggling with customers over a quarter of a cent per pound to create both real and perceived consumer value in the products they were selling.

Had the Monfort suit been successful at the Supreme Court level and the swallowing up of beef packers by conglomerates been stopped, it's doubtful there would have been a meeting and questionable whether Kenny would have changed course. Afterward he was vague about whether it would have changed what he did. When asked by a reporter at the *Greeley Tribune* whether the decision to sell would have been made if they had won the lawsuit, he answered: "I don't know. I can't answer that." They had, however, "lost in the Super Bowl" when they got handed the Supreme Court ruling. And after you lose the Super Bowl, where do you go from there?

At least the money was right. It was a $365.5 million stock exchange. Since the Monfort family owned about 73 percent of the company, it meant a total of $266.815 million in ConAgra stock would go to them. Other stockholders would also benefit, as Monfort stock had been rising and was worth $196 million just before the sale was announced. The $53 million of outside investments at that time were worth nearly $99 million after the sale.

Monfort would have a 10 percent stake in ConAgra, which also purchased E.A. Miller, Inc., a cattle feeder and packer. ConAgra had also bought 50 percent of Swift Independent Holding Corporation, another beef packer. Net sales for the conglomerate in 1987 would hit $9 billion.

Again it proved to be great timing. The company had been very profitable from 1982 to 1987, and was sitting in a strong position to be purchased. They were financially healthy and had even considered taking the company private at one time. They had no need to sell, but if someone came along with the right deal they could listen.

Possibly more important for Kenny, though, was the acquisition was positioned in an attractive way. The Monfort name would be maintained, and nothing would change. (At least that's how it was presented publicly.) Kenny would become the president of the subsidiary called ConAgra Red Meats Company; his son Dick would become the president of that company's Monfort of Colorado. Now instead of having to report to a Board of Directors Ken would be a member of one. "I want to be able to deal with other management people," he told the *Greeley Tribune*. "Me and boards of directors don't always get along."

> "My dad always said to make the best decisions you could make each day and then don't worry about it. I don't think he would be upset with this. It would have been a problem to sell it to someone who wanted to change the name of the company, to change the name on the plants and on the boxes (of beef). But that is one of the pitches ConAgra made. Everything stays the same."
>
> Ken Monfort Quote
> *Greeley Tribune*
> March 6, 1987

There were mixed reactions within the community and within the company when the sale was announced. Long-time employees were confused and concerned, wondering how things would change, and whether those changes would be for the worse. The personnel director at the Kuner Feedlot, Donna Hendron, was quoted as saying "several of our people had tears in their eyes when they learned of the merger. It was seen as the end of an era." And it was.

All of the employees were notified the same afternoon of the merger, either by meeting or by memo. Feedlot nutritionist Bob Reynolds told the *Tribune* that it was the same feeling as in 1970, when the company had gone public. For a company with Monfort of Colorado's history, this was startling news. There was initial anger that "the company had been sold out from under them." If nothing else, it got everyone's attention.

Kenny would try to put the best spin on it he could, saying in a note to employees on March 6, 1987, that the sale was in some respects inevitable, and this was the best thing for everybody. However, he noted that he "certainly cannot promise each of you that nothing will change; some things will. In some areas our responsibilities will increase and in some areas they will probably decrease. These things are, frankly, impossible to forecast."

It had been a difficult decision for him and the Board, the note said, but "in this day of massive corporations with massive financial resources, your company would be better off and our stockholders and employees would be better served by being a very large part of a large company rather than remaining a mid-sized company in our business."

Although kept out of the loop to a large extent initially, Sonny thought the merger had been a reasonable decision. "I don't think the money was the determining factor," he told the *Greeley Tribune*. "He did what he thought was right for the company and his people." Kenny's good friend Paul Hoshiko said the merger wouldn't change him. Sonny said he thought Kenny was now more happy and fun to be around.

According to Kenny, his kids had more problems with the transaction than he did. As he had shown when he had named Sam Addoms president in 1976, he wasn't afraid to turn leadership of the company over to someone else. Kenny went out to dinner the evening the sale was announced and ordered chicken. "And for the first time in my life I didn't feel bad about eating it."

Kenny would remain in that position for two years, but retired in April of 1989 at age 60, turning over the reins of the firm to his 35-year-old son, Dick. He had found that while the work was just as difficult as it had been before the merger, being part of a large conglomerate was nowhere near as fulfilling as being the leader of your own corporation.

Anyway, the promises made by a large corporation while making a deal and the long-term intentions of that corporation are often different. Their approach seemed to be counter to how Kenny had always conducted business. Instead of asking a lot of questions they always professed to know all the answers. There also wasn't a lot of respect shown to Sonny Mapelli by ConAgra brass.

And while they may have said nothing would change, the facts were that things did change, dramatically. He was just expected to deal with it.

> At ConAgra I was asked my opinion on a number of things. Probably at least half of my opinion differed from our chairman. It will come as no surprise that on those occasions he won.
>
> Ken Monfort Column
> *Greeley Tribune*
> Dec. 12, 1990

At one ConAgra board meeting Kenny was the lone dissenter on a vote to acquire another company. After the vote one of the board members came up to him and said they liked those kinds of votes to be unanimous. That may have been the final straw to an independent thinker like Kenny.

Kenny's confidence in his sons was an enormous factor in both his decision to sell and his decision to retire. Prior to 1987 Kenny didn't feel as though he could be out of touch with the company for any extended period of time. After Dick became president and chief operating officer in 1987 that seemed to change. Kenny was confident in Dick's ability to handle everything. In a family-controlled operation, that kind of confidence is important.

Early in their business relationship Kenny had taken a more "hands off" approach to his sons – especially Dick. He had put Dick under other managers, who Dick learned to turn to at critical points. Kenny would allow Dick to flounder a few times before getting involved in a situation. Dick soon developed the reputation as a highly intelligent manager with diligent work habits similar to his father's.

When Dick had been about 10 years old, he got his first taste of the business world when his dad offered him up to cut a patch of grass at the Greeley Packing Plant. Pay him low then work him up, were Kenny's instructions to the managers. Dick had also learned a lot from his grandfather about cattle feeding. He had lived with his grandparents for three or four years when his grandmother was sick and Warren was crippled with arthritis.

Through the years he had gotten more and more involved in the business and became adept at the intricacies it presented. Like his father, Dick had worked in the feedlots and been a cattle buyer. He had worked his way up to packing plant management in late 1979, then been introduced to the corporate environment. His acquaintances saw how he had taken on many of Kenny's mannerisms, talents and qualities, turning into a solid manager who deserved respect from his employees and peers in his own right.

In October of 1987 another 100,000 head feedlot was completed, this one in Yuma, in eastern Colorado, for about $11 million. The lot had been in the works since before the company was sold. In fact, Kenny had designed it from everything he had learned about feedlots to that point. The pens were bigger, allowing more square feet per animal; it was in a location where corn was cheaper; and it was on a railhead so that rail corn could be purchased. The additional feedlot would allow a second shift to be started at the Greeley plant.

But after ConAgra purchased the company it was obvious things were getting further and further away from its roots. In 1988 the company name was changed to merely Monfort Inc.; less than a dozen years later the Monfort name would be dropped entirely in favor of ConAgra.

At his retirement party on June 30, 1989, friends and employees toasted a man they had grown to respect and enjoy. In a book filled with notes and letters those sentiments were captured for posterity. "You have made Monfort Inc. more than a business; you made it a family," employee Jim Blankenship wrote. "I'm proud to have worked for you and your sons."

"It saddens me to see you go," wrote Sue Cassiday. "I want to thank you for all you have done for me and my family. I know we could never repay you for all you have done for us. Kenny, you are a great man. I'm proud to work for you and your company." Bonnie Cassiday wrote that "I have been proud to work for an excellent businessman with integrity, respect for others and the courage and determination to stand up for his convictions."

"You always looked us in the eye and shot straight from the hip and told it as it is," wrote Bruce Holton, who was the personnel manager at the Grand Island plant. "Our employees love and respect you for that." A Laotian employee at that plant, Kdaz Chandravaonz, wrote that "you did not give charity, you gave opportunity. Opportunity to better our lives and the lives of our families. We were part of a company and a community where we feel proud of what we have accomplished with your help and support. For this we will be forever grateful.

"Through your efforts, you have helped many of our people make the adjustment of coming from a foreign land to the United States," he went on. "You have given them self esteem, respect and above all, dignity."

Greeley's Eddie Aragon said "thanks for the many years of employment, education and opportunity that Monfort has given me. Many doors have been opened for me, and I thank you for all of this. Many thanks to you also for the opportunities you have given many Hispanics of this community." Roy Romer, his one-time bicycling buddy turned governor, meanwhile, said to keep in touch. "I need your advice and insight," he wrote.

Kenny spent a good deal of time right after his retirement at the nearby Dunkin Donuts, drinking coffee, smoking cigarettes and chatting with the locals. Although given some golf clubs on his retirement he was not good at the sport, and frankly not that interested. Instead he would enjoy spending time tending to his tomatoes, in which he took particular pride, and his zucchini plants. He had declared in an earlier column that he was "indeed the greatest zucchini grower of all time."

He contended one of the secrets to raising good tomato plants was to wait until they started to curl before flood irrigating them. Taught them character, he said. It also helped to use a lot of cattle manure and be lucky. Perhaps a parallel could be drawn to his philosophy on employee relations.

On his retirement Kenny had time to reflect on his life and how he felt about the decisions he had made through the years. Now that he had a chance to think about it, he was fairly pleased about the way things had come out.

> Life has been kind in getting me involved enough in business and traveling to allow me to know that if I had to do it over again, there are damn few things I would change. I still would have chosen Greeley, although I liked it better at 12,000 to 25,000 population. I still would have gone to Aggies (CSU) although I might have studied harder and finished the last year. I would have bought fewer feeder cattle in 1954, 1962 and 1978. I probably would have tried to keep the business smaller so it was easier to run.
>
> And, of course, there have been some personal and political mistakes along the way. But all in all, I have to be the luckiest guy in the world.
>
> Ken Monfort Article
> *Greeley Style* Magazine
> Winter, 1989

Kenny would donate much of his time, and money, to local efforts both before and after his retirement. One of these was the construction of the Union Colony Civic Center, a project for which he would help orchestrate a $4 million fund drive. Kenny had wanted a guaranteed budget of $8.75 million, but when the price went to $12 million, he had a fit.

He added a disciplined approach to the project, to be sure. His support of the whole project wasn't without reservations. He thought borrowing money for such a venture was foolish.

> I may be either old-fashioned or just old. But I have definite views on what the city should go into debt for and what they should pay for out of cash they accumulate.
> Ken Monfort Column
> *Greeley Tribune*
> Dec. 6, 1989

They did get the price down to $9 million, and reached their goal of $4 million in donations, due in no small part to the $1.4 million donation from Kenny. He wanted to support the project in honor of his mother, who he said would have enjoyed going to concerts at the Center. He was glad to pitch in, he said, as long as he didn't have to go to symphonies himself.

Play Ball

When Colorado baseball fans were looking to bring a major league team to Denver, naturally they thought of one of the state's leading millionaires, Kenny Monfort. They looked at the recent sale of a family-controlled corporation and figured there was a lot of money there to be mined. Kenny was a big sports fan; he was a devoted Denver Broncos booster and had written newspaper columns extolling exploits of the CSU Rams and CU Buffaloes. Who better to show some state pride by buying into a Colorado baseball team? Some believed it was a slam dunk.

After all, sports fans in Denver had been enjoying minor league baseball off-and-on since 1886. The Denver Bears attracted outstanding crowds – in fact, a minor league record 65,666 at one game in the late 1970s. And in August 1990 Colorado voters had approved a ¾-cent sales tax hike to help fund a new stadium by a comfortable margin of 54 to 46 percent.

Local investors were needed to attract the attention of the National League and assure an expansion franchise. When asked whether he wanted to be part of the ownership group by Governor Roy Romer, who was leading the Colorado Baseball Advisory Committee, Kenny said no thanks.

Maybe it wasn't that polite. Someone remembers him saying it was the dumbest thing he'd ever heard, and the word "crazy" was heard more than once. Others said his comments were – to be generous – less than supportive. He was too old and sick to get involved, he told one acquaintance. Kenny also said that he was "not much of a baseball fan." To others he said he'd rather watch paint dry. But more than that, he thought money issues were going to start causing problems for professional sports in general.

"The fans are starting to question the higher and higher ticket prices to watch some stars who are becoming more prima-donnas than athletes," he wrote. "The difference between the college games, with their unpaid although admittedly subsidized athletes, and the pros, with their overpaid superstars, is coming through the video tube. The college kids try harder… And they are fun to watch."

Kenny was puzzled by athletes who thought the then-astronomical salaries they were making were "an insult." When those athletes said the salaries would cause them to not play as hard, he said someone should take "a stand against the prima donnas who may well ruin the goose that is laying the golden egg."

The real reason Kenny turned down an opportunity to invest in the team wasn't his dislike of the sport or the high salaries of the players, however. He just thought it was a risky investment. By all accounts he never gave investment in Colorado's entry into Major League Baseball a second thought.

It was touch and go for the team for awhile, but finally the Colorado Baseball Partnership put together financial commitments of between $80 and $100 million to pay the $95 million franchise fee to establish the Colorado Rockies. And while Kenny wasn't going to get financially involved, he did know someone who might have an interest.

Charlie Monfort was taking Kenny to the airport in 1991 and wanted Kenny's honest opinion. You don't think much of this baseball investment, do you? No, Kenny said, I wouldn't do it for a couple of reasons. First of all, I don't think it's that good of an investment. But second, you're a limited partner. You have no control; no say in what's going to happen. You've got other people running your business, and I just wouldn't invest any of my money in something that I don't have any control over.

Civic leaders were concerned the new team's ownership was primarily out-of-towners, but Colorado is a pretty small state economically. Aside from a few individuals and companies, that's where the money was. Overall the ownership group raised about $140 million for the franchise. Out of 18 groups in 10 cities, Denver and Miami were selected July 5, 1991, by the National League's 26 owners for expansion teams. Six general partners controlled the team; the nine limited partners, including Charlie Monfort, were at the time along for the ride.

The fee for getting a team was steep, even by Monfort standards. Colorado is not home to many large corporations – or wealthy millionaires. Kenny knew that after you had paid the fee owners were still in for some high stakes, not the least of which was paying employees (players) way too much money. Salaries for top baseball players were escalating at incredible rates, and there didn't appear to be any slowing in their contracts, or any ceilings on what good players – and some marginal ones – could make.

To Kenny sport was entertainment, not business, and he wanted to keep it that way. Until he had hurt his knee playing city recreation league volleyball in the early 1960s, he had even considered himself somewhat of an athlete. Now he was just a spectator, but a heavily invested one – at least from an emotional standpoint.

Charlie stayed with it, though. In 1992 Rockies vice-chairman Michael "Mickey" Monus was accused of embezzling funds at his firm, Phar-Mor Inc., and he and his father Nathan gave up about $12.5 million interest in the team. His partner, John Antonucci, the Rockies' CEO, and his father Jack also gave up some of their stock, totaling about $7.5 million. All of a sudden, things were up for grabs.

Now Charlie could eliminate the second of the two concerns his father had expressed to him about investing in the team. Instead of being a limited partner, Charlie would become a general partner and exert some control over how things would be run. Together with Jerry McMorris and Denver entrepreneur Orel Benton, the $21 million in general partnership stock was purchased and control of the team was in local hands. In January 1993, Charlie became a vice-chairman of the Rockies, with Jerry McMorris named as chairman.

On April 5, 1993, they played their first game against the New York Mets in New York's Shea Stadium. Kenny and Myra were on hand, as was Myra's elderly father. The Rockies lost that game 3-0.

The team's return home started with a bang and silenced those who thought Denver wouldn't be a big league city. A crowd of 80,227 saw the team's first home game on April 9, setting a record. By May 9 the team had already reached a million in attendance; by July 28 the Rockies had surpassed three million. They drew 4,483,350 fans to the park in their first year. And in their first season the Rockies had recorded the most wins of any National League expansion team.

Kenny watched with interest, although he didn't regret his decision to stay on the sidelines. (Or, in this case, in the dugout.) And he offered what support he could to both his son Charlie and to his friend Jerry McMorris. He recommended Clark Weaver, who had worked for Kenny at Monfort of Colorado, to become the team's general counsel, and that proved beneficial to the team. It isn't known whether he made any player recommendations, but that would have been highly unlikely and uncharacteristic of him.

Kenny also recommended that Charlie get some advice from Walker Miller, an old friend and attorney who worked for Kenny on personal matters. Miller would later go on to become a federal judge, a position he retired from in 2008.

The early 1990s weren't kind to Rockies ownership. Benton would file bankruptcy and sell his shares to Charlie and McMorris, and to Dick Monfort, who decided to join the general partnership team. Charlie and Dick would eventually buy out McMorris, too, to make them the primary owners in the ball club. In fact, Charlie and Dick now owned the majority of the Rockies stock. Charlie became team CEO; Dick would become Rockies vice chairman.

The team now channels some of the distinctiveness of Dick and Charlie's father: loyalty, fiscal restraint, strong character and integrity. Like their father, the brothers established a thick hide to let the arrows bounce off and they do what they think is right. Both listen and are sensitive to criticism. But in the end, Monfort of Colorado was Kenny's company. Now, the Rockies are their team.

Charlie would remain on board with ConAgra until December 1998; Dick had resigned in June 1995 to get involved in other business ventures.

Chapter 12
The Columnist

If Kenny hadn't gone into business with his father, he thought he might have liked to be a journalist. He had written for his school papers in both high school and college and had freelanced some sports stories to the *Greeley Tribune* in high school for 10 cents a column inch.

He had also written columns for the *Town and Country News*, a free weekly newspaper, from 1971 until Oct. 25, 1979, when he announced he was quitting to spend time on more pressing issues on the work front. He did, however, occasionally submit a column to that paper for the next two years.

In his first column for the paper, Kenny had written that "Tom Gavin and James Reston (*New York Times* columnist) had best watch out." Kenny said he "may not have the… cynical wit of a Gavin or the depth and insight of a Reston, but I am cheap." Tom Gavin was a *Denver Post* columnist with whom Kenny had become friends when he had run for the Colorado legislature in the 1960s.

Gavin fired back a tongue-in-cheek letter: "Cynical wit, your ass! My attorney would call upon you for an explanation of that remark, sir, except that: I have estranged all the lawyers in the state, and thus haven't any; and I would quite likely win the ensuing lawsuit, and take possession of the company, and I have enough people after me without adding the clothespin-nosed environmentalists to the posse. Yours for more sweetness and less light, Thos. Gavin. P.S. This is an indoctrination letter, written solely to familiarize you with the sort of mail you'll be getting, now that you're a columnist. I, of course, will never mention you again publicly, you being a competitor and, worse, now able to strike back. At least in the Greater Ault Metropolitan Area."

Kenny liked to tell people that "I love to read what I write. How else can I find out what I think?" But even Kenny wasn't really sure why he wrote the columns. "I guess I just enjoy it," he wrote. "Sure, I like it when someone comments on an article...especially the favorable comments. But frankly, I even enjoy most of the negative comments."

He had always wanted to be a writer, though, and this was his opportunity to bring those dreams to life – even if it wasn't a real career. Kenny thought it was more likely that he wrote because it gave him something to talk about at the office, meetings, parties or other settings. "I'm not the greatest conversationalist," he said, "and I have a feeling that people resort occasionally to something that appeared in print, under my name, to get a conversation out of what otherwise are long pauses."

When the daily *Greeley Tribune* bought out the *Town and Country News* in the 1980s he arranged to provide a weekly column for the *Tribune* in the 1980s and early 1990s. His arrangement with both papers was the same: He would provide the columns each week, for no pay, and if they felt the topics were appropriate, they would run them. If at any time he didn't feel like writing anymore he could walk away, and if at any time they believed his writing wasn't suiting the needs of the paper they could tell him to go away.

Though he procrastinated in writing them, Kenny took his columns seriously. Often he would sit down behind his typewriter 15 minutes from deadline and pound out a column, handing it off to a runner to be delivered to the paper. Occasionally it wouldn't make it on time.

His early *Town and Country News* columns were often called Random Thoughts, and were truly just that; random ramblings about what was going on in politics, sports or the world. Because Kenny's interests were broad, he kept up on current events and politics and he was well-read, so carrying on about any number of subjects was not hard for him. But the real reason Random Thoughts often was an appropriate title was he always waited until the very last minute to complete his columns, so he rarely had the time to properly flesh out any one idea.

Kenny was proud of what he wrote and rarely changed a word once it got on paper. He had strong opinions about any number of issues, and those opinions were well reasoned, often provocative and almost always discussion-worthy. His folksy writing style and self-deprecating manner weren't for effect; they were natural and genuine Kenny. (He didn't spend enough time on those thoughts for them to be anything else.)

Kenny was a prodigious writer during the 20 years he was contributing pieces to the *Town and Country News* and *Greeley Tribune*. He wrote more than 500 columns, which is a longer run than most columnists get. In honor of his Random Thoughts and in no particular order, following are a few of his ideas that demonstrate his philosophy through the years, as well as some…well…random thoughts. They don't seem to fit neatly into any of the other of this biography's categories. Nevertheless, they are interesting insight into the workings of the mind of Kenny Monfort and provide some additional information about his life.

Random Thought #1: *Kenny thought a bigger, better airport wasn't necessarily a good idea for Denver.* While growth in and of itself wasn't necessarily a bad concept, there was a limit. "How many airplanes can be crowded into one glob of airspace?" he asked the Executive Club at the University of Colorado in 1987. "Is growth associated with being a hub for one, two or three airlines really worth it? How many people do we really want to crowd into this front range?"

Random Thought #2: *There is no cure for the blahs.* How can you tell when you have them? Other peoples' jokes aren't funny. Cold weather is a little colder. Problems get put off. Children get grouched at and the dogs get less attention. Columns become difficult to write and deadlines get difficult to meet. And you really don't even care if you miss the television newscast. The best treatment is isolation. "But that is very difficult when an epidemic is occurring. Barring complete isolation, next best is as little exposure as possible," he wrote.

That's also why some of his columns were a little shorter than others.

Random Thought #3: *Sometimes solutions to societal ills are painful.* "If the biggest problem is our imports of oil, why don't we limit the dollar amount we will pay for that imported oil? This may well force a shortage in the U.S. But that would be something I could understand. I frankly have problems remembering there is a shortage when everyone is wanting to sell me gas."

In an energy poll conducted by Kenny in his *Town and Country News* column of Jan. 30, 1975, more than 76 percent of respondents said they thought the energy crisis would be over within 10 years, while only 15 percent said it would still be a mess and 10 percent said it would lead to war. About 17 percent said the whole thing was contrived by the oil companies, and about 3 percent said the American free enterprise system could fix the problem. "We the American people are a heck of a lot more knowledgeable and willing to face the problem than our representatives believe," Kenny concluded.

Random Thought #4: *Keep those cards and letters coming.* Kenny said he was "appalled" the Pope would express a stand against birth control at a food conference and equally appalled when he said abortion was never justified, even when it's to save the mother's life. "Although I believe wholeheartedly in the right of the Holy Father to air his beliefs, when they are in conflict with what I believe to be the needs of the world in which I live, and in which my children and hopefully my grandchildren live, I reserve the right to comment."

Random Thought #5: *Our country needs to get more respect.* Kenny thought someone needed to start paying attention to the United Nations, because it was in sorry shape and the U.S. picks up a disproportionate share of the bill. "The so-called 'third world,' the maligned, mostly small, mostly new nations of the world have taken control," he said. "I'm not saying that we drop out. I'm just saying we must re-evaluate our commitment in a body that neither appreciates us or respects us."

Random Thought #6: *I'll take part of that action.* Kenny was known to bet on a football game or two. Betting on a football game or two a year, in fact, was his father's only vice. While Warren was good at it, Kenny wasn't; he let his emotions allow him to bet on the CSU Rams and the Denver Broncos. It was up to those who bet with him to settle up at the end of the year, "because I don't ever pay anyone and they have to keep tabs, hoping that after the Super Bowl I will cough up the pesos."

Random Thought #7: *No more chads.* Kenny hated the way elections were becoming impersonal through the use of computers. He had a system of marking his paper ballots in certain ways depending on how he felt about the individuals running. Now? "No emotion, just a mechanical punching of the hole in the wrong place and a one week wait to see who won. Come on, you guys. Let us go back to the paper ballots. Down with computers, sterile elections, social security numbers and all of the other de-humanizing aspects of everyday living."

Random Thought #8: *Sit down and shut up.* Sports shouldn't be taken so seriously – especially high school sports. A couple of end-of-the-year losses by the Greeley West Basketball team elicited some "disgusting" reactions by the parents. "In any athletic contest, someone wins and someone loses," he said. "I hope West will win the tournament. I even more hope that all will treat it like an athletic contest and not really a matter of life and death. Decency can mix with athletics."

Random Thought #9: *That goes for your newspaper, too.* An interview with a *New York Times* reporter ended with the reporter telling Kenny Colorado was a nice place to visit but he wouldn't want to live there. It was a phrase Kenny had used about New York City, until he decided that he didn't even like to visit there.

Random Thought #10: *Wait! I'm not finished!* Although he loved to read, Kenny avoided those books written about people before those individuals had retired or died. One that was making the rounds in the mid 1970s was a book about Henry Kissinger. "Analytical books of political and national figures should wait until their job is done," he wrote. "These 'early' historians write for the buck, not the historical perspective."

Random Thought #11: *This one hurts the most.* The Nixon and the "Squeaky" Fromme enemies lists weren't the only lists Kenny made in his lifetime. Seems as though there was a girl in the fifth or sixth grade at the Buell School and he was on her list, too. He wasn't particularly pleased about being on this one, though. It was her list of boys she disliked.

Random Thoughts #12: *We know it wasn't Myra.* Kenny never lost his sense of humor about some topics. In his May 6, 1992, column for the *Greeley Tribune* he said "strange as it may seem, my wife, dog and I do not frequent motels with fax machines and secretarial services. Often Myra and I have discussed why they will not take us. I believe it to be the dog. She thinks it is the way I dress."

Random Thought #13: *It's hard to carry dead weight.* Downscaling is never easy for any business, but Kenny thought for some it was easier to keep the wrong people. "Companies are discovering that, indeed, they have been overstaffed at the management level... Frankly, company presidents have found it a lot easier to lay off 500 workers they seldom saw than five vice presidents they often saw at work, socially or on the golf course."

Random Thought #14: *Maybe it should have been Sonny and Sunny.* Though he complained some in his columns and occasionally to his family and friends, on most days there couldn't have been a man more appreciative to be on the planet. "I can't think of any place other than Greeley, Colorado in which I would rather live, nor any time better than the latter part of the 20th century. With all the problems, I like my work, my business and the challenges that exist. I'm happy, pleased with and love my family and am fortunate to have many good friends."

Chapter 13
The Educator

If Kenny couldn't make his living as a journalist, he thought he might like to be a teacher, like his parents. Kenny believed education was very important and had made that clear while in the legislature, sponsoring a bill that established the junior college system in Colorado and allowing the creation of Aims Community College in Greeley. He was on the Aims Board when the college was first created.

He also showed his support for colleges in other ways. In September of 1969 as a member of the Colorado Board of Agriculture he urged aid to CSU – although this was more for intercollegiate athletics than for academic programs. The students were facing a hike of $24 a year in student fees to help bail out the athletic department, and were threatening to boycott that increase. Some had suggested eliminating the intercollegiate athletic program instead of raising student fees, but he didn't think that was right, either. Kenny thought it was only fair that the legislature bail the school out of the "mess." College athletes needed to go on to make a living, too.

"No one has yet complained about the $20,000 that it may cost to produce a doctorate degree in engineering for someone who may spend his life on the ABM (missile program)," he was quoted as saying in the Sept. 10, 1969, issue of *The Denver Post*. "No one has yet questioned the $5,000 it would cost to produce another ROTC graduate to replace a Gen. (Lewis) Walt (a controversial Vietnam era military leader). But we get big questions about the $10,000 it costs to produce a Brady Keys, a Fum McGraw or a Jack Christiansen because they end up playing pro football and coaching. Yet all of them have highly marketable talent upon graduation."

(Keys was a football star in the late 1950s who went on to play six years for the Pittsburgh Steelers, while Thurman "Fum" McGraw was a football All-America in the late 1940s who would go on to play professional football and later become CSU athletic director. Jack Christiansen was a 1940s track and football star who played for the Detroit Lions who would be elected to the National Football League Hall of Fame in 1970.)

Kenny also noted the importance of athletics in helping to diversify the student body. Over half of the black students at CSU in 1969 were there on some kind of athletic scholarship, he said, and that if people believed as he did that racial balance was necessary, "credit must be given to the CSU Athletic Department for doing most of the job, inadequate as it is," he said. "There is no better way to make CSU a nice, lily-white school than to start by abolition of intercollegiate athletics."

Elements of teaching seemed to fit Kenny's style. He was personable in one-on-one settings and enjoyed talking in front of groups – after he got the hang of it, of course. In his managerial duties at the packing plant he had made some speeches to his employees (a few easier to make than others) and he made dozens of speeches as a legislator, becoming quite a good orator. Nothing polished, mind you. Just someone you could easily listen to while appreciating some honesty and candor. He often spoke to college-age groups on behalf of the company and enjoyed it.

> "The student would criticize us for worrying more about the quality of our product than about the quality of our life. Sure, we are in a way the Establishment. Our industry has for years been a stronghold of conservative action and conservative beliefs. But it is changing so very fast. Don't relate us with the political system or the educational system. Ours is an industry crying out for and accepting new ideas and methods. This is where the action is. No challenges? Make a feedlot that is odor free. Or train a thousand

butchers from off the farm or from right out of high school or military service. Or even try to finance a bunch of cattle in a new feedlot. No challenges? Baloney."
Ken Monfort Speech
California Livestock
Symposium, Fresno
Summer 1970

He was finally approached in the late 1970s about getting into teaching, and he thought it would not only be challenging but also a lot of fun. The College of Business at the University of Northern Colorado (UNC) asked if he would be a visiting professor, talking about what it takes to be a success in business. The course was a senior level course called Business Policy and was designed to bring together those things students had learned throughout the business curriculum. It was one of the last classes the students would have to take and was very popular. He taught it until the end of the 1979-80 school year.

It was a natural for Kenny, who would identify the major problems managers could face in business situations. He would spice up his classes with stories from his own experiences and the battles he himself had fought. One of the highlights of his class was that Kenny would invite other businesspeople to speak to the classes. Other faculty would often sit in the back of the room for these sessions.

Bill Duff had just joined UNC and had recently met Kenny in the faculty lounge. He was curious about this local businessman and what he brought to his classes that made them such a success with students.

Kenny would give the executive-of-the-day a topic he thought he could handle, then go to the back of the room where he proceeded to sit in a chair and smoke cigarettes. (During those days students and teachers were permitted to smoke in class.) By the time the guest lecturer was done, Ken was sitting there surrounded by cigarette butts and ready to get busy.

He would lead the discussion by challenging the speakers on their views. He would ask a Republican why their views would support a lack of competition, for instance, or a Democrat about anti-government comments they may have made. He would challenge everyone to think – both students and lecturers.

The students would rarely miss these lively and insightful discussions, which always challenged them to think and participate. And the faculty got something out of them, too.

He took a lot of heat for it, but Kenny thought higher education should be run like a business. The Feb. 9, 1983, issue of the *Greeley Tribune* carried an op-ed column by Kenny that equated how companies stayed in businesses and how universities worked. In his simplistic view, it wasn't all that different.

"If some of the products are no longer in demand in our business, we quit making them," he wrote. "If we can sell more of another item we try to make more of that item. I happen to think the same must apply to a university." He went so far as to say universities should shut down departments in fields not in demand by students.

Most institutions of higher learning, however, thought they were anything but a business. "Many believe that a university is the place for scholarly activity, thought and research and that the fact that there is no current demand for their product is no reason to take such drastic action as I describe," he wrote. In that situation, he said, the taxpayer – who had a stake as the consumer of the product the university is producing – should help decide.

"Are our resources such that we should provide for doctorate degrees in philosophy at two or three universities whether there is demand from either students or society for doctors of philosophy? I believe not." He said UNC was then on the right path and "for those who are still teaching the manufacturing of buggies, it will be traumatic."

Among the items he thought government could do without was "vast taxpayer support of colleges, universities, community colleges, etc. that provide us with 100 political scientists, 50 sociologists, 40 psychologists for every one we need, while we are still short of electricians, plumbers and craftsmen of all sorts."

In the past Kenny had seen that the academic community was a leader in society, and he wanted to see it return to that role. During the 1960s many of the civil rights and war protests were from academics. A decade later Kenny saw a big change, and it was disconcerting to him.

It was important to Kenny that academics not get out of step with the rest of society. "If the academics get too out of step with the rest of the people, there will be budgetary effects in higher education, in fact in total education," he wrote. "If the Democratic Party continues to respond to this intellectual elite, to the academic community, and fails to relate to the broader base of constituents, it will fail."

Indeed, Kenny liked what the university had been doing to better meet the needs of society. "I am pleased at what I believe is impressive progress at UNC," he wrote. "Their governing board deserves its share of the credit." He especially appreciated what he saw when it came to its business college. In the 1980s it began eliminating its graduate business programs, focusing instead on building and adding quality to its undergraduate efforts. While many accredited business schools have masters and Ph.D. programs, only a handful offered only undergraduate degrees.

Before the university began its quality initiative in 1983 it had a bigger masters program than the one at the University of Colorado, and offered degrees in nine different business areas. By 1987 the university had eliminated all graduate level programs and reduced the number of undergraduate business degrees to five.

Kenny didn't say it, but it couldn't have hurt his feelings at all. He didn't think much of MBAs, anyway. They thought they knew more than they did, he believed, and wanted to run things too soon instead of learning how things worked in the real world.

More formal education isn't always better than more focused education, he believed. In a speech to the Executive Club at the University of Colorado in 1987, he said that "as we strive, as we should, for economic development within this state, let's (not) channel all of our efforts in job creation to PH.D.s. We need – desperately need – good job opportunities for the mass of our population."

He never seemed too impressed with "experts." Kenny always wanted people around him who not only knew what needed to be done, but who could also make those things happen. He believed education needed to facilitate that business requirement.

It bothered Kenny that America's "best and brightest" were spending their lives "shuffling money, companies and stocks. I just cannot buy the supposed wisdom that we as a people can prosper in an information, financial and service economy with no one producing goods, which are to me the real wealth of our nation," he told the CU Executive Club upon being named the Executive of the Year from that organization in 1987. All of that had a start in the education they were receiving in business school in college.

> "As I look at the degrees, the curriculum, etc., I see an abundance of Finance, Administration and Marketing. Nothing about production. We can administrate the process, finance the process and market it... but we are spending very little time with these students about producing goods, about quality of goods, about managing a workforce. I believe it is a mistake."
>
> Ken Monfort Speech
> CU Executive Club
> 1987

Kenny wasn't similarly encouraged by what he was seeing at CSU. That institution was governed by the Colorado Board of Agriculture, a body that Kenny "loved deeply" and on which he at one time served, as had his father before him. But Kenny believed that because of a politicizing of the appointments to the board it was getting further and further away from its mission. It was, he thought, "the place for Gov. (Dick) Lamm to pay his political debts."

"When I was on that board most of the members were products of the university and also loved it deeply and had no political axe to grind. The same is not true today," he wrote. "It is a political board with almost no ties to the university. I think CSU has lots of problems ahead."

Whether that column made him an immediate pariah at CSU isn't known, but if it did they patched things up fairly quickly. Perhaps it was a $1 million grant by Kenny in 1988 that endowed the Monfort Chair in Agriculture.

In 1988 the university gave him an honorary Doctorate of Science degree for his contributions to the state's agricultural business scene. Though he would never finish his undergraduate degree, he was pleased with being recognized in this manner, and in his remarks to students he said that "when you leave this university you have to learn from others. You do that by reading, by watching and by listening to others."

Kenny was bestowed an honorary doctorate at Colorado State University in 1988

He would also become the first million dollar donor at Colorado State University. And how the gift took place was exemplary of how Kenny Monfort handled his donations.

It was during the early 1990s at an 1870 Club dinner, a gala that CSU conducts to celebrate benefactors who have donated to the university and encourage others to do so. Kenny was sitting at the table with Al Yates, CSU president, and Dick Robinson, the chair of the university's development committee. Kenny suddenly leaned over to Robinson and said, nonchalantly, you know I think I'll give a million bucks to the university. Kenny had been giving it significant consideration and had mulled it over for weeks. He had even mentioned it to Yates at one point. But Robinson was stunned. What did you say?

It wasn't a casual donation, but Kenny didn't want to make a fancy splash of it, either. The university, of course, did hope to make sure people knew this kind of donation was not only possible but was being made by one of the region's best known families.

Kenny and Monfort of Colorado also encouraged their own employees to improve their educations. It was a way of making sure that the people on board had the business education skills the company needed.

Bill Bragg and Cornell "Corky" Swanson were two employees in the early 1970s who went on to meat careers after having their business educations at UNC paid for by the company. After graduating, both entered Monfort management programs that allowed them to further their education with the company and the industry. Each went on to a successful meat career beyond Monfort.

Keeping it Local

With his wife Myra, Kenny had endowed about a million dollars to the UNC business school for its executive professors program in June 1990. This allowed about $50,000 a year to bring well known executives to come to the school and teach. Because Kenny had in the past taught in the same manner, he believed in this program and wanted to support it.

About three months after he became dean of the UNC business school in 1995, Bob Lynch met with Kenny and Myra Monfort in Greeley, laying out a two-page agenda to develop the business school. He wanted to expand the executive professor program, support an entrepreneurship venture, construct a *speaker series, support students in some of their ventures, enrich short-term faculty to allow senior executives to come in for two to three weeks at a time and generally build a reputation for the school. And, by the way, he would like Kenny to contribute $10 million toward this effort.*

Kenny's jaw dropped, and an expletive or two may have been uttered. No one had ever asked him for that kind of money. But he didn't throw Lynch out the door. And he didn't say no. In fact, he ended up taking Lynch to lunch.

It was an enormous request in a city like Greeley, and the university didn't really know how Kenny would react. It certainly wasn't something Kenny would say "sure" to. At the same time, it had the ingredients that Kenny looked for in an investment. It was something that was lasting, something that was needed, and something that would make a difference down the road. He asked penetrating questions about what would be involved, how it would work and how the money would be used.

He wasn't big on putting strings on donations, but he did have a couple for this one. First, he wanted assurances that the money would be put toward developing excellence, not just maintaining programs. And, he wanted to make sure it wasn't used on things the state should be paying for. Darn it, that's why he paid taxes.

When the idea of naming the business school after him came up, he was adamantly opposed to it. There were enough things called Monfort in Greeley, and the family didn't need the continuing exposure. Lynch convinced him, though, that this wasn't about him, it was about the school. The recognized business schools, like the Daniels School of Business at the University of Denver, benefited from having well-known names associated with them. And if not the Monfort name, whose would be better?

The attention to quality that had begun in the 1980s paid off for the university when the business school received the prestigious Malcolm Baldrige Quality Award in 2004. It not only put the UNC Kenneth W. Monfort School of Business on the map, it put Greeley on the map. Kenny would have liked that. He was always encouraging the wealthy to keep their dollars in town, anyway.

Kenny didn't forget the state's largest university, either, and they didn't forget him. In 1988 he was named the Business Man of the Year by the Colorado Academy of Leaders at the University of Colorado Graduate School. He had given the University of Colorado Law School a half a million dollars, mostly because Myra had earned her degree there.

Chapter 14
The Conclusion 1991-2001

Kenny loved Greeley, and couldn't imagine living anywhere else. It had a good city complex, streets, businesses, experts, restaurants, people, volunteers – he couldn't have been happier calling Greeley home. In 1989, in fact, the city was bestowed a designation as an "All American City" by the National Civic League and Kenny thought that was just right.

> After looking around, thinking a little and listening a lot, I have decided that we damn well deserved the designation. This is a great city. It really has everything that we normal people might want.
> Ken Monfort Column
> *Greeley Tribune*
> July 18, 1990

The city, in fact, had been singled out before for its beauty and charm. Thomas R. Marshall, who served as vice president under Woodrow Wilson from 1913-1921, had called it and Phoenix, Arizona, "the two prettiest cities in the U.S."

"I never wanted to live anywhere else," Kenny told the *Longmont Times Call* on March 26, 1989. He believed Colorado couldn't be beaten as a state, and he appreciated it even more after he had been away.

Most of all, though, he liked the people. They were nice to be around. In his last *Town and Country News* column for 1977 he said he wanted to thank readers because there had been "kindness from many. You know, the common everyday acts of being friendly, smiling and kind. As we get a little older we appreciate those things more. Those are the things that make it a joy to live in

Greeley, Colorado rather than being one of the multitudes in one of the cities in America."

Kenny took car trips through the region almost every spring to see how the wheat, corn and alfalfa fields were doing, talk with other feedlot owners or as an "attitude adjustment" for rotten business conditions. While he liked to drive, these were business trips to him. Kenny would base decisions on what he discovered out in the country.

These trips were usually through Kansas, Oklahoma, the Texas Panhandle, New Mexico, Nebraska or other states. On May 30, 1974, he reported two key observations on a trip he had just taken to readers of his column. One was "don't try to find a room without a reservation in Bartelsville, Oklahoma, at eight at night." And the second was that "Colorado is particularly beautiful, as always, after a trip like this one."

Though he loved the city and the state, he didn't hesitate to speak up when he thought the city or city officials were on the wrong track. He told the Lion's Club on Sept. 6, 1965, that the city should possibly use incentives to lure more business to Greeley. His message to the *Greeley Tribune* was that its editorials about the city's smell didn't help the city's prospects either. He said if he had been a Chamber of Commerce manager at another competing city he would have saved and broadly shared those articles.

> I, like my father, am a perpetual optimist. I keep being amazed that even with our nation's debt load and our ability to elect the wrong people, the sun does, indeed, come up in the morning, the crops do grow, the children do feed me on Father's Day.
>
> Ken Monfort Column
> *Greeley Tribune*
> June 24, 1992

By the time 1991 rolled around, Kenny and Myra had retired part-time to Longboat Key, Florida, near Sarasota. It wasn't for the weather. He always considered Greeley home and would have preferred to stay there. But in his physical condition it was just too hard to breathe at the altitude, which in Greeley is nearly 4,700 feet.

Kenny had Chronic Obstructive Pulmonary Disease (COPD) caused partly by his case of rheumatic fever as a youngster and greatly aggravated by his smoking through the years. People with COPD have a hard time getting enough oxygen into their bloodstream. Part of his COPD included emphysema and chronic bronchitis, conditions that would eventually take his life.

Kenny's family history on lung issues wasn't good, either. His parents had exhibited signs of asthma-type problems, and his sister Margery had died from respiratory disease in 1988. Warren also had a severe case of arthritis that caused him to be stooped for much of his later life. But it was really Kenny's smoking that had made life most miserable for him in the 1990s. Sonny had hounded Kenny mercilessly about the smoking. He should have listened to Sonny.

Kenny was on oxygen most of the time now. It was late 1994 and the breathing problems were becoming more and more troublesome. But he was going back to Greeley anyway. Sonny needed him.

Sonny had been on chemotherapy for more than three years for the cancer that had ravaged his body. There wasn't much time left. Sonny's wife Nomie had brought a hospital bed into their townhome, giving it a fitting view of the golf course. Every day for a week Kenny would sit on one side of the bed and Myra the other. Sonny was too weak to say much of anything, so Kenny and Myra did the talking. It was a comfort to both Sonny and Nomie. And probably Kenny and Myra, too.

They said their goodbyes in the early morning hours of Jan. 19, 1995. It was like losing a brother all over again.

Kenny had gone through the pain of losing loved ones after extended illnesses before. His mother on Jan. 24, 1972; his father on Sept. 23, 1978; his older sister on April 13, 1988. His nephew,

Rick Wilson, Margery and Lloyd Wilson's son, had died of leukemia on March 3, 1970, at the tender age of 19. Those deaths, too, were expected. None would be easy to bear. Death never is.

In Kenny's case it was a matter of bringing it on sooner than necessary. Yes, you need to enjoy life, but at what ultimate cost? How many years had he lost to cigarettes? "I feel dumb about it because I knew better," Kenny said in one of his last columns in the *Greeley Tribune*. "I tried to quit, but not hard enough, so now I get to pay the price." He didn't want to preach, though, because obviously it hadn't helped him. But if you asked him whether you should smoke, "unless your name is Saddam Hussein, I would say no."

He was the same friendly person in Florida as he was in Colorado, but some friends there were special. Sal Randisi was in that category. Randisi and his wife Hilda lived three houses away from Kenny. Sal had a similar sense of humor. The couples enjoyed spending many days together along the coast.

He sat down next to the tall man at the homeowners association meeting and introduced himself. It was late 1991 and he felt a duty to his community to be there. But Randisi didn't consider it fun. Neither did the neighbor by his side. They enjoyed sharing humorous asides about the goings on at the meeting, then made plans to go off to lunch with the wives. Hilda and Myra hit it off, too. Randisi thought there was just an aura about this man. These are going to be our friends, he told Hilda.

And they were. Randisi would run business ideas by Kenny, who would enjoy talking about them and give him advice. Never in a "this is the rule" way, mind you. Kenny's business thoughts were carefully weighed and always appreciated and respected.

Myra and Hilda would shop at the same stores, often buying similar outfits for their husbands. Sometimes they would wear the same things as they went out to lunch or on outings, causing some of their acquaintances to call them "the twins." That was funny, since Kenny had a good 14 inches on Sal.

They talked on a daily basis – about the stock market, politics, sports, you name it. Nothing deep. Kenny was retired, after all.

It seemed as though every day was an adventure, and with Kenny these adventures were fun and enjoyable. Kenny was lighthearted and had a casual quality about him that made people smile. They were as close as friends could be and would do anything for each other. But age and health are two things your friends can't do anything about. *I wish I had known the man 10 years earlier,* Randisi thought. *Just another 10 years with the man.*

Kenny knew what it took to be a business success, but didn't flaunt the success he had. Though he was glad to share his views, he appreciated the positions that others took and tried to see the value in them.

The investment club was on its way back from the trip to Japan in the early 1980s, and everyone was happy and laughing. It had been a great trip, coordinated by Seigi Horiuchi, who had initiated many of the Monfort Japanese contacts for the company. Several of the participants were giving Kenny a hard time about how little he had spent on the trip, and generally how cheap he was.

Your money is wasted on you, said friend Leonard Prothe. He took off one of his new shoes. It was a pair made of alligator skin that he had purchased while in Japan. Look at these, he said, glancing at the scuffed pair Kenny had on. You could have a pair like this if you wanted. You just don't know how to spend your money.

After the announcement was made that the business school at UNC would be renamed the Kenneth W. Monfort School of Business, Prothe called his good friend to congratulate him. To what do you think you owe this honor? Prothe asked. Kenny thought for a moment. It was because I never bought those alligator shoes.

I want my family to know what to do. I want to avoid pain unless that pain is necessary to a healthy ongoing life. I do not wish to lie in a coma or be pounded on or be put through the contortions that come with the aid of a respirator. I want my doctor or doctors to know this. I want it in my will, on my driver's license and, if need be, they can carry this column around with them, although I trust and hope that it will be out of date by the time it is needed.

I want the good people who are my wife, children and doctor to be able to decide these things without the threat of court action or a "Quality Control" rehash by hospital or the government.

And, I love to eat. And I love to drink coffee, water, lemonade and a periodic scotch. If my affliction results in a coma or something like that, I don't want to be starved to death or to die from lack of liquids. Some laws believe this kind of death is acceptable while a nice little shot that ends it immediately is wrong.

I couldn't disagree more. And, if the time comes when I feel that my life should end due to illness and/or pain, I will not deem my own actions a suicide.

Ken Monfort column
Greeley Tribune
August 1, 1990

Kenny fell into a coma three days after undergoing heart surgery to fix a heart valve in May 1997. His cardiologist in Greeley, Randy Marsh, M.D., had ordered the surgery, having abruptly pulled Kenny from a treadmill test due to his fragile condition. The surgery was performed at the Cleveland Clinic in Cleveland, Ohio. He was in a drug-induced coma off-and-on for three weeks.

On waking from the coma Kenny's first words to his teary-eyed wife Myra were, Why didn't you just let me go? I couldn't let you go, she said. I just got you back.

It was a difficult time for Myra, who was devoted to Kenny and would do anything she could to make him happy. He was the love of her life, she would say, and the care she gave to Kenny the remaining four years was further demonstration of that fact.

Having used his bridge game to gauge his condition, Kenny had hated it that his game went to hell after he got sick. Other than

Kenny with (from left) Dick, Kyle, Kaye and Charlie in 1998

that, though, he didn't complain. Heck, he told others, I always just liked to sit around anyway.

Kenny had always wondered whether he would have had the courage his brother had. His last four years proved he did.

The year 1996 was a tough year in terms of health for Kenny Monfort, but it was a tough one for Jerry McMorris, as well. McMorris's son Mike was having a rough time. Born with cystic fibrosis, Mike wasn't expected to reach 2 years of age. But here it was 30 years later. Mike had been able to do the things a young man of his age had wanted to do, but this year he would hit the roadblock his family had expected decades before. A true warrior, Mike passed away at the age of 32.

One of the calls McMorris received after Mike's death was from his friend Kenny Monfort, who couldn't ease his pain but who offered tremendous support and said all of the right things. It was a call that could stay with you through the years, helping salve a wound that could never be fully healed. If Kenny cared, you always knew it.

It was a cold blustery day as more than 1,500 attended the Greeley memorial service held for Kenny Monfort on Wednesday, Feb. 7, 2001, five days after he had passed away at age 72. Flags at the Colorado State Capitol Building flew at half-staff throughout the day and parking fees in the city of Greeley were waived. Dick Monfort gave the eulogy, saying his father had been "my friend, my mentor, and the best man I ever knew."

A service had already taken place in Sarasota, and had been attended by more than 350 people. Kenny's former employee Joe Meilinger, now a deacon in the Catholic Church, performed both memorials, and Myra gave the eulogy in Sarasota. At both services were people from all walks of life. Hundreds of Kenny Monfort stories filled the air as people laughed and cried about the man who had touched their lives in so many different ways.

Ike Kelley was not going to miss the memorial service. In his 50s at the time, it was his years with Kenny Monfort in Greeley in the early 1970s that he had always remembered most fondly. Kenny had been like a second father to him, teaching him a lot and treating him with respect. Black like Ike or white like Kenny, it made no difference. We may come from different cultures but are all the same under the skin, really. Just guys working hard, being fair and trying to enjoy life.

At the service Ike and hundreds of others weren't ashamed to cry. Great men touch people like that, Ike believes. They leave pieces of themselves that can be both appreciated and shared. In Kenny's case it's those pieces that create both the lasting legacy and the hope for our future as a society. He was an enormously gifted man with an incredibly humble presence whose life made an impact on many others. Kenny would be remembered for many things, but his humanity said it all.

Hank Brown, in a Feb. 6, 2001, *Greeley Tribune* tribute to his longtime friend and associate, gave him the highest praise possible, calling him "the finest human being I ever met in my lifetime. He was the brightest person I ever met, but didn't feel a need for others to acknowledge it." The life of Kenny Monfort, he said, "shines as an example to all who knew him. He led by example, not by rhetoric."

Greeley Resident Ed Phillipsen experienced it only once, but it was an experience he wouldn't forget. Writing in a guest column in the Feb. 10, 2001, *Greeley Tribune* Phillipsen remembered the cold 1976 day he was stranded along the highway, late for class and a middle-aged man stopped to pick up this long haired student in the military fatigue jacket.

They chatted into town about his Vietnam experience and other things. The specifics were long forgotten, but Phillipsen remembered "feeling warm, comfortable and grateful for his interest in me and for his generosity of spirit." It wasn't until years later that he realized who had given him that ride, the man who had said to "just call me Kenny."

In a touching tribute, Phillipsen said Kenny was a "great man for great reasons. He was also a great man for simple reasons. He cared about an ordinary man who was cold and late for school." He believes Kenny's legacy should not be just his philanthropy, but the way he showed how to contribute time to the common good in smaller ways. There's great honor to the man through these kinds of simple gestures.

Ken Monfort once wrote that about the most that can be said of any of us when we're gone is that the lives of others are at least a little better because we had once lived.

> "I have no idea whether we were placed on this earth to enjoy life or to make a difference. For most of us lucky enough to be here, it's all the same. We can enjoy life and make a difference."
>
> Ken Monfort Interview
> *Greeley Style* Magazine
> Winter 1989

There are those who will judge other people by the shoes they wear. If you did that with Ken Monfort, you could have found yourself way off base.

And yet there were some hints in those often scuffed-up shoes about the man inside. Comfortable, humble, easy to be around, unpretentious. He was an old shoe kind of guy. If you found him wearing a mismatched pair? Well, that just demonstrated he was willing to look at both sides of an issue. He was open-minded and unprejudiced, most of the time coming to the conclusion there were good and bad points of any argument. Might as well have one of each.

After all, he had another pair just like 'em at home.

Epilogue
The Gift

Sam Addoms stood on the porch of his retirement home in the mountains near Walden, Colorado. He quietly regarded the bull moose grazing lazily on a nearby hillside. It was late afternoon in the Fall of 2007, and the sun shone on the Medicine Bow Mountain Range in the distance.

After a few moments of gazing at the scene, Addoms made the observation that the moose and the view were gifts of having a retirement home here in the majestic mountains of Colorado. You'd receive gifts like them every day. They were hard to quantify, but easy to appreciate. Bright stars on cloudless nights, clean air, peace and quiet, wildlife in its natural habitat or views that stretched as far as the eye could see. At 68 years of age and in good health, it was a retirement that could be valued by Addoms for the feelings these kinds of daily gifts generated.

After his resignation from Monfort of Colorado Addoms had gone on to other roles, the last as president, CEO and chairman of start-up Frontier Airlines in 1994, from which he would retire in 2007. It had been his rapport with both employees and customers that allowed the Denver-based company to spread its wings and succeed, especially in Colorado.

Part of that ability had been honed with Kenny Monfort. Addoms considered Kenny, who valued employee relationships, a mentor and teacher. Hmmm. Are Frontier Airlines, its employees and customers better off for having some of Kenny's attributes rub off on Addoms?

And what about another of Kenny's associates, Hank Brown? He went on to serve a distinguished 10 years in the U.S. House of Representatives and six as a U.S. Senator. He had been a popular, hard working and dedicated public servant, championing the reduction of costs of regulation and taxes on American business and improving the welfare system. Kenny was also mentor to Brown. How much of Kenny rubbed off on him?

How about Brown's subsequent career, as president of the University of Northern Colorado and later the University of Colorado? What hand did Kenny the Educator have in Brown's illustrious service in those roles?

And what of Monfort salesman Ike Kelley? He had gone on to run for Lieutenant Governor of Colorado in 1993 and been appointed to positions by two U.S. presidents. Without Kenny? Who can say.

What about the thousands of others who were touched by Kenny in similar or lesser ways? What kind of positive impact did he have on their lives, and what did that impact have on the lives of others through the years?

Kenny's gifts of kindness, generosity, education and integrity are worth considering. It was also, Addoms mused, a gift Kenny provided to his children when he sold the Monfort business in 1987. No, it wasn't about the money. Sure that was significant. But there was enough money there whether or not the business was sold.

No, the gift was the freedom the sale created. Charlie had expressed to Kenny at least once that he really didn't want to be in the business. Kenny had said the same thing to his father. His daughters, Kyle and Kaye, were not involved in the business, but were fundamentally linked to it and always would be as long as it remained essentially a family business. Dick was the only one who seemed completely content on the path that had been cleared for him.

During his prime years at Monfort of Colorado Kenny had also expressed the thought that if he could he would prefer to give the stock away and do something else with his life. But his sense of responsibility – not to mention the IRS – would have frowned on that kind of action.

That was the kind of freedom that escaped Kenny Monfort during his lifetime. The sale created for his sons and daughters the freedom to do whatever they wanted, not what they felt a responsibility to do.

In the grand scheme of things the aspiring journalist turned successful businessman certainly didn't have much to complain about. Yet dreams aren't always made of dollars. And good health can't be bought by them.

The Gift of Freedom. Now there's a concept! It would have appealed to Kenny the Democrat. And to Kenny the Republican. Both shoes fit.

Sources

Much of the information in the chapters, especially the incidents in paragraphs printed in italics, was provided by acquaintances, co-workers, friends and family interviewed from October 2007 to August 2008. These individuals are identified in the Acknowledgements section.

In addition to the sources identified in the text, following are some of the key sources for information:

Chapter 1

The *Town and Country News* of Sept. 18, 1975 and Feb. 23, 1978 provided information for this chapter. Information about the wedding was obtained from the *Greeley Tribune* of Wednesday, Nov. 25, 1949. Photos: Page 6, courtesy of Kyle Futo.

Chapter 2

Much of the information in this chapter is from interviews conducted and an unpublished manuscript written by the late William Hartman, Ph.D., at the University of Northern Colorado in 1971. Greeley information is from *The Greeley Story* by Peggy A. Ford. *Development of the Colorado Cattle Feeding Industry*, an undated article by W.D. Farr in the 1995 book *A Journey Back*, by John K. Matsushima and W.D. Farr, provided much of historical perspective for cattle feeding in the area. Photos: Pages 14, 16 and 17 courtesy of Kyle Futo.

Chapter 3

Weather information came from the Weld County site on the Internet. The W.D. Farr and John Matsushima book *A Journey Back* again provided valuable information on early 20th century cattle feeding. A column by Ken Monfort in the May 29, 1975, issue of the *Town and Country News* and an interview of him in the Jan. 6, 1991, *Denver Post* also contributed information for this chapter. Photos: Page 32 courtesy of the *Greeley Tribune*; pages

35 and 37 courtesy of the UNC Kenneth W. Monfort Library, and page 39 courtesy of Kyle Futo.

Chapter 4

Again, *A Journey Back* was used for details on the beef packing and cattle feeding industries. The Congressional Record of Oct. 7, 1966, provided the information on Bert Bandstra, while other facts were gleaned from an interview with Kenny Monfort by Steven Dittmer in *CALF News* published April 2001, a *Greeley Tribune* article of April 13, 1964, and Ken Monfort letter in the company newsletter of November 1969. The Monfort of Colorado prospectus from 1970 also provided significant information. Photos: Page 45 courtesy of Bud Middaugh; page 46 courtesy of the *Greeley Tribune*, page 48 courtesy of the City of Greeley Museums, Permanent Collection; pages 50 and 68 courtesy of the UNC Kenneth W. Monfort Library.

Chapter 5

An article called *The Greeley Story* by Peggy A. Ford was instrumental in providing facts about Greeley's early years. Steve Dittmer's two-part interview with Ken Monfort, this one in the April 2001 issue of CALF News, provided tremendous insight. *Denver Post* and *Greeley Tribune* articles of Sept. 3, 1967 and Sept. 6, 1968, respectively, held information on Kenny's political aspirations, and many *Town and Country News* columns contained his views, including the ones providing material from the following dates: June 8, 1972; May 24, 1973; January (date unknown), 1973; Oct. 25, 1973; Feb. 21, 1974; Aug. 8, 1974; Sept. 5 and 12, 1974; Oct. 10 and 17, 1974; March 6, 1975; July 3, 1975; Nov. 7, 1974; Oct. 9, 1975; April 15 and 29, 1976; Sept. 23, 1976; Nov. 4, 1976; Dec. 16 and 23, 1976; Jan. 20, 1977; Feb. 10 and 24, 1977; Sept. 22, 1977; Oct. 6, 1977; Feb. 16, 1978; May 11, 1978; June 1 and 29, 1978; July 20, 1978; Aug. 10, 1978; Oct. 26, 1978; Nov. 9, 1978; Jan. 11, 1979; Feb. 15, 1979; March 1, 1979; May 10, 17 and 24, 1979; July 26, 1979; July 3 and 31, 1980; Aug. 14, 1980; Sept. 11, 1980; Nov. 6, 1980; Feb. 3, 1981; and March 26, 1981. Columns from the *Greeley Tribune* of Aug. 10, 1983 and June 20, 1990 were also used, as were articles from that publication on Nov. 1, 1990 and June 24, 1992. An undated 1971 Ken Monfort column from the *Town and Country News* dealing with international relations also was referenced. Photos: Pages 87 and 88 courtesy of the UNC Kenneth W. Monfort Library; page 110 courtesy of the *Greeley Tribune*.

Chapter 6

Meatpackers and Beef Barons: Company Town in a Global Economy is by Carol Andreas and was published by University Press of Colorado in 1994. Two *Town and Country News* columns, one from March 15, 1973 and the other from Feb. 3, 1977, provided views expressed in this chapter. Other information came from a *Rocky Mountain News Sunday Magazine* interview of May 3, 1987.

Chapter 7

A reporter for *Fortune Magazine* came across one of the urinal signs and reported on it in the magazine's January 1973 edition. The other was observed by the author. Other information for part of this chapter was from a Ken Monfort column in the company newsletter's March/April 1971 edition.

Chapter 8

Town and Country News columns of Nov. 2, 1972; July 5, 1974; Nov. 26, 1976; Aug. 11, 1977; Jan. 4, 1979; and Dec. 13, 1980 were sources for this chapter, as were *Greeley Tribune* columns of May 18, 1983; June 8, 1983; and Oct. 3, 1990. An article in the *Denver Post* dated Jan. 6, 1991, and one in the *Town and Country News* dated July 25, 1974 were also used. An undated 1972 column from the *Town and Country News* provided information on his religious views. Photos: Page 173 courtesy of the UNC Kenneth W. Monfort Library, page 176 courtesy of the *Greeley Tribune*.

Chapter 9

Sources for this chapter included *Town and Country News* columns of April 6, 1972; May 4, 1972; Dec. 6, 1972; and May 19, 1977. A *Greeley Tribune* article of Aug. 10, 1967, also contributed. Photos: Page 182 courtesy of the City of Greeley Museums, Permanent Collection.

Chapter 10

Extensive information on the Greeley meat plant strike was derived from Greeley Tribune articles on the issue from July, 1979 to March, 1980. The *Meatpackers and Beef Barons* book (see Chapter 6 sources) was again referenced in Chapter 10. The *Town and Country News* columns consulted for this chapter included those in editions dated March 28, 1974; Oct. 2, 1975; Aug. 24, 1978; Nov. 16, 1978; July 5, 1979; Aug. 7, 1980; and Jan. 1, 1981. An article from the *Denver Post* dated Jan. 6, 1991 also was used, as was information from a Ken Monfort column in the company's May 1966 newsletter. Photos: Page 223 courtesy of the *Greeley Tribune*.

Chapter 11

Two of Ken Monfort's *Town and Country News* columns, from March 29, 1979, and Aug. 28, 1989, were among the sources for this chapter, as was a *Greeley Tribune* article of March 29, 1987.

Chapter 12

The majority of information for Chapter 12 came from Ken Monfort's columns in the *Town and Country News* – especially those that contained "Random Thoughts." Among the columns consulted were from issues dated Nov. 27, 1973; Dec. 6, 1973; Aug. 22, 1974; Oct. 24, 1974; Nov. 28, 1974; Dec. 20, 1974; Jan. 1 and 9, 1975; April 3, 1975; Sept. 11, 1975; Dec. 18, 1975; March 4, 1976; April 8, 1976. A *Greeley Tribune* article of Dec. 18, 1991 was also a source for the chapter.

Chapter 13

Columns from the *Town and Country News* dated Aug. 7, 1975, and Oct. 23, 1975, were among those providing information for Chapter 13. Photos: Page 257 courtesy of the *Greeley Tribune*.

Chapter 14

An undated 1971 column from *Town and Country News* by Ken Monfort was a source for this chapter, as were two other of his columns from that publication dated May 30, 1974, and Dec. 29, 1977. Photos: Page 267 courtesy of the UNC Kenneth W. Monfort Library.

Epilogue

The interview with Ken Monfort by Steve Dittmer in *CALF News* dated April 2001 was a source for information on the relationships between the generations of Monfort men.

Acknowledgments

Dick Monfort gave his approval to start research for this book on Sept. 27, 2007, the day after the Colorado Rockies had won their 10th straight game in a dash for a 2007 National League West Division playoff spot. (They would win their 11th in a row that night and go on to play in the 2007 World Series.) He sounded genuinely more excited about getting a book about his father underway than about his team's potential prospects for a World Series appearance.

Without his support, and the support of the entire Monfort family, this book would not have been written. In addition to their honest and candid memories, the family's foundation paid for out-of-pocket expenses incurred in the writing of this book, which allowed it to be researched, written and edited in a more timely manner than it would have been otherwise.

The late Bill Hartman, head of the Journalism School at the University of Northern Colorado, interviewed Warren and Edith Monfort and some of their employees in 1970-71, using those interviews to write a manuscript that was never published. A significant portion of Chapter 2 is based on that material, of which I was unaware before starting this book. Dr. Hartman not only turned out to be a tremendous help on this biography, he was my journalism advisor at UNC and a great supporter of mine while at the university and afterward. I will always be grateful to him.

Special thanks to my wife Chris, who was my first editor and my biggest advocate, and who also came up with the idea for the biography's title. Curt Olson was a meticulous and careful editor for the manuscript and the book is much better as a result of his input. Betty Anne Redson and Carol Storey also read, edited and provided outstanding feedback on the book.

The cover was designed by my friend Joe Kerr of Del Rey Oaks, California, a truly gifted artist and graphic designer. He has bailed me out on projects numerous times, and this one just adds to my indebtedness.

Kenny's friend and fellow legislator Rich Gebhardt was relentless in his quest to track down details of the "mismatched shoes" incident and I thank him for both his time and his efforts. He went above and beyond the call of duty.

More than 90 people contributed their time and memories during interviews for this book. Most of those interviews were taped. Follow-up phone calls for clarification were kindly taken and questions generously answered. Many thanks to each of those individuals, listed below.

Thanks to Peggy Ford, research coordinator at the Greeley History Museum, and her assistant Ann Norman for their assistance in securing publications and documents that provided a historical foundation for Kenny's life. Mike Leonard at the Kenneth W. Monfort School of Business provided help in securing additional Monfort information, as did Sarah Naper at the UNC Michener Library. Other librarians at the Michener Library were also very accommodating and my thanks go out to these frequently unappreciated and talented professionals.

Special appreciation to Bill Jackson of the *Greeley Tribune* for files on Kenny and his family; to Don Mueller for his briefcase full of company documents; to Myra Monfort for photos of Kenny, especially in his later years; to Nomie Mapelli for her extensive scrapbook of clippings and information from her husband Sonny's life; to Rudy Schlotthauer for his binder of company newsletters; to Mike Haskett for his file of Monfort clips and information; and to Tom Weiler for his wonderful scrapbook of clippings and mementos of his Monfort years.

Interview subjects:

Sam Addoms
Jim Alles
Bill Benton
Shirley Bernhardt
Jay Boedekker
Bill Boekel
Rod Bowling
Pat Braddy
Bill Bragg

Hank Brown
Doug Carey
Royce Clark
Paul Clayton
Mike Croot
Dean Davis
Bruce Deifik
John DeMoney
George Doering

Bill Duff
Larry Eaton
Dave Evans
Bill Farr
Bob Fillinger
Charlene Fillinger
Duane Flack
Peggy Ford
Kyle Monfort Futo
Lucille "Lucky" Gallagher
Steve Garcia
Rich Gebhardt
Randy Geist
Mark Gustafson
George Hall
Wayne Harrison
Mike Haskett
Lynn Heinze
Dallas Horton
Jean Hoshiko
Burke Hurt
Bill Jackson
Ike Kelley
Lloyd Kindsfater
Larry Knee
Dick Lamm
Matt Larson
Torben Lenzberg
Harold Lesser
Marilyn Lesser
Kenny Lloyd
John Lussenhop
Bob Lynch
Shirley Mangum
Nomie Mapelli
Steve Mason
John Matsushima

Jerry McMorris
Gene Meakins
Joe Meilinger
Bud Middaugh
Pat Monfort Miller
Walker Miller
Manly Molpus
Charlie Monfort
Dick Monfort
Myra Monfort
Rick Montera
Don Mueller
Kay Norton
Bob Parris
Patty Penfold
Norm Peterson
Mike Purtill
Sal Randisi
Bob Reynolds
Roy Romer
Mike Sanem
Rudy Schlotthauer
Phil Seng
Gerald Shadwick
Lew Sullivan
Corky Swanson
Dave Swanson
Joe Tennessen
John Todd
Bob Tointon
Dave Vinsonhaler
Kaye Monfort Ward
Clark Weaver
Bill Webster
Tom Weiler
Albert Yates

Ken Monfort's Awards and Honors

1963	Named one of State's Three Outstanding Young Men by Colorado Jaycees
1969	Portrait of Nation's Most Successful Packer-Feeder, Meat Magazine
1970	Employer of the Year in Colorado, Governor's Committee on Employment of the Handicapped
1970	Colorado Conference United Church Award, Leadership in the Employment of Persons from Minority Groups
1972	Greeley-Weld Association for Retarded Children
1973	Conservation Award by Greeley Chapter of Trout Unlimited for Ecology Program
1973	Commercial Cattle Feeder of the Year, Feedlot Magazine (with Warren Monfort)
1974	Award of Excellence, Colorado Correctional Association for Working with Probationers and Parolees
1975	Honor Award, Environment Monthly Magazine for Environmental Excellence
1975	Certificate of Merit, Colorado Epilepsy Foundation for efforts in helping persons with epilepsy work in dignity
1978	Grand Marshal, Greeley Independence Stampede Rodeo
1979	Man of the Year Award, Colorado Meat Dealers Association
1985	Agri-Business Achievement Award, National Food & Energy Council, Inc., for efficient use of energy
1986	Colorado Business Award, Northern Colorado Region, Colorado Association of Commerce and Industry
1987	Colorado State University, Stockman of the Year (awarded to Warren Monfort in 1967)
1987	Executive of the Year, University of Colorado Graduate School
1988	Honorary Doctorate Degree, Colorado State University
1988	Colorado 4-H Alumni Award for contributions to state's youth
1988	National 4-H Alumni Award
1988	Top Choice Award, Colorado Cattle Feeders Association
1989	Inducted, International Stockmen's School Hall of Fame, Houston, Texas
1989	Inducted, Colorado Academy of Leaders, Colorado Education Foundation
1989	Master of Agri-Marketing Award, Rocky Mountain Chapter of National Agri-Marketing Association
1989	Humanitarian Award, United Way of Weld County
1990	Jerry Litton Memorial Award for Achievement in Agriculture, CSU, Alpha Gamma Rho Fraternity
1991	Outstanding Philanthropist of the Year, National Philanthropy Day in Colorado
1993	Weld Distinguished Citizens Award, Boy Scouts of America
1994	Inducted, Colorado Business Hall of Fame
2001	(Posthumous) William E. Morgan Alumni Achievement Award, CSU

State and Community Service

Democratic State Representative, Weld County (Colo.), 1965-1969
Colorado State Board of Agriculture

Industry Service

Vice Chairman, American Meat Institute, 1970
Member, Cattlemen's Beef Promotion and Research Board, 1986
Vice Chairman, American Meat Institute, 1987
Chairman, American Meat Institute, 1988

Directorships

Greeley National Bank
Affiliated Bankshares of Colorado
Colorado Cattle Feeders Association
Governor's Commission on Mental Health and Mental Retardation
Boy's and Girls Clubs
Boy Scouts
Girl Scouts
Rotary Club
YMCA
Salvation Army
Governor's Business Advisory Committee
Co-Chair, NAACP Freedom Dinner
Aims Community College

Ken Monfort's Philanthropy

Kenny Monfort's legacy is much more than a collection of his financial donations and gifts. Nevertheless, he shared his parents' belief in generosity to those who need help. And millions of people continue to benefit from his munificence.

The majority of contributions were made quietly, with no fanfare or publicity. From 1985 until the time of his death, documented records show that various charitable groups and organizations received about $33 million from Ken Monfort and the Monfort Family Charitable Foundation. And every year since his death, more and more is added to this part of his legacy through the family foundation and the Kenneth and Myra Monfort Charitable Foundation.

"We could have had someone different, someone who wouldn't share his money," noted former Greeley Mayor George Hall. "But we were lucky. We got Kenny."

Following is a list of some of those benefiting from his generosity.

Aims College Foundation
Adoption Exchange
Almost Home
American Cancer Society
American Lung Association
Ami Anderson Medical
ARC of Colorado
Arthritis Foundation
Bonell Center
Boys and Girls Club
Boy Scouts of America
CR Classics
CSRA of Greeley
Cap Cure
Catholic Charities
Celebrity Casino Night
Child Abuse Inc.
Children's Diabetes
Children's Education Fund
Children's Theatre
Choices of Greeley
Colorado Christmas
Colorado Farm Show
Colorado 4-H Youth Fund

Colorado State University
Connections for Independence
Courthouse Inc.
Creative Arts Center
Community Foundation
Dream Team of Greeley
Eaton Baseball Association
Eaton Elementary Beautification
Eaton First Cong.regational Church
Town of Eaton
Elks Youth Baseball
Education Foundation
FFA Foundation
First Congregational Church
First Steps of Greeley
Friends of Lincoln Park Library
Galeton PTO
Girl Scouts of America
Greeley Area Community Trust
Greeley Art Mart
Greeley Civic Center
Greeley Island Grove Park
Greeley Center for Independence
Greeley Central High

Greeley Chamber Orchestra
Greeley Children Chorale
City of Greeley
Greeley Food Clearing House
Greeley Independence Stampede
Greeley Jaycees
Greeley Philharmonic Orchestra
Greeley Polio Plus
Greeley Police Department
Greeley Swim Team
Greeley Transition House
Greeley West High
Habitat for Humanity
Headfirst Foundation
Highland Day Care
Highland Recreation
Hispanic Coalition Voice
Humane Society
Island Grove Treatment
Junior Achievement
Latin American Education Foundation
Linn Grove Cemetery
Lincoln Park Flower Pro.
LULAC Dollars for Hispanic Scholars
Make A Wish Foundation
March of Dimes
Marollino Eddie Aragon Scholars
Meals on Wheels
Michener Library Foundation
Monfort Children's Clinic
Mountain View Academy
NC Heat Baseball
N. Colorado Animal League
N. Colorado Bookmobile
N. Colorado Center on Deafness
N. Colorado Medical Center
Parental Child Learning Center of Greeley
Partners of Greeley
Pierce Senior Citizens Inc.
Platte Valley City Center
Poudre River Trail
Right to Read of Greeley
Rotary Club Foundation
Salvation Army
Santa Cops
Senior Center of Greeley
Schaffer Rehabilitation
Sunrise Health Clinic
Tennis Association of Greeley
Union Colony Charter School
Union Colony Civic Center
United Way
University of Colorado
University of Northern Colorado
Weld Fund for Choice
Weld Santa Cops
Weld School District Re-1
Weld Veterans Memorial
Weld Food Bank
Weld Opportunity School
Weld School District 6
Windsor Historical Society
A Woman's Place

Index

Abortion, 114
Adcock, Harold, 57
Addoms, Sam, 127, 139, 199, 201, 219, 235, 271
Aims Community College, 251
Amalgamated Meat Cutters Union, 50
American Meat Institute, 136
Anderson, A.D., 194
Angelotti, Robert, 106
Army Air Force, 5, 6
Avery, Bert, 31
B.B., 176
Bandstra, Bert, 51
Beef imports, 53
Beef Promotion and Research Board, 137
Benton, Bill, 24
Big Five packers, 193
Boeddeker, Jay, 49
Boekel, Bill, 46
Bowling, Rod, 137
Box speech, 130
Bragg, Bill, 161
Brown, Hank, iv, 62, 93, 100, 104, 110, 119, 134, 144, 225, 269, 271
Capital punishment, 170
Capitol Pack, 44, 45, 48
Carey, Doug, 146
Carter, Jimmy, 99, 100, 102, 104, 105, 107
Chicago Mercantile Exchange, 123
Chronic Obstructive Pulmonary Disease, 263
Cigarettes, 132, 155, 156, 160, 238, 253, 264
Circus wagons, 201
Civil Rights Act, 77
Colorado A&M, 2, 5, 7
Colorado Board of Agriculture, 26, 251, 256
Colorado Rockies, 242
Colorado State Fair, 36
Colorado State Normal School, 14
Colorado State University, 2, 26, 56, 66, 88, 137, 165, 180, 183, 257, 285, 287
ConAgra, 229, 231, 232, 233, 234, 236, 237, 244
Constitution, U.S., 114
Corn ensilage, 68
Corn flakes, 55
Cost of living adjustments, 151
Croot, Mike, 155
Democratic Convention, Colorado, 82
DES, 222, 223
Doehring, George, 229
Dominick, Peter, 84, 85, 90, 91, 145
Dos Rios, 66
Drake, Justus, 225
Ducks Unlimited, 160
Duff, Bill, 253
Eat Crow Club, 109
Enemies list, 96, 97, 121, 179
Energy crisis, 191
Environmentalism, 189
European Trip, 9
EXCEL, 230
Farmers Spur, Colorado, 6
Farr, W.D., 31, 275
Feldman, Maurice, 49
FIFO. See LIFO accounting
Fillinger, Bob, 132, 157
Flavorland Industries, 212
Food and Drug Administration, 222
Ford, Gerald, 72, 97, 98, 179
Foreign policy, 116
Foreman, Carol, 105
Fromme, Lyn "Squeaky", 179
Futures trading, 124, 125
Gallagher, Lucky, 133, 147
Gavin, Tom, 87, 245
Gebhardt, Rich, i, 83, 158, 282
Gilcrest feedlot, 65
Grand Island plant, 107, 148, 155, 204, 206, 212, 213, 219, 223, 224, 226, 230, 238
Greeley High School, 3, 5, 6, 7, 35, 57

Greeley National Bank, 26, 30, 131, 229, 286
Greeley Odor Control Committee, 180
Greeley, Colorado, history, 13
Harper, Mike, 229
Hart, Gary, 99, 103, 109
Heinze, Lynn, 133
Herdman, Don, 159
Hogan, Mark, i
Holman, Currier J., 194
Hoshiko, Paul, 235
Hurt, Burke, 60
IBP, 143, 150, 195, 196, 198, 199, 205, 206, 223, 230, 231
Iowa Beef Packers, 196
JOBS program, 190
Johnson, Lyndon, 79, 80, 82, 83, 86
Kadlecek, Jim, 112
Kappa Alpha Theta, 3
Kelley, Ike, 141, 268, 272
Kennedy, John F., 75
Kennedy, Robert F., 78
Kenya, 82
King, Martin Luther, 78
Kissinger, Henry, 98, 250
Knee, Larry, 25, 60
Ku Klux Klan, 76
Kuner feedlot, 161, 184, 187, 210, 234
KUSA, 135
Lamm, Dick, 98, 100, 103, 108, 120
Lance, Bert, 100
Lenzberg, Torben, 136
LIFO accounting, 40, 127
Lloyd, Kenny, 123
Longboat Key, Florida, 262
Love, John, 95
Lucas, Ward, 135
Lynch, Bob, 258
Malcolm Baldrige Quality Award, 259
Mansfield, Mike, 93
Mapelli Bros. Co., 59
Mapelli, Eugene M., 72
Mapelli, Herman, 70
Mapelli, Mario, 71
Mapelli, Neoma Robinson, 70
Mapelli, Sonny, 69, 72, 108, 155, 179, 202, 219, 225, 236
Marsh, Randy M.D, 267
Matsushima, John, 20, 36, 56, 275
McClearn, William C., 69
McGovern, George, 93, 96
McMorris, Jerry, 268
McNichols, Steve, 87, 88, 90, 91
Meakins, Gene, 2, 3, 4, 207
Meat grading, 105
Meat inspection, 105
Meilinger, Joe, 143, 146, 160, 161, 268
Memorial service, 268
Michener, James, 177
Miller, Gurdon, 21
Monfort Food Distributing Company, 68
Monfort Girls, 87
Monfort Gold, 129
Monfort International, 57
Monfort Provision Co., 56
Monfort Transportation Co., 201
Monfort, Charles, 11, 12, 14, 17, 18, 19, 107, 133, 179
Monfort, Charlie, 39, 87, 136, 164, 174, 175, 242, 243, 244, 272
Monfort, Dick (brother), 4, 6, 18, 33, 34, 36, 37, 177
Monfort, Dick (son), 39, 174, 223, 231, 232, 234, 236, 244, 268, 272
Monfort, Edith, 8, 15, 16, 17, 18, 19, 20, 22, 25, 26, 27, 33, 34, 61, 62, 63, 76, 80, 153, 160, 281
Monfort, Kaye, 39, 174, 176, 272
Monfort, Kyle, 38, 75, 87, 174, 272, 275, 276
Monfort, Margery, 4, 18, 19, 63, 263, 264
Monfort, Myra, 156, 175, 176, 243, 250, 258, 260, 262, 263, 264, 267, 268, 282, 287
Monfort, Pat, 3, 4, 38, 46, 75, 88, 94, 161, 163, 166, 167, 174, 175, 176, 177
Monfort, Pella, 11, 12
Monfort, Warren, 8, 11, 12, 14, 15, 16, 17, 18, 19, 20, 21, 22, 23, 24, 25, 26, 27, 29, 30, 31, 32, 33, 34,

35, 36, 37, 38, 39, 40, 41, 43, 44, 48, 49, 51, 60, 61, 62, 63, 64, 68, 76, 80, 81, 118, 125, 139, 153, 155, 160, 171, 182, 183, 200, 237, 249, 263, 281, 285
MOPAC, 54
Mueller, Don, 162, 200, 282
National Labor Relations Board, 107, 209
National Organization for Women, 169
National Western Stock Show, 36, 72, 225
Newton, Marcus, 159
Nixon price freeze, 120, 141
Nixon resignation, 97
Nixon, Richard, 93, 96, 97, 98, 100, 121, 179
NLRB, 209, 217, 218, 224, 227
Oregon Cattlemen's Association, 129
Organic movement, 189
Osborne, George "Rosie", 57
Park Congregational Church, 3
Parris, Bob, 143, 160
Peacenik, 82
pollution, 179, 185
Poudre Provision Co., 57
Profit sharing, 61
Prothe, Leonard, 265
Randisi, Sal, 264
Reagan, Ronald, 104, 116, 168
Red Steer Restaurant, 20
Religion, 13, 80, 115, 147, 170, 176
Rheumatic fever, 131, 153, 263
Rocky Mountain Discount, 143

Romer, Roy, 8, 9, 71, 238, 241
Sarge, 176
Saturday Night Massacre, 97
Schlotthauer, Rudy, 156, 158, 282
School districts, 67
Seigi Horiuchi, 136, 265
Shoes, alligator, 265
Shoes, mismatched, i
Sigma Phi Epsilon, 2, 4, 5
Six, Robert F., 69
Sodman, Wayne, 99
Spencer Foods, 200, 231
Strickland, Ted, 100
Swanson, Viola, 6
T-Bone Club, 26
Tennis shoes, green, 165
Thomas, Steve, 210, 217, 219
UFCW, 50, 206, 207, 213, 218, 224
Union Colony Civic Center, 240
United Nations, 248
Urban, John, 208
Vietnam War, 82, 84, 85, 92, 113, 145
Watergate, 93, 97
Weaver, Clark, 131
Webster, Bill, 162, 172
Weld County Fair, 36
Weld County, Colorado, 29
Welfare programs, 168
Wheeler, John R. P., 87
Wilson & Co., 122
Wilson, Rick, 264
Wiseman, Frederick, 171
World War I, 17
Yates, Al, 165, 166, 257
Yuma feedlot, 237